American Essays: Mak

CHARLES TOMLINSON

*American Essays:
Making It New*

CARCANET

First published in Great Britain in 2001 by
Carcanet Press Limited
4th Floor, Conavon Court
12–16 Blackfriars Street
Manchester M3 5BQ

Copyright © Charles Tomlinson 2001

The right of Charles Tomlinson to be identified
as the author of this work has been asserted by him in accordance
with the Copyright, Designs and Patents Act of 1988

All rights reserved

A CIP catalogue record for this book
is available from the British Library

ISBN 1 85754 476 5

The publisher acknowledges financial assistance
from the Arts Council of England

Set in Monotype Bembo by XL Publishing Services, Tiverton
Printed and bound in England by SRP Ltd, Exeter

To Brenda

Acknowledgements

Acknowledgements are due to publishers and editors of magazines who have previously printed some of the material in this book: Cloudforms, Editions Rodopi, Interim Press, New Directions, *The New Review*, *Parnassus*, Penguin Books, *The Times Literary Supplement*, University of California Press, University of Keele Tapes. My essay on Marianne Moore is reprinted with the permission of Simon and Schuster from *Marianne Moore: a collection of critical essays*, edited by myself. Copyright © 1969 by Prentice-Hall Inc.

Contents

Foreword	ix
Poetry in America	1
On First Reading Pound	8
Eliot, Pound and *The Waste Land*	17
Reading *The Waste Land*	22
Williams's Thousand Freshets	27
Marianne Moore: Her Poetry and her Critics	38
Wallace Stevens and the Poetry of Scepticism	53
The Integrity of George Oppen	70
A Rich Sitter: Lorine Niedecker	75
Elizabeth Bishop: *The Complete Poems*	79
Poetry and Friendship:	
Elizabeth Bishop, Marianne Moore and Robert Lowell	86
Eye and Ear in the Verse of James Laughlin	91
Black Mountain Revisited	98
From Amateur to Impresario: Charles Olson	108
Some Americans: A Personal Record	
1 Beginnings	117
2 Objectivists: Zukofsky and Oppen	144
3 A Late Greeting: O'Keeffe	163
4 Dove Sta Memoria: In Italy	174
Sources	195
Index of Names	197

Foreword

I found my own voice as a poet by learning from four Americans, a woman and three men – Marianne Moore, Wallace Stevens, Ezra Pound and William Carlos Williams. Williams joined this company late, since his work was hard to come by in England. The rest was chance. A 1942 selection of Pound had lingered on the shelves of a local bookshop in the Midlands where I was born. I had browsed through it for some two years and finally bought it in 1944. The next year a second-hand copy of Michael Roberts's *Faber Book of Modern Verse* appeared in Heffers of Cambridge and the purchase of that finally put Pound into context for me, somewhat later than Hopkins and not far from Marianne Moore, my next discovery. Wallace Stevens also appeared there with four poems, and 'The Emperor of Ice-Cream', with its arresting title, focused my attention on him. An American friend inquired what literature I would like him to bring across the Atlantic and I asked for Stevens' *Harmonium*.

In the 1950s my American-influenced poetry received several prizes from *Poetry (Chicago)* and finally its editor nominated me for a travelling scholarship which took me to the States and resulted in my meeting Miss Moore and Williams whose poems in the meantime I had managed to borrow from another doctor-poet, Gael Turnbull. Subsequently I also met that splendid American painter, Georgia O'Keeffe, whose fame by now has crossed the water. The outcome of this, the first of many subsequent journeys to and across America, was a prose work, *Some Americans*, which appeared twenty years ago. It was well received then, but has long been out of print. So when Michael Schmidt suggested I combine it with a selection of my essays on American poetry, I jumped at the opportunity. Thus, the present volume contains the first appearance of a selection of my criticism.

The essay on Pound here goes back to my first reading of his work and reaches forwards to subsequent readings – of the Cantos and of Pound's translations. I now saw that an original poet may be at his most original when translating the work of others. On turning to the work of Marianne Moore, I realized the depth of Pound's own surprise and wonder when he came upon her poems and when, misled by the words of 'Melancthon', 'Black / but beautiful my back' (Moore is describing an elephant), he wondered if he had indeed discovered a poet of 'Ethiopian hue'. Her diction remains a lesson to any poet in the use of prose cadences and a guarantee that sources like *Scientific American* or the Bell Telephone leaflet, *The World's Most Accurate Clocks*, need not be shied away from. When W.C. Williams declared that 'Anything is good material for poetry', he had written his classic essay on Marianne Moore (1925), describing her 'Marriage' as 'an anthology of transit', 'a swiftness that passes without repugnance from thing to thing'. Evidently what Williams means by 'without repugnance' is the kind of inclusiveness indicated by Marianne Moore when she writes, 'nor is it valid / to discriminate against "business documents and / school books"; all these phenomena are important.' Already these poets of the early years of the century were establishing a basis for Charles Olson's approach in his own work and in his postwar manifesto, *Projective Verse*: first and foremost, verse must keep moving through a trajectory, as Williams had already said, and not 'sink decoratively to rest'. That, of course, had always been the intention behind traditional poetry. But after Williams and Moore, variable lineation and verse patterns become the focus where somatic energies can declare themselves in an increased attention to the syllable. Between Moore's syllabics and Olson's 'place of the elements and minims of language' where the syllable is declared king, there exists a devious but connecting pathway. The same direction is followed in a poem close to Pound's early Chinese translations, Wallace Stevens' 'Thirteen Ways of Looking at a Blackbird', another anthology of transit using a rapidly varied series of short stanzas, very different from Stevens' excessively circular syntax of cogitation in some of his later 'philosophical' poems.

In reading these Americans – and obviously Eliot's *The Waste Land* was part of the same experience – I felt that I was in touch with a source of power and utility, as I did not feel with the work of my English contemporaries (though Hopkins's previous innovations of line and metre had arrested my attention). The word 'utility' here implies that new technical possibilities had entered the language via American poetry and that I, as an Englishman, was not debarred from using them. Williams at times seemed to identify this newness and what he referred to as 'measure', with 'the American idiom', sometimes even 'the American language'. But clearly Williams's 'measure' and the poem as 'an anthology of transit', offered both challenge and promise for the English writer too.

Although these poets, of an older generation than myself, are all dead, they remain contemporaries in that they initiated a new poetic phase whose resources are still present and ready for use.

Poetry in America

American poetry is a very easy subject to discuss for the simple reason that it does not exist. This italicised passage (unattributed) appears in Book Three of William Carlos Williams's *Paterson*, Williams having excerpted it from an article of George Barker's published in *Poetry London* in 1948. Tackled almost twenty years later by Mike Weaver, then in the preliminary stages of his book on Williams's American background, Barker cheerfully responded, 'Certainly it is a remark that, in and out of my cups, I made several times too often in those days. Myself I don't think it disputable that American poetry is beginning to happen now.' *Beginning* to happen? – the year is 1966. In 1994 the subject is coming apart at the seams and contained with difficulty in Jay Parini's and Brett C. Millier's wide-ranging *Columbia History of American Poetry*. The volume runs to over eight hundred pages and will long go on giving us food for argument, but little reason to suppose that this history was not in full flood by 1966.

When I first read the Barker quotation in *Paterson*, unaware of its author, I took it to be merely a piece of (probably British) arrogance, as indeed it turned out to be. However, I am no longer sure that this is the way Williams meant it to strike us, but rather as supporting his own contention that the American poetry he was inaugurating, written in the mode of twentieth-century modernism and what he aggressively called 'the American language', was indeed hardly underway. It had to cope with the sell-out to Europe, as he saw it, of Eliot and Pound, and re-root and replenish itself on the often thin soil of American locality – in his case, that of New Jersey. And *The Columbia History* makes perfectly clear how, after Williams, much American poetry – from the Beats to the blacks, to the emergence of other ethnic poetry in English and the anti-paternalists among women poets – the irreducible and unavoidable fact of America, political, psychological and geographic, or people's not infallible perceptions of the fact, looms as centrally as it had for Whitman.

Whether this makes for good, bad or indifferent poetry is the job of the literary historian to try to assess. In the present volume some honestly undertake that task, others politely mouth the agreed shibboleths and reiterate what F.R. Leavis used to call currency valuations. But present-day critics have long since buried the name of Leavis, as they have that of another critic and poet, the American Yvor Winters. The latter might have provided an interesting, resistant and acerbic presence in this history, but he doesn't get included. The reason – it is difficult to believe no one would have taken on the job of attempting to evaluate Winters – is hard to fathom. His work, as Parini tells us, 'has been hard to place'. He gestures towards Robert Pinsky's 'homage to Winters in his essays and poems' and that is that.

But to return to George Barker and non-existent American poetry, and to how it began to exist for the interested British reader. Barker's generation and my own found their way into American poetry as a chiefly twentieth-century affair – we had forgotten bits of Longfellow glimpsed at school, and we were suspicious of Whitman – via our reading of Michael Roberts's *Faber Book of Modern Verse*, a book whose subsequent re-editings disguised the shapely intelligence of Roberts's original choice. Barker, whose own early poems rode in that anthology, ought surely to have spotted the extraordinary range of the Americans Roberts had lighted on. Williams was, of course, missing, as he almost always was in those days, and for some reason there was no Robert Frost, perhaps because of the absence of such tokens of modernism as Roberts was looking for (an absence that caused him to reject Edward Thomas, though Wilfred Owen was included on the showing of those half-rhymes and modern-sounding assonances). Roberts, however, already included in 1936 many of the poets who have survived to the stock-taking of *The Columbia History* and some – Aiken, Cummings and Laura Riding – who are given unaccountably short shrift in 1994. Roberts had picked out all three of the above along with Crane, H.D., Eberhart, Vachel Lindsay, Marianne Moore, Ransom and Tate and the then (on this side of the water) very elusive Stevens. (Vice-president of the Hartford Accident and Indemnity Company, Stevens is noted on Columbia's publicity leaflet as 'the much beloved, insurance salesman-poet, Wallace Stevens'.)

If Roberts's selection, in its battered third printing, led undergraduates like myself to explore a wider range of American poetry, working backwards from the twentieth century, it was F.O.

Matthiessen's *Oxford Book of American Verse* of 1950 that brought one into the wide-open spaces that are to be explored by Parini's team of literary critics and historians – his writers are sometimes both together, though occasionally one has the feeling one is being told about 'causes' or treated to special pleading, and that literary discrimination is in abeyance. Diane Wood Middlebrook on the over-rated Anne Sexton drove me back to Helen Vendler's excellent piece in *The Music of What Happens* (1988) where distinctions of literary quality are being made over the course of Sexton's work. Indeed, Vendler expresses there feelings I came to experience when confronted by some of the more predictable jargon from gender studies in *The Columbia History*. As she writes, 'Nor will it do to hail any poet, finally, as a "woman" poet (or a "gay" poet). Every poet is in the end only one sort of poet – a poet of the native language. The poet does well by perception in vesting it in language, or does not. The poem finds a language for its experience, or does not. Sometimes Sexton found that language.'

If Matthiessen's anthology helped open out a growing interest in the whole range of American poetry, it was Roy Harvey Pearce's critical study *The Continuity of American Poetry* of eleven years later that ambitiously elucidated connections, looked at forgotten authors – Bryant, Longfellow, James Russell Lowell, Whittier, Lanier –, characterized the different geniuses of Whitman and Dickinson, and brought focus to the roles of Pound and Williams. This was one critic's attempt to take on single-handed most of the territory covered by *The Columbia History*, though the thirty-year gap has left much subsequent work for comment and enquiry. There is some virtue in having the literary history of a given phase written by one person, as readers of Johnson's *Prefaces, Biographical and Critical, to the Works of the English Poets* soon discover. And it was Johnson, after all, who invented the genre, literary history, that is being practised by Pearce and by the numerous contributors to the Columbia compilation.

Jay Parini has his worries about the many points of view displayed here and opens the book with a quick look at everybody, and, after a pat on the head, sends them each on his or her way. There occurs some phrase-making of the blurb kind in this introduction: 'It might easily be argued that she is the central poet at work in America today' (on Adrienne Rich); 'Her compacted poems are bullets aimed straight at the heart, and they kill', this on Dickinson whose 'intensely wrought lyrics splinter in the reader's eye'. There is also some honest anxiety about the justifiability of a plurality of views, something Roy Harvey Pearce was not obliged to consider. 'These chapters are arranged chronologically, and represent what the editors consider important aspects of American poetry. Nevertheless,' – and here we prick up our ears – 'each chapter should be taken as one critic's point of view: necessarily subjective, rooted in the critic's position in the evolution of the culture as a whole.' Is criticism so bound to the evolutionary and subjective as to need an editorial health warning before we can assume that all worthwhile critics should be in possession of many years of reading experience, of some sense of the literary canon, and have tested their subjectivities against their spouses, colleagues and students over a long period?

After the preliminaries, it is good to get into the body of the book with Francis Murphy's excellent account of Anne Bradstreet and Edward Taylor. (It is now politely assumed by all that American poetry begins with Bradstreet, though an equally good case could be made for George Sandys whose pioneering translation of Ovid's *Metamorphoses* was completed in 1626 while he was Treasurer of the Virginia Colony. But let that pass.) Murphy is incisive and handles the contrast of the style of these two poets well. There is a somewhat Johnsonian savour to his phrase on the opening lines of Taylor's 'The Preface' to *God's Determination* – 'lines that first captured the imagination of Taylor's readers, and no one who has written about him since has failed to quote them', which he does:

> Infinity, when all things it beheld
> In Nothing and of Nothing all did build,
> Upon what Base was fixt the Lath, wherein
> He turn'd this Globe, and riggalled it so trim?...
> Who Lac'de and Fillitted the earth so fine,
> With Rivers like green Ribbons Smaragdine?...
> Who Spread its Canopy? Or Curtain's Spun?
> Who in this Bowling Alley bowld the Sun?

It is the sound of poetry once more brings over the flavour of an epoch, dire in itself, in Carolivia Herron's often moving second chapter, 'Early African American Poetry'. Paul Laurence Dunbar (1872–1906), the most popular African American poet of his day, has his own well-tuned version of 'Go down, Moses':

> Now ole Pher'oh, down in Egypt,
>   Was de wuss man evah evah bo'n,

>   An'he had de Hebrew chillun
>   Down dah wukin' in his co'n;
>   'T'well de Lawd got tiahed o' his foolin',
>   An' sez he: I'll let him know –
>   'Look Hyeah, Moses, go tell Pher'oh
>   Fu' to let dem chillun go.'

Phillis Wheatley (1753?–84), shipped as a child to the Boston slave-market at the age of seven, proved – much to the delight and pride of her owners, the Wheatley family – to be a literary prodigy. She mastered English and by her teens Latin and was translating Ovid. Pope and Milton were her formative influences. Her ill-health caused the alarmed Wheatleys to send her to England for convalescence. There her poems were published and she returned with a valuable edition of Milton given to her by the mayor of London – returned one is glad to say, to her freedom. Others were less fortunate. George Moses Horton (1797–1880) 'sought, begged and wrote for his freedom from the North Carolina Horton family for most of his life'. He finally got it at the age of sixty-five. He, too, must have been a man of spirit and a believer, not only in liberty, but in poetic discipline:

>   True nature first inspires the man,
>   But he must after learn to scan,
>   And mark well every rule;
>   Gradual the climax then ascend,
>   And prove the contrast in the end
>   Between the wit and fool.

I was less persuaded by the evidence Herron has to offer on African American epics. George Marion McClellans's *The Legend of Tannhäuser*, written in the blankest of blank verse ('In horror-stricken tones the nobles cried...'), may well be, as she says, 'the most successful work in the genre', but verse like this isn't much of an adjunct to the Muses' diadem.

A number of these thirty-one chapters are of quite exceptional interest. My first candidate, in order of appearance, would be Dana Gioia's 'Longfellow in the Aftermath of Modernism'. Modernism had little use for the kind of narratives that Longfellow excelled in and which brought him a small fortune – two thousand pounds a year more than Tennyson. Gioia makes a persuasive case for these poems and the need for a revaluation that would correct the blindspots of later writers who are our immediate literary ancestors. He points with some irony to the fact that two of the greatest modernists, Eliot and Pound, were anticipated by Longfellow in his shift of the poet's frame of cultural reference from Anglo-American to European literature – German, Spanish, French, Danish, Italian. Longfellow, like Pound, was also a translator and Pound (Longfellow's grand-nephew, as Gioia reminds us) represents him in his anthology *Confucius to Cummings* with a translation from Saint Teresa of Avila. 'Longfellow's vision of the American poet's international role was central to both Pound and Eliot', writes Gioia, 'and it remains a dominant force in poetry (locked, of course, in eternal dialectical opposition with nativism). Although Eliot did not take his mission directly from Longfellow, he developed it in the Harvard humanities curriculum that Longfellow helped create.' Gioia takes note of the over-copiousness of too many of Longfellow's offerings, but the variety of his prosidy, his ability to tell a story directly and the faithfulness of his best translations – his versions of Goethe's Wanderer's Night Songs matching rhyme for rhyme – all argue for the permanence of his contribution to American poetry. 'You'll have to go a long way round if you want to ignore him,' concludes Gioia.

One might say the same of Longfellow's contemporaries Bryant, Whittier, Holmes and J.R. Lowell, for whom no space is found in *The Columbia History*. Pearce thought Whittier's long narrative *Snow-Bound* 'a great poem' and a case might be made also for *The Pennsylvania Pilgrim*, some of the ballads (particularly *Maud Muller*) and the blank verse prelude to *Among the Hills*, a prelude finer than the poem it introduces. With this, one is already in the grimness of Frost country:

> ... how hard and colourless
> Is life without an atmosphere. I look
> Across the lapse of half a century,
> And call to mind old homesteads, ...
> Within, the cluttered kitchen-floor unwashed,
> (Broom-clean I think they called it); the best room
> Stifling with cellar damp, shut from the air
> In hot midsummer ...

The kind of level of excellence found in Gioia turns up again with William Pritchard on T.S. Eliot, W.S. Di Piero on 'the essential relation between the political order and the poetic imagination' in Pound and George Oppen – other important Objectivists do not appear in this history: Reznikoff, Rakosi and Niedecker, likewise Mina Loy; Patricia Wells makes a thoughtful case for the poetry of Robert Penn Warren and Helen Vendler still finds new and enlightening things to say about Wallace Stevens after long years of practice. What is admirable about all these articles is their tone, balanced and often witty, not irritably bristling with partisan intensities, a delight to read in themselves.

Among much fascinating work on the modern era, a theme started by W.S. Di Piero left me hungry for its development. A one-man history would have had to go on to substantiate (as no doubt he can) the following perception of things: 'I sometimes think the intense personalism of American poetry in recent decades, with its psychological fussiness and maniacally modest self-absorbtion, is one sign of the failure of belief in the possibility of poetry as truly public music.' This provocative statement glimmers with suggestion. Fully articulated, it could well help define one's too frequent dissatisfaction on opening American poetry reviews today.

On First Reading Pound

I can say at once where it was I first read Pound. In what seems now a remote historical period, the mid-1940s – before accountancy had invented the term 'shelf life' for books – I had gone back several times to the shelves of a bookshop in the Midlands where I was born, and had browsed through the pages of *A Selection of Poems* of Ezra Pound (Faber and Faber, 1942).

Books, then, would often remain on the same shelves for a long time, and you could become quite familiar with the contents of interesting works over the months and even years. Such was the case with Pound.

I must describe the little volume: it had a yellow cover with navy-blue lettering on it. It was priced at two shillings and sixpence – half a crown. It was the Sesame Books selection, and for me the series was an 'Open Sesame' not only to Pound, but to several other poets, including Edward Thomas and Lawrence.

The problem about the Pound was this. It cost half a crown and it was in paperback. For another sixpence I could have bought the Everyman hard-bound *Thus Spake Zarathustra* by Nietzsche, about whose 'Übermensch' our German teacher had told us. It was war-time and we had gone on learning German at school and hearing from this highly intelligent Jewish refugee from Hitler's Germany about both Nietzsche and Rilke.

But what has learning German from a cultured refugee at a provincial high school to do with reading Ezra Pound for the first time, you might well wonder. Rather more than one would immediately suppose. For, with the arrival of the refugees in the late 1930s and early 1940s, there occurred in Stoke-on-Trent a complete change in the cultural atmosphere, a whiff of internationalism, and for the first time one heard records of Bruckner and of Brecht's *Threepenny Opera*, and one saw books of woodcuts by Franz Masreel and Feininger and of paintings by Klee and Kandinsky. In a curious way, and because of the cultural time lag in our district of potters' kilns, one was re-living, however fragmentarily, the cultural history of the earlier years of the twentieth century. I was even reading the plays of Maeterlinck, culled from the secondhand trays of that same bookshop, imagining that *Interior* and *The Death of Tintagiles* were 'the latest thing'. (Imagine my surprise when in 1992 I heard an academic from the University of London claiming *Interior* as a forerunner of the plays of Samuel Beckett.) Maeterlinck, Brecht, Kandinsky – an unfamiliar mixture for Stoke in 1944! And precisely at that moment, I first began reading Pound.

I had no real notion of what Pound's role had been in the revolution of twentieth-century modernism. I approached him totally without preconception, unsure whether he was alive or dead, since nobody I knew ever talked about him. I had no information about Imagism or Vorticism and was wholly unacquainted with critical theory. What sank in? I was struck by the presence of the prose phraseology and the clarity of diction in several of Pound's poems and also by the way he divided his lines. I could have had no idea at that date that Pound's breaking of his lines, his fragmenting of phrases into units of articulation and units of prosody, would reinforce what I was later to find so intriguing in Pound's close friend, William Carlos Williams – namely, often quite long sentences broken up into phrases, each phrase or fragment given a line to itself, in a verse form of clear facets, a sculpting of the verse line (however syllabically brief it might be) so that it could stand aesthetically firm in its own right and in relation to the rhythmic pattern that ran straight through the poem. That lesson was preparing, as I first read and was captivated by 'The Garden' – a lesson, as Williams was to put it, in how the poet must turn his verses 'this way, then that at will'.

It was the shape of the lines drew me again to the three Chinese poems from *Cathay* in the Sesame selection, but particularly to 'The River-Merchant's Wife'. Here, there was once more a prose rhythm rather different from what I had been taught to think of as poetry. The poem had roughly one statement per line, and one line clearly set out after another. It seemed a happy release from ti-tum, ti-tum, ti-tum, ti-tum, ti-tum:

The River-Merchant's Wife: A Letter

While my hair was still cut straight across my forehead
I played about the front gate, pulling flowers.
You came by on bamboo stilts, playing horse,
You walked about my seat, playing with blue plums.

And we went on living in the village of Chokan:
Two small people, without dislike or suspicion.

At fourteen I married My Lord you.
I never laughed, being bashful.
Lowering my head, I looked at the wall.
Called to, a thousand times, I never looked back.

At fifteen I stopped scowling,
I desired my dust to be mingled with yours
For ever and for ever and for ever.
Why should I climb the look out?

At sixteen you departed,
You went into far Ku-to-yen, by the river of swirling eddies,
And you have been gone five months.
The monkeys make sorrowful noise overhead.

You dragged your feet when you went out.
By the gate now, the moss is grown, the different mosses,
Too deep to clear them away!
The leaves fall early this autumn, in wind.
The paired butterflies are already yellow with August
Over the grass in the West garden;
They hurt me. I grow older.
If you are coming down through the narrows of the river
　Kiang,
Please let me know beforehand,
And I will come out to meet you
　　　　　As far as Cho-fu-Sa.

This poem, along with 'The Garden', began my education in the poet's conscious use of prose cadences. I had received inklings of this when listening to certain songs of Debussy in which he sets to music poems of Paul Verlaine. Already, thanks to my splendid teacher of French, Cecil Scrimgeour, I knew some of these poems by heart. What I had not been prepared for was the way they would sound when translated literally into English. At the BBC concert I am thinking of, long lost in the mists of yesteryear, the announcer read these lyrics in an English version. I have no idea who translated them and perhaps the translations were of no literary value. What impressed and over-rode the immediate question of such value was the shock of lyrical poems being rendered into quite plain prose statements, the suggestion of the way such statements might constitute an actual poem. I became addicted to such pre-concert renderings and fancied I heard something similar in poems like Pound's 'The Condolence' (also in the Sesame selection) where the keen prose edge came as a tonic to the ear:

> We were in especial bored with male stupidity …
> We were not exasperated with women,
>   for the female is ductile.

Whatever the justice of that last phrase, justice – and also mere meaning – were once again over-ridden for me by the way the eighteen syllables of this statement were tossed off with such nonchalance, the phrase nicely divided by and pivoted on the comma after 'women'. (Here was something that preluded the pleasure of future years when one came upon the multi-syllabled dexterity in Canto LXXVIII of 'and those negroes by the clothes-line are extraordinarily like the figures del Cossa / Their green does not swear at the landscape'.) Like Chaucer, Wyatt and Donne, as I was soon to learn, Pound in 'The Condolence' was incorporating into his work the cadences of prose speech, the prose speech of his own century – my century – and free of rhyme. It was that freedom from rhyme also which made a big difference in 'The Condolence'.

My juvenile reading of 'The Condolence' and of 'The River-Merchant's Wife' could scarcely have told me that, years ahead, Donald Davie, with whom I enjoyed the first rational talks on Pound I was to have, would write of the poetry of *Cathay*: 'It was only when the line was considered as the unit of composition, as it was by Pound in *Cathay*, that there emerged the possibility of "breaking" the line, of disrupting it from within, by throwing weight upon the similar units within the line.'

Think of the simple expressiveness in 'The River-Merchant's Wife' of her line about the paired butterflies: 'They hurt me. I grow older.'

When in 1981 I gave the Clark Lectures at Cambridge, I quoted the Davie passage to reinforce my sense that (and here I quote myself) 'from Pound's moment of discovery, [often] the writer's attention is to continue to rest on the line as poetic unit [not the metrical foot] – as in William Carlos Williams, in George Oppen and in the Black Mountain poets'. As I explain in *Some Americans*, Pound's description of the sea in Canto II, in the Sesame Books selection, stayed with me, haunting me with a sense of new possibilities and with the realization that I'd have to look up quite a few things to understand this poet. What was 'hyaline', who was 'Tyro', how could 'black azure' exist?

The thing about Pound – and certain other poets, come to that – is that he impels one to search out in nature the effects he evokes. I discovered Pound's seascape when, almost ten years later, I went to live in Italy and could corroborate before the very sea and in the very light he was recalling, the felicity of his 'glass wave'.

One was also instigated to find out what his references to the contents of certain works of art actually implied. My first experience of this was also prompted by the Sesame selection which contained 'The Picture':

The eyes of this dead lady speak to me,
For here was love, was not to be drowned out.
And here desire, not to be kissed away.

The eyes of this dead lady speak to me.

Was this poem, then, addressed to a corpse? Did the second line imply she had died by drowning? Was the picture one of Ophelia, perhaps? It could scarcely be that, I realized, as my eyes drifted to the foot of the page and read '*Venus Reclining*, by Jacopo del Sellaio (1442–93)'. For some reason I supposed that this picture must be in the National Gallery where, as far as I knew, most of the Italian pictures outside of Italy were to be found. In 1945 I went up to London to be interviewed for a scholarship and persuaded my father, who accompanied me, to visit an art gallery for the first and last time in his life. Most of the National Gallery was closed, so no hope of finding Jacopo del Sellaio. But as I trailed disconsolately out of the building my glance fell upon a book published at five shillings in 1930 and still on sale at that price fifteen years later. It was entitled *National Gallery: Illustrations to The Catalogue, Volume, I, Italian Schools*. Clearly this must contain the clue to the appearance of the picture I was looking for. I borrowed the five shillings from my father, promising to repay out of future pocket money, and without bothering to look inside, purchased the magic volume. It was a storehouse of visual knowledge and illustrated several hundred paintings which I eagerly investigated on the return journey by train. But no Jacopo del Sellaio. I was puzzled by his absence. *Venus Reclining*, now renamed *An Allegory*, is certainly in the national collection. Perhaps it was missing from the 1930 catalogue because in 1929 it had been de-attributed and assigned to 'Follower of Botticelli'. Perhaps it had been lying in limbo? At any rate, this was the first piece of 'looking up' I did instigated by the author of *The Cantos*, an early piece of research to be followed by others less frustrating – expeditions to see what the del Cossa frescoes looked like in the Palazzo Schifanoia, Ferrara; to Mantua to see 'Gonzaga his heirs and his concubines', first learned of from Canto XLV in the Sesame selection; to San Zeno in Verona to find that capital in the crypt signed *Adamo me fecit* according to the same Canto. Yes, Pound was the sort of poet who made you go and find out for yourself. What I found in the half light of the San Zeno crypt was that the full quotation ran:

> ADAMINUS.
> DESCO
> GEORG
> IO. ME
> FECI
> T.

Not so long after first looking into Pound, in the autumn of 1945 I went to Cambridge where a few of the mysteries might have been cleared up. Not a word. For all Cambridge knew, Pound might never have existed. There was, of course, the highly interesting and rather grudging section in Leavis's *New Bearings*, but nobody actually *spoke* of Pound. It was Eliot, among the modernists, who carried the day. It was Eliot you read. And with all the reading required to get through just a fragment of our immense literature, I lost sight of Pound, although the passages I have mentioned were growing radioactive under the black azure of the mind's lower depths.

It was not until the appearance of Hugh Kenner's *The Poetry of Ezra Pound* in 1951, a pioneering study that ventured out onto its limb in the middle of the Eliot era, that I got back to Pound and *really* (as it were) read him for the first time – read him, that is, *in extenso*, including the criticism, and even then it took a long time to sort it all out into anything resembling intelligibility. Kenner had quoted some key passages from the criticism – hard to come by, of course, until it was reissued in selection in 1954. I remember gratefully the following:

> 'Artists are the antennae of the race.' They are the registering instruments, and if they falsify their reports there is no measure to the harm that they do.

Or, again, on the function of literature in the State:

> It has to do with the clarity of 'any and every' thought and opinion. It has to do with maintaining the very cleanliness of the tools, the health of the very matter of thought itself. Save the rare and very limited instances of the plastic arts, or in mathematics, the individual cannot think or communicate his thought, the governor or legislator cannot act effectively or frame his laws, without words, and the solidarity of these words is in the care of the damned and despised literati. When their work goes rotten – by that I do not mean when they express indecorous thoughts – but when their very medium, the very essence of their work, the application of word to thing goes rotten, i.e., becomes slushy and inexact, or excessive or bloated, the whole machinery of social and individual thought and order goes to pot.

Kenner made it possible for one to at least dig into *The Cantos* at salient points and then venture on alone, sometimes to be turned back by the impenetrability of the poet.

In editing *The Oxford Book of Verse in English Translation*, I began reading Pound yet once more – and again for the first time! This first time was all of Pound's translations, though I'd read them in bits and pieces over the years. It became quite clear, as one covered the ground, that – if a choice had to be made among the great translators – Dryden and Pound came out at the top, for sheer variety and memorableness. Of course, Pope, whom Pound didn't much care for as a translator, runs pretty close, as the author of our greatest eighteenth-century poem, Pope's *Iliad*. Pope and Dryden opened, via translation, a serious dialogue with paganism – Dryden, in particular, as he ranged through Ovid, Lucretius and Virgil. Dryden's Venus, as she emerges from his translating activities with these poets, is as vibrant as Pound's Aphrodite in *The Cantos*. Now Greek and Latin, for Dryden and Pope, were seldom allowed to pull English off its familiar course as Chinese does for Pound. Serious as their dialogue with paganism was, at a linguistic level the pagans were thoroughly homogenized and Englished. Pound, on the other hand, right from *Cathay* to the late Confucian anthology, allows his original text to influence both verse form and word order. As I have suggested in the introduction to the Oxford book,

> [in translation the] writer is thrown up against a new scale of things, adding to his awareness of alternatives in literary expres-

sion, an awareness which carries over to his reader ... One hears English being drawn into a dialogue with other cultures, as when Pound in Canto LII, translating the Chinese Book of Rites, gives us in magnificent processional rhythms something English and something irreducibly foreign and distant.

What is striking about Pound's choice of text for translation here, is the way he lights on and makes available for us, a document where sacred rites are concerned with, not (say) the life after death, but the union of the sacred and the practical amid the seasonal changes of this world. I close with some extracts from Pound's sacramental year. The style in which they are presented is a summation of poetic qualities I had been groping my way towards understanding in that Sesame Books selection when I was eighteen years of age – an inevitability of ear; a perspective on the world through myth where myth does not become a woozy Jungian self-indulgence; and a compactness of utterance which yet reaches out beyond the individual voice and the time-bound instance:

> Know then:
>   Toward summer when the sun is in Hyades
> Sovran is Lord of the Fire
>   to this month are birds
> with bitter smell and with the odour of burning
> To the hearth god, lungs of the victim
>   The green frog lifts up his voice
>   and the white latex is in flower
> In red car with jewels incarnadine
>   to welcome the summer
> In this month no destruction
>   no tree shall be cut at this time
> Wild beasts are driven from field
>   in this month are simples gathered.
> The empress offers cocoons to the Son of Heaven
>   Then goes the sun into Gemini
> Virgo in mid heaven at sunset
>   indigo must not be cut
> No wood burnt into charcoal
>   gates are all open, no tax on the booths.
> Now mares go grazing,
>   tie up the stallions
> Post up the horsebreeding notices

>   Month of the longest days
> Life and death are now equal
>   Strife is between light and darkness
> Wise man stays in his house
>   Stag droppeth antlers
> Grasshopper is loud,
>   leave no fire open to southward ...

So it continues for another two pages, enriching a canto which begins with vituperation and anti-Semitism, Pound at his crudest and most doctrinaire. Whole passages have been blanked out in the 1950 edition of *Seventy Cantos*, presumably at the insistence of the publisher, perhaps of Eliot himself. Re-reading sections where the balance of the Cantos is askew, I have often found myself locating a litter of beautiful fragments previously hurried past in an effort to outpace the crudity of Pound's obsessions. The whole work ends or peters out with *Drafts and Fragments of Cantos CX–CXVII* and precisely with his own admission, 'that I lost my center fighting the world'. This happened earlier than he had been willing to admit, while trying to convince a petty tyrant of the relevance of his monetary theories to social harmony:

>   The dreams clash
>   and are shattered –
>   and that I tried to make a paradiso terrestre

The shattered paradise is still there in his own mind. Its presence on paper is what makes *Drafts and Fragments* such a moving close to a literary career.

Eliot, Pound and The Waste Land, *The Narrative of a Relationship*

Eliot and Pound: Eeeldrop and Appleplex (Eliot's name for them), Possum and Brer Rabbit (Pound's). Hence Pound's epistolary onset: 'Waal Possum, my fine ole Marse Supial', and Eliot's 'Caro lapino' – a Frenchified Italian noun you will not discover in the Cambridge Italian Dictionary. Eliot was both possum and parson to Pound, so that when Pound found little to like in *Old Possum's Book of Practical Cats*, he wrote: 'Sez the Maltese dawg to the Siam cat / Whaaar' zole Parson Possum at?' To the clerical Eliot, Pound wrote in the tones of God the father: 'Filio dilecto mihi'. Eliot was duly respectful, 'Ezzum Pound, Sir'. Pound was both respectful and teasing: 'Waal my able an sable ole Crepuscule'.

As Pound's publisher, Eliot could wear two masks at once, that of the Reverend Eliot and Mr Faber-and-Faber: 'In virtue of the authority given to me as a Director of this firm, I give you my blessing for 1934, expiring on December 31st.' When Pound began to wander into fascism, Eliot was able to convey tender and earnest concern through this tone of banter which Pound had set going in their correspondence: 'Rabbit I don't much mind what you do as long as you don't go involve yourself with that Mosley / that is only a place fit for Bad rabbits.' But Pound was not to take advice from the friend he addressed as 'Eminent Udder'.

I suppose the only other correspondent of Eliot's who attempted such a jokey style with the poet was Groucho Marx, Eliot's 'most coveted pin-up', as he said. Groucho, when Eliot and he exchanged photographs, wrote to him: 'I had no idea you were so handsome. Why you haven't been offered the lead in some sexy movies I can only attribute to the stupidity of the casting directors.'

But Pound's *own* epistolary high-jinks were serious. In the 'ole Crepuscule' letter, he was trying to get out of Eliot an essay on drama and he wanted it in a less guarded style than he felt Eliot was prone to: 'It needn't be *long*, as I know you're lazy. But also it needn't be in that keerful Criterese which so successfully protekks you in the stinking and foggy climik again the bare-boreians ...'

As Eliot said of him: 'He would cajole, and almost coerce, other men into writing well: so that he often presents the appearance of a man trying to convey to a very deaf person that the house is on fire ... He has always been, first and foremost, a teacher and a campaigner.' It was the campaigner for Eliot's release from Lloyd's bank who wrote to the majestic Amy Lowell (she having refused to contribute to Pound's fund): 'Aww shucks! dearie, ain't you the hell-roarer, ain't you the kuss.' The campaigner also speaks when he asks her elsewhere: 'Before it is too late, do you wish to repent and be saved?' With comparable verve, he took H.G. Wells to task for implying that Italy was one of the backward nations. This is Pound the teacher, rather than Pound the campaigner, selecting what he called the radiant gist – though whether this gist quite proves what he meant to teach is another matter: 'I have also seen two females in combat in Kensington back street with admiring throng of refeen'd lower clawrs henglish and a comic male (about your build) telling one of 'em, the winner, "You 'adn't orter strike a wumman."'

Pound's letter style is catching. Eliot caught it in his replies and (at least once) in the tone of his criticism – in the essay on 'Ezra Pound: his metric and poetry.' Pound felt that Eliot's 'epistolatory', as he called it, revealed another man: 'Eliot was constantly ALIVE in private letters, at least to me', he says. He had doubts about Eliot's more public persona. 'Why do you think I baptised him?' he inquired of Charles Olson and replied to his own question: 'The possum: ability to appear dead while it is still alive.' Pound felt, no doubt unfairly, that Eliot's review *The Criterion* represented the deader side of Eliot: 'KIYRypes!!! I keep on readin at this Morterarium ...'

When Eliot asked Pound to write an article for *The Criterion* on – of all people – Robert Bridges, Pound wondered, after much resistance, if he mightn't do something on (say) Bridges' relations with Hopkins 'for an article that wdn't be as *dull* ... as merely trying to yatter about wot he wrote.' He posted this, then next day dashed off another to Eliot: 'NO!! my dear Sathanas: On reflection I see that it wd be whoredom, and not even en grande cocotte ... I did not instantly expect to find the EVIL one lurking under yr weskit. But so was it.'

Years before, Pound had recognized Eliot's talent from a first look at the manuscript of *Prufrock*. He specified the terms of their relationship (according to Hugh Kenner) as follows: 'You let me throw the brick through the front window. You go in at the back door and take the swag.'

Pound's role as activist on Eliot's behalf took the form of getting his poems published, offering to put up the money himself for a first book, inventing a scheme of financial contributions that aimed at buying Eliot's freedom to create, taking the pen out of Eliot's hand and – not rewriting his poems exactly – but, as Eliot explained, by some extraordinary combination of ear, intuition and intelligence, making Eliot aware of what it was *he* wanted to say. The first extensive collaboration that we have evidence of is the restructuring of Eliot's 'Whispers of Immortality'. Pound slashed and recast and Eliot followed his lead. Pound is brisk in his suggestions: 'Omitting fourth stanza of the present Nth variant ... wash the whole with virol and leave in hypo. At any rate, I think this would bring us nearer the desired epithalamium of force, clearness and bewtie.'

'Force, clearness and bewtie' were what Pound helped bring to that mass of materials which, late in the day, came to be called *The Waste Land*. The rediscovery, then publication of *The Waste Land* manuscript, practically fifty years after it had gone astray, point to Pound's decisive role. Dryden had reworked the verse of younger colleagues. Pope had helped old Wycherley. Johnson wrote the last four lines of Goldsmith's *Deserted Village* and the last nine lines of his *Traveller*. We have no documentary evidence of anything in the whole history of poetry on the scale of Pound's interventions in *The Waste Land*. As he triumphantly wrote to Eliot, bursting into verse:

> *Sage Homme*
>
> These are the poems of Eliot
> By the Uranian Muse begot;
> A Man their Mother was,
> A Muse their Sire.
>
> How did the printed Infancies result
> From Nuptials thus doubly difficult?
>
> If you must needs enquire
> Know diligent Reader
> That on each Occasion
> Ezra performed the Caesarean Operation.

... It is after all a grrrreat liiiterary period.

Eliot speaks of the 'sprawling chaotic poem' 'which left his [Pound's] hands reduced to about half its size, in the form in which it appears in print'. There were the wholesale slashings: the first fifty-four lines – a night on the town led by a name-sake 'old Tom' – is crossed out in Eliot's hand, conceivably prompted by Pound. Pound gets indubitably to work on the seventeen quatrains written in the heroic stanza of Dryden's *Annus Mirabilis* (Eliot had just reviewed Mark Van Doren's *The Poetry of John Dryden* and seems to have 'caught' the stanza form from there). These seventeen stanzas are peppered with Pound's suggestions and crossed through with his excisions, and are finally compacted into the episode of Tiresias, the typist and the house agent's clerk with Dryden left far behind. A 69-line imitation of Pope's *Rape of the Lock* disappears. Eliot records of this: 'Pound once induced me to destroy what I thought an excellent set of couplets; for, said he, "Pope has done this so well that you cannot do it better; and if you mean this as a burlesque, you had better suppress it, for you cannot parody Pope unless you can write better verse than Pope – and you can't" …' 'Death by Water' – namely the ten lines on Phlebas the Phoenician – had formerly been an episode of 92 lines before Pound got at it. Eliot, somewhat dejected, suggested that Phlebas himself ought, perhaps, to go too. And, as so much of the poem had disappeared, 'Do you advise,' he wrote to Pound, 'printing "Gerontion" as a prelude …?' Pound's reply: 'I do *not* advise printing "Gerontion" as preface … I DO advise keeping Phlebas. In fact I more'n advise. Phlebas is an integral part of the poem; the card pack introduces him, the drowned phoen. sailor. And he is needed ABsolootly where he is. Must stay in.'

Once he'd arrived at what is now entitled 'What the Thunder Said' Pound stayed his hand and wrote at the top of this the final section, 'OK from here on *I think*'. Among the many minute particulars incorporated by Eliot into his text, one notes that the cock, which speaks French (Co co rico!), was shorn of its adjective, 'black', by Pound. 'Too penty' he'd written at one point. Or was it 'too purty'? Mrs Eliot, editing the drafts, flew to Venice to inquire of Pound. 'Penty', he affirmed. Mrs Eliot asked him to write down 'penty' and 'purty'. 'Penty' tallied perfectly with the marginal annotation. And it means? Too much like a pentameter line. Here Pound was surely off the mark – as he sometimes was – and Eliot – as he frequently did – dug in his heels and we still have the incomparable line about the nightingale: 'Filled all the desert with inviolable voice'. Sometimes things worked the other way round and Pound actually restrained

Eliot from cutting: 'OK, ... STET, ...Type out this *anyhow*'.

And so we arrive at Pound's triumphant letter:

'The thing now runs from "April ..." to "shantih" without a break. That is 19 pages, and let us say the longest poem in the English langwidge. Don't try to bust all records by prolonging it three pages further ...Complimenti, you bitch. I am wracked by the seven jealousies ...' Eliot wanted to use Pound's squib 'Sage Homme', plus one other, as epigraphs. Pound dissuaded him. When, a little later on, Pound began a new canto with: 'These fragments you have shelved (shored)' with its glance at Eliot's 'These fragments I have shored against my ruins', Eliot was growing cautious: 'I object strongly on tactical grounds to yr. 1st line. People are inclined to think that we write our verses in collaboration as it is, or else that you write mine and I write yours.'

Though Eliot sought Pound's advice about 'The Hollow Men', the great phase of collaboration was over, signalled by that famous dedication to *The Waste Land*: 'For Ezra Pound il miglior fabbro' – the compliment from *Purgatorio* to Arnaut Daniel: 'Fu miglior fabbro del parlar materno' – 'He was the best craftsman of the mother tongue'. And so ended a chapter of literary history.

After Eliot's death, the 81-year-old Pound was approached by *The Sewanee Review* for a memorial of his friend. He wrote:

> His was the true Dantescan voice – not honoured enough and deserving more than I ever gave him.
>
> I had hoped to see him in Venice this year for the Dante commemoration at the Giorgio Cini Foundation – instead: Westminster Abbey. But later, on his own hearth, a flame tended, a presence felt.
>
> Recollections? let some thesis writer have the satisfaction of 'discovering' whether it was in 1920 or '21 that I went from Excideuil to meet a rucksacked Eliot. Days of walking – conversation? literary? ... Who is there now for me to share a joke with?
>
> Am I to write 'about' the poet Thomas Stearns Eliot? or my friend 'the Possum'? Let him rest in peace. I can only repeat, but with the urgency of 50 years ago: READ HIM.

'On his own hearth, a flame tended.' The tender of the flame was Valerie Eliot. Let hers be the final word – from the acknowledgements to her splendid edition of *The Waste Land* drafts and fragments: 'It is a pleasure to thank Mr. Ezra Pound, "a wondrous necessary man" to my husband ...'.

Reading The Waste Land

'Read with your ears', said Gerard Manley Hopkins to his friend Robert Bridges, trying to persuade the latter, the Poet Laureate-to-be, that Hopkins's poetry, once you could *hear* it, was not unintelligible. Bridges had read Hopkins's 'Wreck of the Deutschland', and responded to that by saying he had no wish to do so a second time. So perhaps he never heard that poem? Can we hear Eliot's *The Waste Land*? Our case is rather different from Bridges'. So much has been written about *The Waste Land* that we can't get at the poem's acoustics for all the commentaries. If you're just starting on Eliot, you may find that commentaries are already being thrust at you, or that, nervous, you rush for enlightenment to those famous notes at the end of the poem, only to be disappointed.

One shouldn't try to clear up *The Waste Land* too soon. Obviously, you might want to know who Tristan and Isolde were. But even if you don't know what *Bin gar keine Russin, stamm' aus Litauen, echt deutsch* means – and you're sure to find out, sooner or later – its very unintelligibility on a first reading is part of the poem's drama. This is a poem that, like the rapid cutting in some films, only releases its larger meanings as you re-experience it, as you hear it again. A lot of Eliot's poetry deals with protagonists who find it difficult, like Prufrock and Gerontion, to say just what they mean. One needs to be patient with them and with the poems in which they appear, as they try to spit out the butt-ends of their days and ways. In fact, the very spitting out is again part of the poetry's drama, if our ears attend to it sharply enough. If we *hear The Waste Land*, putting aside for the moment the hunting down of all literary allusions, the difficulties of speaking out and thus making things meaningful become the very heart of the drama. The pace of *The Waste Land* is all the time giving us a dimension of the poem's meanings. It's a poem that keeps hesitating between stasis and release, that keeps feeling about for ways out of a dead end, that will suddenly break free, only to be cornered once more, and that finally ends up in mid-air, as it were, wanting to earn the peace of the Sanskrit blessing with which it closes, even reaching out *towards* that peace across the silence at the end.

This is a poem full of silences, stretches of blank paper. At times the silences express – and this is something we hear too – the frustration. At other times they intimate the sort of wordlessness that could be rich with meaning – 'Looking into the heart of light, the silence'. I've said that this is a poem that keeps hesitating between stasis and release, and sometimes things work the other way round, of course. Frequently the poem's movement seems psychologically clogged, and an intelligent reading can bring this out, without being exaggeratedly actorish about it. Take the opening. The rhythmic character of the poem declares itself in the very first word – 'April is the cruellest month'. April – not January, February or March. And in distinguishing the name of the month, a reader, to some extent, brings out that word, which, as one goes from its heavy first syllable, trailing away on its second, enforces a rhetorical pause before moving forward. 'April is the cruellest month, breeding…' One is at the line's end, with another two-syllable word, 'breeding' – going from heavy to light – and after this, the line's end itself as the meaning continues over, it seems to enforce a breath-pause: 'breeding / *Li*lacs'. There's something almost unwilling about that 'breeding'. Then one notices that the following lines mostly end similarly on present participles – 'mixing', 'stirring', 'covering', 'feeding'. If, of course, a reader tried to mark all these pauses with an equally heavy unwillingness, the effect would be monotonous. Our intelligence informs us that what all these present participles add up to is a curious amalgam of energies that want to go, and yet the words falling at the end of lines on a weak accent are also being retarded. These participles carry on the effect of that first word, 'April', with its reined-back promise – 'the cruellest month'. An alert reading has to decide on the degree of retardation the voice must make.

That hesitation between movement and stasis, between words and silence, gets many unexpected variations throughout this poem, which is a poem of many voices. There's that curious phrase in 'A Game of Chess', about the woman's hair that 'under the brush, spread into fiery points, / Glowed into words, then would be savagely still'. The first glowing into words of the poem that belongs to a recognizable voice is that of Marie, after the opening passage about the seasons. Marie is excited and vivacious, but she too retreats into a routine that suggests unspoken insecurities: 'I read, much of the night, and go south in the winter'. A space of blank paper blots out her voice, and the voice that follows hers sounds like that of a biblical prophet. It even uses a phrase, 'Son of man', that God addresses to the prophet Ezekiel. This alternation of voices was indicated in Eliot's rejected title for the opening section of the poem: 'He do the Police in Different Voices'. This early title was culled from Dickens' *Our Mutual Friend*, where old Betty Higden tells us about her adopted foundling, Sloppy. 'I do love a newspaper. You mightn't think it, but Sloppy is a beautiful reader of a newspaper. He do the Police in different voices.' If, like Sloppy, we read it aloud, *The Waste Land* compels us to do it in different voices. They are the voices of Marie, of the hyacinth girl and the man who addresses her, the neurotic woman who demands of another man that he 'Speak' to her. There are Tiresias, the two women in the pub scene, the voice of Madam Sosostris, to name only a few. Rendering them requires tact. I like Alec Guinness's Madam Sosostris, a preposterous and overblown fake. But he's less successful with Marie, I think, whom he makes speak with a heavy Austrian accent and call a sled a 'schled'. Curiously enough, Madam Sosostris, for whom Eliot indicates a *foreign* accent ('Tell her I bring the horoscope myself') Guinness renders in straightforward English, though very plausibly. Eliot is sparing with any phonetic indications, but surely the pub scene must be done in Cockney. Guinness opts for a curious sort of Loamshire. Eliot's own reading is chary of performing in demotic English of any sort.

Eliot's reading of *The Waste Land*, as of his other poems from 'Prufrock' to *Four Quartets* may sound monotonous to some ears, but it is at any rate chaste, not busily interpreting every nuance by heavily underlining. It deliberately avoids the histrionic. The only reading I know by Eliot that ventures to impersonate voices is the one he did of 'Sweeney Agonistes'. It seems curious, perhaps, that this poet who always admired Elizabethan and Jacobean drama, who wanted to write plays himself, and had some success in doing so, should have gone for a very neutral rendering of a poem like *The Waste Land*. Initially, it was a poem conceived, of course, on the page, and there are many typographical effects, of spacing, for example, that immediately catch the eye and affect one's silent reading of the text, yet would be lost when read aloud. In the pausing sort of reading one gives to a poem, when one reads it by eye, there are ambiguities of stress and intonation that reading aloud often simplifies. On the other hand, an intelligent oral rendering of the poem – clearly, 'performance' would be the wrong word – fulfils a basic human impulse, to murmur almost any poem aloud as we read it, to feel out its shapes on the tongue and to inform one's browsing mind with some sense of its overall shape when heard.

I began by mentioning Hopkins. Eliot's impersonality in *The Waste Land*, his almost numbed sense of himself, is clearly very different from the rhapsodic orchestration of parts of 'The Wreck of the Deutschland' where word-patterns are delightedly offered to the ear, sentences swayed this way and that like the rhythms of some great baroque church made audible. Obviously, you could never read Eliot as you would read Hopkins. As I've said, one's reading requires tact and not heavyweight acting. One needs to bring out, however, that the poem has a soundscape, going through all those different human voices to the mythical singing of the Rhinemaidens, 'Weilala leia', to all those bird sounds that suggest everything between mere noise and myth once more, the transformation of Philomela who has had her tongue cut out, into a nightingale that can sing.

The poem itself wants to get from inarticulateness and frustration to wholeness and song. But it knows that it must pass through fragmentation in the attempt to arrive there. So, along the way are all those snatches of other people's lives, other people's voices, and these bird-cries that perhaps have some sort of meaning, if only one could hear it, or are merely an echo of our own desperate gibberish. 'Twit twit twit / Jug jug jug jug jug jug'. 'Drip drop drip drop drop drop drop'. 'Co co rico co co rico'. Eliot as a small boy was a devoted birdwatcher, and all through his work birdsong is often used to suggest a frontier between ordinary reality and the visionary. Was ever any poem so full of bird noises as *The Waste Land*? At the very end a voice from Roman culture asks, 'When shall I be like the swallow?' ('Quando fiam uti chelidon?') The cataract of quotations, of which this is one, that closes the poem, confronts the ear with sounds in an assortment of languages. Although these are expressive of fragmentation and the desire to overcome it, the fragments themselves contain worlds of meaning, once we can listen beyond the mere noise they make. Despite the crisis at the centre of all this, these sounds from the Tower of Babel are strangely enjoyable, are thrilling both to say and hear. Art is like that. It permits us to confront alienation and disunity, and metamorphose them into a curious rejoicing. We rejoice partly in the artist's ability to so order things, or to hold them in such powerful *dis*order as at the climax of *The Waste Land*.

This climax, commandingly oral, bids the ear to attend, right from the terrifying voice of the thunder: 'DA'. DA is one of the most primitive sounds a human voice can make. And yet, at the same time, we know it means 'Give', an act that can begin to reconstitute our wholeness as we forget ourselves in giving. We need to hear the primitive directness of DA, and the way it echoes on and around those literary fragments at the close that are fragments of the European mind. It's as though the thunder-clap, the root word DA, as it grows into the command 'Datta', then 'Dahaydvam', ('Sympathize') and 'Damyata' ('Control'), is being brought to bear on the task of knitting up once more what is fragmentary. 'DA' – if we became aware of its true meaning – could put us into control once more.

What is significant about the final words of *The Waste Land* is that none of the words in the European heritage or in the Christian tradition could bring alive, within the poet's imagination, the peace he wants to find: 'Shantih shantih shantih'. Perhaps our own initial dumbfounding by these words – how, one asks, should one begin to pronounce them even? – tells us more than Eliot's note. When the poem was first published, he cautioned us that '"The peace which passeth understanding" is a feeble translation of the content of "Shantih"'. Later editions, when presumably Eliot the Christian was trying to square what he had once said with what he now believed, inform us that '"The peace which passeth understanding" is our equivalent to this word'. Both these statements cannot be true. So perhaps the sound we hear, or that at first we don't know how to say, and which literally passeth understanding, conveys to us more than Eliot's note.

By and large, I'm grateful for his notes to the poem. They tell us where to go. Eliot has nothing snobbishly to hide. Indeed, he gives us reading matter for years to come, and listening matter too if we follow up his references to Wagner. Notes and commentators only become a problem if we let them overpower the acoustic dimension of the poem itself, a dimension that comes from the different voices, the different languages, the bird-calls. We have to re-learn our primary innocence as we read the poem again and again. Perhaps one of the advantages of hearing it read by someone else is that we must surrender ourselves to its pace and progress, not questioning overmuch, but relishing the clash and strangeness as it builds up to the mighty climax, beginning with DA, at once primitive and at the root of great complexities.

Williams's Thousand Freshets

It was Ezra Pound, that indefatigable discoverer of talent, who first seized on the essential elements in Williams's poetry. Introducing Williams's second, still tentative, volume, *The Tempers*, in 1913, Pound quoted one of Williams's similes where he speaks of a thousand freshets:

> ...crowded
> Like peasants to a fair
> Clear skinned, wild from seclusion.

Pound has instinctively isolated here elements thoroughly characteristic of this poet's entire venture – poetic energy imagined as the rush of water; not so much Wordsworth's 'spontaneous overflow of powerful feelings', but feelings 'crowded', forcing and yet constrained by their own earth-bound track; a certain rustic uncouthness whose end is a celebration and which wears the stamp of locality. 'The only universal', as Williams was to say later, 'is the local as savages, artists and – to a lesser extent – peasants know.'

The most interesting of Williams's early volumes, *Al Que Quiere!*, appeared in 1917, the same year as T.S. Eliot's *Prufrock and Other Observations*. Pound was there to salute the arrival of both volumes and to differentiate them:

> Distinct and as different as possible from the orderly statements of an Eliot ... are the poems of Carlos Williams. If the sinuosities of Misses Moore and Loy are difficult to follow I do not know what is to be said for Mr Williams's ramifications and abruptnesses. I do not pretend to follow all of his volts, jerks, sulks, balks, outblurts and jump-overs; but for all this roughness there remains with me the conviction that there is nothing meaningless in his book, *Al que Quiere*, not a line...

Perhaps Pound overstates the 'roughness' of Williams, but, in pointing out the 'jerks, balks, outblurts and jump-overs', he has arrived at one of the earliest and most accurate formulations of what

Williams's verse was about. Not only is 'locality' (a sticking to New Jersey when Pound and Eliot had chosen European exile) the geographic source of Williams's poetry, but 'locality', seen as the jerks and outblurts of speech rendered on to the here and now of the page, is the source of his lineation. In the imaginative play of Williams's poems, where the attention is frequently turned upon outward things, the sound structure of the poems which embody that attention is an expression of strains, breath pauses, bodily constrictions and releases. Thus Williams's 'locality' begins with a somatic awareness, a physiological presence in time and space, and this in quite early poems. When he starts on his longest poem, *Paterson*, in the mid-1940s, it is the remembrance of the act of walking through a given terrain which propels some of its best stretches, the gerund 'walking' itself used as a repeated motif and, at one point, checked against the descriptions of an article, 'Dynamic Posture', from *Journal of the American Medical Association*: 'The body is tilted slightly forward from the basic standing position and the weight thrown on the ball of the foot, while the other thigh is lifted and the leg and opposite arm are swung forward (fig. 6B) ...' A sentence from later on in this article (quoted by M. Weaver in his *William Carlos Williams, The American Background*) would doubtless have appealed to Williams in his identification of poet and walker: 'The good walker should be able to change pace, stop, start, turn, step up or down, twist or stoop, easily and quickly, without losing balance or rhythm...' The Williams poem finds analogies for most of these movements.

The relation between subject and object appears in Williams in a series of images of physical strain – a poem from *Al Que Quiere!*, 'Spring Strains' feels out its own balks and resistances against those of the scene outside where the swift flight of two birds is challenged, as:

> the blinding and red-edged sun-blur –
> creeping energy, concentrated
> counterforce – welds sky, buds, trees,
> rivets them in one puckering hold!

At the close, the birds exert their own counterforce of speed and lightness, breaking out of the riveted landscape

> flung outward and up – disappearing suddenly!

– the poem imparting a verb-like force to its combined prepositions, 'outward and up', and ending, as so often in Williams, on a dangling clause that pulls the main clause towards incompletion and asymmetry.

This predilection for the open-ended and asymmetrical leaves Williams free to accept the suggestion of his surroundings with their evidence of overlap and relativity –

> roof out of line with sides
> the yards cluttered
> with old chicken wire, ashes,
> furniture gone wrong;
> the fences and outhouses
> built of barrel-staves
> and parts of boxes...

Instead of wishing simply to reform the poor ('It's the anarchy of poverty / delights me...'), he senses there is a point where the imagination, partaking of this anarchy, could dance with it, could 'lift' it to an answering form, but a form fully responsive to the waywardness and inconclusiveness of daily realities. The broken fringes of the city in 'Morning' witness a sort of heroism among 'diminished things', humorously absurd:

> And a church spire sketched on the sky,
> of sheet-metal and open beams, to resemble
> a church spire...

Williams hears in all this, and in the profusion of natural fact, a kind of music – 'a vague melody / of harsh threads', as he says in 'Trees' where the tree which first catches his eye is 'crooked', 'bent...from straining / against the bitter horizontals of / a north wind', the jump-overs at the line breaks enacting the pressure of that straining. There is no romantic fusion of subject and object possible in this nature poem: the voices of the trees may be 'blent willingly / against the heaving contra-bass / of the dark' but the contra-bass remains contra, the crooked tree warps itself 'passionately to one side' and the poem still presses forward as Williams adds 'in [its] eagerness', the poem like the tree dissociating itself from a blent music for that 'melody / of harsh threads'. 'Bent' puns and rhymes eagerly against 'blent' in this piece.

When Williams in his turn paid tribute to Pound, he saw the poet – himself and Pound included – as seeking a language which 'will embody all the advantageous jumps, swiftnesses, colours, movements of the day...' He was praising the collage elements in the poetry of Pound's *A Draft of XXX Cantos*, but the terms of his praise ignore those other elements of archaism and of the *musée imaginaire* that Williams distrusted in his friend. Both Pound and Eliot, or so Williams felt, had lost contact – it was a word whose meaning he was to go on exploring – with their American roots: they had sold out to Europe that American renaissance of which Pound himself had spoken, one which he had prophesied would 'overshadow the quattrocento'. It was an old story, for the trend of the American mind 'back to Europe' had grown in its appeal in nineteenth-century America. Williams, who feels the pull himself in his first novel, *A Voyage to Pagany*, reflected towards the end of his life:

> The novels of Henry James featured this seeking of Europe by the heiresses of America. He himself, for complex reasons...fled to the assurances of Victorian England. It was understandable, it was even admirable in him. He became a distinguished citizen in the republic of letters and a great artist. But he left another world behind. He abandoned it.

Williams's poetry and novels explore an America his two most powerful contemporaries also left behind, in the raw merging of American pastoral and urban squalor. He described his struggle to make articulate that world, in *Paterson*, as 'a reply to Greek and Latin with the bare hands'. Williams exaggerates, of course, and as he himself well knew his insistence on 'contact' and 'locality' needed for its completion an awareness that was also European – the kind of awareness he recognized immediately in the reproduction of a painting by Juan Gris, with its cubist sharpness, its almost fastidious handling of a world of broken forms. 'Contact' had been Whitman's word: 'I am mad for it to be in contact with me,' says Whitman of nature in *Song of Myself*. So is Williams. The difference lies in the *eruditus* of that *tactus eruditus* he speaks of in one poem. 'A fact with him', says Kenneth Burke, 'finds its justification in the trimness of the wording.' Whitman is a great poet, but he is never trim. Trimness was something Williams could recognize and applaud in Juan Gris's 'admirable simplicity and excellent design'.

When he speaks in the prose parts of *Spring and All* (1923) of Whitman, the company he puts him into is that of two great Europeans, Gris and Cézanne, announcing that 'Whitman's proposals are of the same piece with the modern trend toward imaginative understanding of life'. At this point, the imagination for

Williams was identified with the cubist re-structuring of reality: modern poetry with its ellipses, it confrontation of disparates, its use of verbal collages – a device both Pound and Eliot had used – provided direct analogies. In *Spring and All*, after a rapid transition from Gris, Cézanne and Whitman to Shakespeare, Williams tells us of the last named: 'He holds no mirror up to nature but with his imagination rivals nature's composition with his own.' Shakespeare, too, could be made to belong to the moment of cubism. This seems a far cry from 'a reply to Greek and Latin with the bare hands'.

Kenneth Rexroth, in an excellent and too little known essay, 'The Influence of French Poetry on American' (reprinted in the Penguin critical anthology, *William Carlos Williams*, edited by the present writer) has commented on Williams's cubist allegiances and expresses the relation between these and Williams's stress on localism – 'place' and 'contact' – with great perspicacity:

> Williams could be said to belong in the Cubist tradition – Imagism, Objectivism, the dissociation and rearrangement of the elements of concrete reality, rather than rhetoric or free association. But where Reverdy, Apollinaire, Salmon, Cendrars, Cocteau and Jacob are all urban, even megalopolitan, poets of that Paris which is the international market of objects of *vertu*, vice, and art, Williams has confined himself in single strictness to the life before his eyes – the life of a physician in a small town twenty miles from New York. In so doing, his localism has become international and timeless. His long quest for a completely defenseless simplicity of personal speech produces an idiom identical with that which is the end product of centuries of polish, refinement, tradition and revolution.

On the face of it, the inheritance Williams brings to cubism seems to be very close in spirit not only to Whitman but also to Emerson and Thoreau. If 'contact' is re-explored, so is Emerson's attachment to the vernacular: 'the speech of Polish mothers' was where Williams insisted he got his English from. 'Colleges and books only copy the language which the field and work-yard made,' said Emerson. Williams's famous 'flatness' comes not from the field, but from the urban 'work-yard' of New Jersey. As Hugh Kenner writes of Williams's characteristic diction: 'That words set in Jersey speech rhythm mean less but mean it with greater finality, is Williams's great technical perception.'

Emerson seems to have prepared the ground for Williams's other war-cry, 'No ideas but in things' with his 'Ask the fact for the form'. Thoreau sounds yet closer with: 'The roots of letters are things.' Again Emerson tells over things – 'The meal in the firkin; the milk in the pan; the ballad in the street; the news of the boat...' – in the shape of a list very like Williams's 'rigmaroles', as he calls his poems. 'Bare lists of words,' says Emerson, 'are found suggestive to an imaginative mind.' When Williams, long after Emerson and after Whitman's application of this, constructed 'list' poems, he came in for suspicion, as in the interview which he prints as part of *Paterson 5* and in which, defending what amounts to a grocery list that forms the jagged pattern of one of his later poems, he concludes: 'Anything is good material for poetry. Anything. I've said it time and time again.'

Paterson 5 came out in 1958. Years before, Williams had formulated his kind of poem made out of anything and with a jagged pattern, in the 1920 preface to *Kora in Hell*, when he wrote that a poem is 'tough by no quality it borrows from a logical recital of events nor from the events themselves but solely from the attenuated power which draws perhaps many broken things into a dance by giving them thus a full being'. He was often to return to the idea of poem as dance. If as with Emerson, Williams seems to 'ask the fact for the form', the form, once it comes, is free of the fact, is a *dance above* the fact. After *Kora in Hell* he had another shot at the formula in the prose of *Spring and All*, where he concludes of John of Gaunt's speech in *Richard II* that 'his words are related not to their sense as objects adherent to his son's welfare or otherwise, but as a dance over the body of his condition accurately accompanying it'.

J. Hillis Miller in his book *Poets of Reality* has argued that Williams marks an historic moment for modern poetry in that his work sees the disappearance of all dualism. If it is not from dualism it is yet from a duality that much of the interest of his work arises; the words 'accurately accompany' a perception of the forms of reality, they dance over or with these forms, but it is the gap between words and forms that gives poetry its chance to exist and to go on existing. Williams's most truncated and Zen-like expression of this fact comes in the tiny

> so much depends
> upon
>
> a red wheel
> barrow

> glazed with rain
> water
>
> beside the white
> chickens

What depends on the red wheelbarrow for Williams is the fact that its presence can be rendered over into words, that the perception can be slowed down and meditated on by regulating, line by line, the gradual appearance of these words. The imagination 'accurately accompanies' the wheelbarrow, or whatever facets of reality attract Williams, by not permitting too ready and emotional a fusion with them. When things go badly the imagination retreats into a subjective anguish –

> to an empty, windswept place
> without sun, stars or moon
> but a peculiar light as of thought
> that spins a dark fire –
> whirling upon itself... ('These')

But when the dance with facts suffices, syntax, the forms of grammar, puns, the ambiguous pull between words unpunctuated or divided by line-endings, these all contribute to – accompany – the richness of a reality one can never completely fuse with, but which affords a resistance whereby the I can know itself.

One has in Williams's best verse a vivid sense of what Olson calls 'the elements and minims of language', down to the syllabic components or 'the diphthong/ae' ('To Have Done Nothing'). It is this drama of elements, played across the ends of frequently short lines, which gives to Williams's 'free verse' its cohesiveness, and intensifies what Olson calls

> The contingent motion of
>   each line as it
>   moves with – or against –
>   the whole – working
>   particularly out of its immediacy.

Williams insisted that he did not write free verse, of course. As early as 1913 he was saying: 'I do not believe in *vers libre*, this contradiction in terms. Either the motion continues or it does not continue, either there is rhythm or no rhythm.' In the same essay ('Speech Rhythm', quoted by Weaver, pp. 82-3), Williams writes that, in an

Odyssey, 'rightly considered', 'no part in its excellence but partakes of the essential nature of the whole':

> This is the conception of the action that I want. In the other direction, inward: Imagination creates an image, point by point, piece by piece, segment by segment – into a whole, living. But each part as it plays into its neighbour, each segment into its neighbour segment and every part into every other, causing the whole – exists naturally in rhythm, and as there are waves there are tides and as there are ridges in the sand there are bars after bars...

This intuitive conception of the kind of poetic writing he sought gets closer to essentials than Williams's later and self-defeating attempts to define the 'variable foot', that 'relative measure' which ends by being what Williams said *vers libre* was, a contradiction in terms. It is 'the contingent motion of / each line' and what Robert Creeley has referred to as the 'contentual emphases' of each line that give life to Williams's verse, rather than any prosodic notion of feet. These emphases are brought to bear most consistently perhaps in relatively short poems. *Paterson* has its incidental finenesses, but there are stretches when one feels, as in others of the more lengthy pieces, that the dance has broken down. At the same time, some of the longer poems, unachieved as a whole, frequently contain passages of great brilliance. Yvor Winters is reminded by Williams of the brevity of a Herrick, which is to narrow Williams's range somewhat unduly; after all, he is capable of the extended range of poems like 'The Crimson Cyclamen' and 'Elena'. The shorter poems are certainly more proof against the meditative self-regard which elsewhere often makes for sentimental proliferation. Even a poem initially as fine as 'The Orchestra' runs aground on the most banal professions of innocence.

Williams may not have been capable of the unity of *The Waste Land*, but, as Octavio Paz insists, introducing his translations of Williams in *Veinte Poemas*, 'The greatness of a poet is not to be measured by the scale but by the intensity and the perfection of his works. Also by his vivacity. Williams is the author of the most *vivid* poems of modern American poetry.' And the vivacity arises, one might add, from the unexpectedness of Williams's apparently wayward forms. How, for example, in 'Raindrops on a Briar', did one get from the opening statement to those water-drops 'ranged upon the arching stems / irregularly as an accompaniment', and yet wasn't that devious track the poem's most exact way of saying what it had to and by a superb use of form?

Williams's attitude to form rather resembles his attitude to friendship, which should be, he says, 'dangerous – uncertain – made of many questionable crossties, I think, that might fail it. But while they last, give it a good cellular structure – paths, private connections between the members – full of versatility.' This passage comes from Williams's *Autobiography* – Chapter 49, 'Friendship'. In Chapter 50, 'Projective Verse', it is silently transfigured into an ideal of artistic form, and this ideal is seen as part and parcel of Williams's conception of locality. Chapter 50 is, in many ways, pivotal to the book, for, in using Charles Olson's conception of 'composition by field', Williams does so – and very tactfully – against an implied background of why his forms were not readily understood in his own country or ours, why 'The Criterion had no place for me', why Eliot's *The Waste Land* had seemed to him 'the great catastrophe to our letters…Eliot had turned his back on the possibility of reviving my world'. That world seemed to Williams to receive its recognition in Olson's 'Projective Verse' essay, with its preference for an explorative, syllable-based verse and its invitation 'to step back here to this place of the elements and minims of language…to engage speech where it is least careless – and least logical'. In Chapter 50 Williams juxtaposes 'this place of elements' with an *actual* place – and the leap is beautifully justified in the chapter as a whole – with the painter Charles Sheeler taking over a small stone house on a ravaged New York estate and making of it 'a cell, a seed of intelligence and feeling security'. 'The poem,' says Williams, 'is our objective, the secret at the heart of the matter – as Sheeler's small house, re-organised, is the heart of the gone estate of the Lowes…' Sheeler and his Russian wife and what they do with the local conditions are vibrant with meaning for Williams as a poet, and the form of the chapter lays bare that meaning: 'It is ourselves we organise in this way not against the past or for the future or even for survival but for integrity of understanding to insure persistence, to give the mind its stay.' Coming, as it does, in the last lap of the book, this makes a fine conscious formulation for the many years of groping with potentials of language and it balances four-square in the American locality a mind that had gone back to it armed – despite Williams's frequent protests – by Europe. The figures who stand out in those autobiographical pages are Joyce and Brancusi as well as Sheeler and Demuth: Paris counterpoints Rutherford and New York.

Of all the American modernists Williams was the most tardy in receiving recognition. His writing lifetime was dominated by the literary criteria of T.S. Eliot and the New Criticism, in neither of whose terminology was there a place for the kind of thing Williams was concerned with doing. Parker Tyler imagines Williams explaining why T.S. Eliot's theory of the objective correlative was not for him and where its shortcomings lay: 'My theory of poetry was that it arises from immediate environment, and in the case of *my* environment, America, the poetic formulas for familiar (or 'objective correlative') emotions did not exist. Why not? Because the emotions themselves, and the very imagery of their implicit situations, were elusive and unformed.'

To name what possessed no name, to avoid surrendering oneself 'into the inverted cone of waning energy...[and] fly off at last into nonentity, general deracinate conclusions', were the tasks that Williams had recognized early on – earlier, in fact, than the 1913 essay, 'Speech Rhythm', quoted above. *How* early one realizes in his accounts of his undergraduate poem (which he burned) about the prince who is abducted and taken to an unknown country – Williams's inarticulate America – to wake confronted by all the problems of language and cultural identity that Williams himself was to face: 'No one was there to inform him of his whereabouts and when he did begin to encounter passers-by, they didn't even understand, let alone speak his language. He could recall nothing of the past... So he went on, homeward or seeking a home that was his own, all this through a "foreign" country whose language was barbarous.'

This myth would seem to lend itself to a long psychic alienation. But one sees Williams breaking through by meeting the demands of day-to-day existence, never too involved in himself to feel the ballast of place, people and things. The source of his resilience recalls his hero, the Jesuit Père Rasles, among the Indians, of *In the American Grain*: 'This is a moral source not reckoned with, peculiarly sensitive and daring in its close embrace of native things... For everything his fine sense, blossoming, thriving, opening, reviving – not shutting out – was tuned. He speaks of his struggles with their language, its peculiar beauties, "je ne sais quoi d'énergique", he cited its tempo, the form of its genius with gusto, with admiration, with generosity.'

The myth of the prince and the necessity of a counter-statement to it underlie Williams's work. In his *Autobiography*, the counter-statement reappears in the final pages when he drives out to look at the site of the poem, *Paterson*: 'The Falls let out a roar as it crashed upon the rocks at its base. In the imagination this roar is a speech or a voice, a speech in particular; it is the poem itself that is the answer.'

Marianne Moore
Her Poetry and Her Critics

I

In an age when major poets such as Eliot and Yeats have treated nature with an imperiousness that, at times, recalls their symbolist forebears, Miss Moore is ready to accord to objects and to animals a life of their own. 'She is lavish and meticulous,' Robert Lowell has said. 'Her excellence is woman's I think in its worldly concreteness...' This quality, which makes her so different from Eliot and Yeats and draws her closer to the universe of Pound and Williams, depends on an outward-looking interest in fact and detail. Thus, when she came to review Williams's *Collected Poems, 1921–31*, she chose among her instances for approval to quote the specific resistance of:

> a green truck
> dragging a concrete mixer
> passes
> in the street –
> the clatter and true sound
> of verse –

and, further on in the same essay, we are given the following piece of meticulous observation from Williams:

> And there's the river with thin ice upon it
> fanning out half over the black
> water, the free middlewater racing under its
> ripples that move crosswise on the stream.

The first quotation would appeal readily to a poet who, like Miss Moore, elects to celebrate and to qualify (here she begins to differ from Williams) the irreducible, mechanical presence in 'To a Steam Roller'. With her, the presence becomes a moral presence, or one that begets nuances of thought where a moral atmosphere asks for definition:

> The illustration
> is nothing to you without the application.
>   You lack half wit. You crush all the particles down
>   into close conformity, and then walk back and forth
>   on them.
>
> Sparkling chips of rock
> are crushed down to the level of the parent block.
>   Were not 'impersonal judgment in aesthetic
>   matters, a metaphysical impossibility', you
>
>   might fairly achieve
>   it...

This ethical extension of fact itself is all her own, and it is something that, as we shall see in the animal poems, distinguishes her approach as fabulist from that of La Fontaine. And for La Fontaine, unlike Miss Moore, the sheer quiddity of animal existence is but a minor concern.

The second quotation from Williams, with its careful attention to the appearance of the iced river, finds its parallel in Miss Moore's capacity to see in an artichoke 'six varieties of blue', and also in the way 'A Grave' has room, in its sombre trajectory, for those firs 'each with an emerald turkey-foot at the top'. Similarly, the same trees in 'An Octopus' gain definition by the borrowing of Ruskin's phrase, 'each like the shadow of the one beside it'. Discriminations are present in Miss Moore for 'making out', as James would say, the way the thing looked. They are also present for sheer exuberance or humour and simultaneously for an imaginative deepening of the poem's moral implications. In 'Four Quartz Crystal Clocks' this alliance of humour and penetration occurs with great charm. The poem appears to deviate at a tangent with the entry of the lemur student, but this turns out, after all, to be precisely to the point:

> Repetition, with
> the scientist, should be
> synonymous with accuracy.
>   The lemur-student can see
>   that an aye-aye is not
>   an angwan-tibo, potto, or loris...

The unity here of humour and insight, fusing in that notion of accuracy which is being presented, is possible to the kind of poet for whom there is no war between science and poetry, and for whom fact has its proper plenitude. It is this plenitude that supplies the meaningful basis both of poetry and of Miss Moore's earliest interest, biology. She hints at her sense of this unity in her *Paris Review* interview with Donald Hall, where she says: 'Precision, economy of statement, logic employed to ends that are disinterested, drawing and identifying, liberate – at lest have some bearing on – the imagination, it seems to me.' It is no surprise to learn from this same interview that she had once thought of taking up medicine, that, in short, she should have found compatibility with two of the least abstract of the sciences. Biology clearly provides a common ground on which eye and mind could come together in harmony. Like Dr Williams's own medical studies and practice, 'drawing and identifying' for Miss Moore in some measure served perhaps to structure and to release the poetic impulse. 'Structure' is as important to her as 'release', for there is a science of art, and in Miss Moore's own art it is related to care in observing as well as to her scrupulousness over sources and quotations. Samuel Johnson himself, in unexpectedly Moore-like fashion, with his enthusiasm for on-the-spot observations and the noting down of them, saw the affinity of scientific with moral concern, when he wrote, in *A Journey to the Western Islands of Scotland*:

> He who has not made the experiment, or who is not accustomed to require rigorous accuracy from himself, will scarcely believe how much a few hours take from certainty of knowledge, and distinctness of imagery; how the succession of objects will be broken, how separate parts will be confused, and how many particular features and discriminations will be compressed and conglobated into one gross and general idea.

'Particular features and discriminations' stand at the heart of any Moore poem. Yet what of the imaginative flight that goes from the particular to the achieved work of art? How do fact and imagination, at its broadest stretch, learn, in Williams's phrase, to 'lie / down together in the same bed', for, though related, they are obviously not synonymous. The poems of wild life are instructive here. They insist often on a primary descriptive accuracy as the ground base for ultimate vision, as in 'The Jerboa':

> By fifths and sevenths,
> in leaps of two lengths,

> like the uneven notes
> of the Bedouin flute, it stops its gleaning
>   on little wheel casters, and makes fern-seed
>   foot-prints with kangaroo speed.
>
> Its leaps should be set
> to the flageolet;
>   pillar body erect
>   on a three-cornered smooth-working Chippendale
>   claw – propped on hind legs, and tail as third toe,
>   between leaps to its burrow.

Or, as in 'The Paper Nautilus', we are provided with the details of the way the nautilus 'constructs her thin glass shell' to rear her progeny:

>   Giving her perishable
>   souvenir of hope, a dull
>   white outside and smooth-
>   edged inner surface
>   glossy as the sea, the watchful
>   maker of it guards it
>   day and night; she scarcely
>
>   eats until the eggs are hatched.
>   Buried eight-fold in her eight
>   arms, for she is in
>   a sense a devil-
>   fish, her glass ramshorn-cradled freight
>   is hid but not crushed.

And the description of the process concludes with the beauty of a world of fact ramifying out into that of imaginative possibility:

>   the intensively
>   watched eggs coming from
>   the shell free it when they are freed, –
>   leaving its wasp-nest flaws
>   of white on white, and close-
>
>   laid Ionic chiton-folds
>   like the lines in the mane of
>   a Parthenon horse...

In both 'The Jerboa' and 'The Paper Nautilus' an ideal of ethical preference inserts itself among the facts, just as it did in a different way in Miss Moore's presentation of the steam roller, and in this insertion the imaginative power kindles to cast light on both the fact and the ideal. In 'The Jerboa', its habitat, the desert, is preferred to the opulence of the pharaohs because of the ascetic ideal of the animal's freedom, a freedom which Miss Moore characterizes as 'abundance' against the 'too much' of ancient Egypt. In 'The Paper Nautilus' the mode of protection accords with the ethical extension that 'love / is the only fortress / strong enough to trust to'. Elsewhere, as in 'The Frigate Pelican', man receives his ethical placing simply by the poet's registering that, as Lawrence puts it, 'he is not the measure of creation'. Lawrence, too, was writing about the animal world, and in 'Fish', from which the quotation comes, man is measured by being confronted with 'the water-horny mouth … the water-precious, mirror-flat bright eye' of the fish. In Miss Moore's 'The Frigate Pelican' 'we' (that is, we human sight-seers) are placed as we 'watch the moon rise / on the Susquehanna', but 'this most romantic bird', the pelican 'flies / to a more mundane place, the mangrove / swamp to sleep'. We do wrong to humanize everything, to accept only on our own terms the jungle night-fall, 'which is for man,' she writes, 'the basilisk whose look will kill; but is / for lizards man can / kill, the welcome dark'. Man, the 'less limber animal', with his practical mottoes, must accommodate himself to sea, jungle, frigate pelican, and lizard, and the ethical and the imaginative are one in Miss Moore's animal poems in urging this accommodation.

Different in mode from 'The Jerboa' and 'The Paper Nautilus' and also from 'The Frigate Pelican' is a poem like 'Bird-Witted' where the imaginative sharpening comes from an accurately close fit between incident and words. The poem stays close to the incident, the words miming its movements:

> With innocent wide penguin eyes, three
>   large fledgling mocking-birds below
> the pussy-willow tree,
>   stand in a row,
> wings touching, feebly solemn,
> till they see
>   their no longer larger
>   mother bringing
> something which will partially
> feed one of them.

> Toward the high-keyed intermittent squeak
>   of broken carriage-springs, made by
> the three similar, meek-
>   coated bird's eye
> freckled forms she comes; and when
> from the beak
>   of one, the still living
>   beetle has dropped
> out, she picks it up and puts
> it in again.

Hugh Kenner comments in detail on this same poem, in his essay 'Meditation and Enactment' (*Poetry*, May 1963) and, if he is correct, besides heeding the Emersonian prescription, 'Ask the fact for the form', Miss Moore is perhaps also engaged in taking up a challenge of Ezra Pound – to equal the bird sounds of Arnaut Daniel. The imaginative effect here is one of mimesis rather than transfiguration or the kind of ethical extension we have encountered elsewhere. The polar opposite of 'Bird-Witted' occurs in 'Melancthon', the poem about an elephant, though 'about an elephant' scarcely says much of the poem's real subject. The title 'Melancthon' (Melancthon was a Protestant theologian of the Lutheran Reformation) already alerts us with its obliquity to the controlled fantasy which sets it apart from the poems we have so far discussed. Here the more-than-animal speaks, which is an unusual occurrence in Miss Moore's poetry. Its protestant virtues come, by the middle of the poem, to symbolize the fully human as against 'the / wandlike body of which one hears so much', with its fragile prettiness and glassy egotism.

'Melancthon' takes us to the heart of Miss Moore's imaginative exploration of her moral world, a world where spontaneity and order are not at odds and where the marriage between them results in 'spiritual poise' rather than the 'external poise' of 'the wandlike body'. An objective symbol of the values proposed in 'Melancthon' is to be found in the description the poet gives us of the little town in 'The Steeple-Jack'. It is the symbol of a social and also a natural mean. The town makes no attempt to impress; it possesses 'spiritual poise':

> ...The church portico has four fluted
>   columns, each a single piece of stone, made
> modester by white-wash. This would be a fit haven for
> waifs, children, animals, prisoners...

> It could scarcely be dangerous to be living
> > in a town like this, of simple people
> who have a steeple-jack placing danger-signs by the church
> when he is gilding the solid-
> > pointed star, which on a steeple stands for hope.

Nature is present in 'the sweet sea air', the 'water etched / with waves as formal as the scales on a fish', in the sea-gulls, the lobsters, the storm that 'bends the salt / marsh grass, disturbs stars in the sky and the / star on the steeple', in 'the trumpet vine',

> > fox-glove, giant snap-dragon, a salpiglossis that has
> > spots and stripes; morning-glories; gourds,
> > > or moon-vines trained fishing-twine
> > at the back
> >
> > door...

But, to use the subtitles of 'The Jerboa', it is natural 'Abundance', not 'Too much':

> > ...There are no banyans, frangipani, nor
> > > jack-fruit trees; nor an exotic serpent
> > life. Ring lizard and snake-skin for the foot, or crocodile;
> > but here they've cats, not cobras, to
> > > keep down the rats. The diffident
> > little newt
> >
> > with white pin-dots on black horizontal spaced
> > > out bands lives here; yet there is nothing that
> > ambition can buy or take away.

In this setting 'the hero, the student, / the steeple-jack, each in his way, / is at home.' The student perceives the presence of the human mean beside the natural in 'an elegance of which / the source is not bravado' that characterizes the architecture of the town, 'the antique / sugar-bowl-shaped summer house of interlacing slats', the church spire and its portico 'made modester by white-wash'. The imaginative harmony of civilization and nature in the scene is made doubly telling by the intermingling of human and natural attributes in each other's sphere: the waves are 'formal', the pitch of the church spire is 'not true' as though it had grown there rather than been built.

I have so far spared the reader any discussion of Miss Moore's use of syllabic verse forms. But this is something that immediately distinguishes her poetry and that embodies and reinforces by technical means our sense of that relationship between freedom and formality which we have already sketched. It is the effect of Miss Moore's syllabic measures which permits Robert Lowell to say, 'Marianne Moore is an inventor of a new kind of English poem, one that is able to fix the splendor and variety of prose in very compressed spaces.'

Already, before World War I, an interest in syllabic form had spread through American poetry. There was, for example, the work of Adelaide Crapsey domesticating the Japanese tanka and haiku with her invention of the five-lined cinquain. This consisted of lines of two, four, six, eight, and two syllables, as in 'Triad':

> These be
> Three silent things:
> The falling snow...the hour
> Before the dawn...the mouth of one
> Just dead.

'Triad' is conventional stuff beside Miss Moore's syllabics, with their variation of line length and unpredictability of rhythmic pattern. Thus the stanzas of 'Melancthon' run to a syllable count of four, six, thirteen, and thirteen, but we are conscious at the same time of their open-endedness, the sense of rippling on from one verse to the next:

> ...the blemishes stand up and shout when the object
> in view was a
> renaissance; shall I say
> the contrary? The sediment of the river which
> encrusts my joints, makes me very grey but I am used
>
> to it, it may
> remain there; do away
> with it and I am myself done away with...

Here, we have a rhyme scheme, also reinforced by syllabic count, which compels us to pick out and pronounce 'a' so that it chimes with 'say' and also to give the kind of attention to 'it may / remain there' that we give to Donne's 'he that will / Reach her...' We are, among other details, made by the syllabic lay-out to take cognizance of the humbler components of language, the 'to it' and the 'with it'.

In 'The Hero' the very uncertainty of the hero's quest is caught up into the irregularly patterned syllabics:

> We do not like some things, and the hero
>   doesn't; deviating head-stones
>   and uncertainty;
>   going where one does not wish
>   to go; suffering and not
>   saying so; standing and listening where something
>   is hiding. The hero shrinks
> as what it is flies out on muffled wings, with twin yellow
>   eyes – to and fro –

The full effect of this uncertainty of count – an uncertainty without limpness, with imaginative pressure behind it – depends on a foil throughout the poem created by rhyming the first line of each stanza with the last two on the sound 'o'. Thus 'so' and 'grow' in the last two lines of verse one are taken up by 'hero' in verse two (quoted above) and re-echoed by 'yellow' and 'to and fro' at the end, a device repeated in all six stanzas. Here an unexpected placing of rhyme words works together with the syllabification to produce a curious ebbing away from known to unknown and a final return.

The effects of Marianne Moore's syllabics and her rhyming has been well described by Robert Beloof in an article that has received little attention, namely his 'Prosody and Tone' (*The Kenyon Review*, Winter 1958). There the aim is to examine the interaction of these two, prosody and tone, and Beloof sees her syllabic technique as principally tending 'to minimize the sense of metric regularity'. He sums up:

> The sparseness of rhyme sets, the redoubling of the sense of run-on line by ending lines with unimportant words or hyphenations, the leaping between somewhat extreme lengths of line – these are all devices to minimize a firm sense of line as a rhythmic unit. The basic rhythmic power and beauty exploited by syllabic poetry lies traditionally in this firm sense of length of line which becomes a rhythmic unit used contrapuntally against the rhythm of the phrase. She uses this contrapuntal technique to a degree, but it is minimized. Her manipulation of syllabic prosody makes a somewhat unique contribution to the historic use of this form in the devices by which, as we have described, she accomplishes this minimization.

The minimization of which Mr Beloof speaks is illustrated at the beginning of 'Virginia Britannia', where the swaying and leisurely rhythmic effect prepares us for a poem with that 'true sauntering eye' Thoreau asks for, going from shore, to churchyard, to tomb:

> Pale sand edges England's Old
> Dominion. The air is soft, warm, hot
> above the cedar-dotted emerald shore
> > known to the red bird, the red-coated muskateer,
> > the trumpet-flower, the cavalier,
> > the parson, and the wild parishioner. A deer-
> track in a church-floor
> > brick, and a fine pavement tomb with engraved top, remain.
> The now tremendous vine-encompassed hackberry
> > starred with the ivy-flower
> > shades the church tower;
> And a great sinner lyeth here under the sycamore.

Mr Beloof concludes, and rightly if we bear the above quotation in mind, that the syllabic poetry of Miss Moore 'is made to *sound* very much like her free verse poems...' – like, that is to say, 'Marriage', 'Silence', 'A Grave'. His remarks go a long way toward explaining the characteristic feel of Miss Moore's verse and the source of her originality. This originality is, at the same time, a question of content and also an extending of tradition. If she is 'an inventor of a new kind of English poem...able to fix the splendor and variety of prose in very compressed spaces', she does, in her own way, what has long appealed to poets – namely, makes available to verse the materials and cadences of prose speech and prose writing. Chaucer did it. Wyatt did it. Miss Moore does it with the speech and writing of her own day. Her raids on prose are as audacious as theirs and perhaps more so when she insists, 'nor is it valid / to discriminate against "business documents and / school books"; all these phenomena are important'. Thus 'Silence' consists of two extended prose quotations – one from a Miss A.M. Holmans' recollections of her father, the other from Prior's life of Edmund Burke. 'Four Quartz Crystal Clocks' transpired from a foray into a leaflet, *The World's Most Accurate Clocks*, put out by the Bell Telephone Company, but one would never mistake the result for anything other than Miss Moore, as fact is scrutinized by those 'sharpened faculties which require exactness' which she has admired in another poet; 'we know,' she says:

> ... that a quartz prism when
> the temperature changes, feels
> the change and that the then

>   electrified alternate edges
>   oppositely charged, threaten
>   careful timing; so that
>   this water-clear crystal as the Greeks used to say,
>   this 'clear ice' must be kept at the
>   same coolness. Repetition, with
>   the scientist, should be
>   synonymous with accuracy...

After the scientist, we move in this poem to the lemur student, the aye-aye, angwan-tibo, potto and loris. Indeed, we never quite know where we are going to in one of Miss Moore's pieces, nor where the next leap will take us. If she respects 'logic employed to ends that are disinterested', hers is a logic scarcely foreseeable or linear. In this she is at one with that interest in 'the intersection of loci' common to Pound, Eliot, and Williams. Thus Williams, who approved of 'Marriage' as 'an anthology of transit', could describe his own poems as 'rigmaroles'. The word would happily describe many a Moore poem, as would his formulation of what a poem is and does: it is 'tough ... from the attenuated power which draws perhaps many broken things into a dance by giving them thus a full being'.

In 'Marriage', the dance of broken things – the fragments of omnivorous reading and looking, rather than the urban detritus of Williams – can comprise a phrase from a review of Santayana's poems ('...something feline ...something colubrine...') in the *New Republic*, a memory of a Persian miniature, cymbal music, a quotation on waterfalls:

>   And he has beauty also;
>   it's distressing – the O thou
>   to whom from whom,
>   without whom nothing – Adam;
>   'something feline,
>   something colubrine' – how true!
>   a crouching mythological monster
>   in that Persian miniature of emerald mines,
>   raw silk – ivory white, snow white,
>   oyster white and six others –
>   that paddock full of leopards and giraffes –
>   long lemon-yellow bodies
>   sown with trapezoids of blue.

> Alive with words,
> vibrating like a cymbal
> touched before it has been struck,
> he has prophesied correctly –
> the industrious waterfall,
> 'the speedy stream
> which violently bears all before it,
> at one time silent as the air
> and now as powerful as the wind'.

Half the pleasure of the poems lies in their 'anthology of transit', in the way we are conducted irresistibly in, say, 'Then the ermine', from the Duke of Beaufort's motto, through Lavater's pysiography, and finally to violets by Dürer; or, in 'Tom Fool at Jamaica', in the way prophet, schoolboy, and Victor Hugo all serve as prelude to a rhapsody on a race-horse:

> Look at Jonah embarking for Joppa, deterred by
> the whale; hard going for a statesman whom nothing could
>   detain
>   although one who would not rather die than repent.
>   Be infallible at your peril, for your system will fail,
> and select as a model the schoolboy in Spain
>   who at the age of six, portrayed a mule and jockey
>   who had pulled up for a snail.
>
> 'There is a submerged magnificence, as Victor Hugo
> said.' *Sentir avec ardeur*; that's it...

In 'Marriage' and also in 'The Octopus' – a poem from the same phase which presses into service The National Parks Portfolio, details of Greek philosophy, not to mention an item from a list of useful inventions (i.e., glass that will bend) – the broken things, assembled into the dance of the whole, work with a power that is often centrifugal and recalls the apparent disconnections of those 'chains of incontrovertibly logical non-sequiturs' which Miss Moore finds in Williams, thus returning him the compliment in her essay on him in *Predilections*. A new unity, won from the apparently intractable, is a measure of the creative force that permeates these poems of hers where originality and freedom stand on the other side of the equation from decorousness and rectitude. Her best poems are the resolutions of tough moral elegance. If she is self-reliant like the cat, her self-reliance is outward-going like her interest in detail.

Her morality, like her technique, is put on its mettle by facing difficulties imaginatively.

II

Critical writings about the work of Miss Moore fall into two sharp divisions: clear-minded essays – Eliot and Kenner are cases in point – where an exact perception of what she is about eschews all floridness; and, on the other hand, a host of 'tributes' in which the poet is reduced to the status of a kind of national pet and where the intellectual stamina finds no answering attitude in the appreciator but calls forth instead sentimental rhapsodizing. One of the more depressing thoughts to cross the mind of anybody who has read such criticism in bulk is to wonder whether Marianne Moore has not suffered more from lax adulation than almost any other significant poet of our century. Perhaps the reason for this lies as much in the nature of the work as in the nature of Miss Moore's more indulgent public. This work is morally 'armoured', like some of her favourite animals, but suppose that armour should come to seem quaint, a carapace of knowing quiddities? This is the way many people have apparently read it, and this is the basis for Miss Moore's popular success. Thus the one potential defect in a brilliant oeuvre passes for its virtue in a body of critical writing that seldom engages with the reality.

Robert Duncan, in his 'Ideas of the Meaning of Form' (*Kulchur* No.4, 1961), puts the matter keenly when, speaking of the type of poem which has earned Miss Moore a wide public in the pages of *The New Yorker*, he writes:

> These poems were practices meant to insure habitual virtues. Vision and flight of the imagination was sacrificed to survival in terms of personal signature... What had been boney insistences and quirks of protective structure now become social gestures of fuss and lapse, a protest of charming helplessness.

Duncan instances 'Hometown Piece for Messrs. Alston and Reese', 'Enough', and 'In the Public Garden' as illustrations of a sacrifice of 'character to the possibilities of what America loves in public personality'. One could also perhaps trace the limitation in Miss Moore's style back to poems like 'Propriety', first gathered into the *Collected Poems* of 1951, where the effect of spontaneity is consciously worked out and there is a resultant lack of significance in the form of what is offered:

> Some such word
> as the chord
> Brahms had heard
> from a bird,
> sung down near the root of the throat;
> it's the little downy woodpecker
> spiralling a tree –
> up up up like mercury...

The effect here is to simplify and to sentimentalize. Stylistically it represents a kind of self-parody:

> ...Brahms and Bach,
> no; Bach and Brahms. To thank Bach
> for his song
> first, is wrong.
> Pardon me; ...

The order and the spontaneity no longer coalesce: the order becomes merely typographical dexterity and the spontaneity the exploitation of a willed simplicity. 'Propriety' illustrates a loss of stylistic decorum within Miss Moore's chosen limits. Two other much longer poems, 'In Distrust of Merits' and 'Keeping Their World Large', show what happens when she ventures outside of them. Both attempt to deal with the theme of war, and both fail because the feeling is no longer contained. Her characteristic and remarkable achievements derive from an impersonality in the means of the poetry which, in fact, permits the fusion of both personal and impersonal in their most significant form. There occurs no invitation to 'feeling' because the means do not admit of such. In her two wartime pieces, however, the means admit of little else:

> They're fighting, fighting, fighting the blind
> man who thinks he sees –
> who cannot see that the enslaver is
> enslaved; the hater, harmed. O shining O
> firm star, O tumultuous
> ocean lashed till small things go
> as they will, the mountainous
> wave makes us who look, know
>
> depth.

It is precisely in the avoidance of an over-elaboration of the rhetorical machinery and of an inviting coyness of diction that makes for the unwavering balance of her finest work. In the less admirable poems, the coyness, as in 'Propriety', and the public rhetoric, as in the above quotation from 'In Distrust of Merits', seem to have struck a bargain satisfactory to both, yet disconcerting to the reader.

One pauses to register the nature of the defect because an anomaly arising from it has too often gone unnoticed: here is a poet whose public image is now perhaps only slightly less famous than that of Allen Ginsberg, but whose most characteristic and sound work would, from all appearances, have ensured a long and healthy unpopularity. Pound saw in the verse, in 1919, 'an arid clarity', certainly not something that would have recommended it to the bosom of a nation, and he described it, unexpectedly, as bordering on despair. Eliot, when he introduced her poems in 1935, recognized that her originality represented qualities not generally assimilable, that her 'feeling in one's own way' would be mistaken for frigidity. Thirty years later it is precisely 'humanity', 'warmth' 'delightfulness' that are attributed to these poems, the charge of frigidity having vanished beneath the weight of approval. The true standard of Miss Moore's excellence and the difficulties which ensue once this singular and apparently self-sufficient talent unbends to make friends with the audience are recalled to us by Hugh Kenner when he writes in 'Meditation and Enactment':

> One might sort Miss Moore's poems into those that observe, meditate, and enact ..., the rigorous pattern a dimension of meditation and enactment; those that soliloquize, like 'A Grave' or 'New York', and have as their center of gravity therefore the speaker's probity and occasional tartness; and those (rather frequent of late) that incite, that set themselves to *exact*, appropriate feelings about something public. For her public occasions Miss Moore seems a little dependent on the newspapers: 'Carnegie Hall: Rescued' has her inimitable texture, but the sentiment of the poem is extrinsic to that texture.

Wallace Stevens and the Poetry of Scepticism

When in 1943 Yvor Winters (1900–68), in *The Anatomy of Nonsense*, commented on the poetry of Wallace Stevens, he referred to 'a combination of calm and terror' that 'will be found in only one other poet in English, in Shakespeare as one finds him in a few lines of the more metaphysical sonnets'. With the appearance in the 1950s of *Selected Poems*, one discovers Winters' high estimate being endorsed by Donald Davie in a review entitled 'Essential Gaudiness': 'He is indeed a poet to be mentioned in the same breath as Eliot and Yeats and Pound.' Winters' piece had had for its title 'Wallace Stevens, or the Hedonist's Progress', containing reservations about that 'essential gaudiness' which Davie was to go on to salute. Davie himself, when he reprinted his own essay in *The Poet in the Imaginary Museum* (1977), registered in a footnote: 'I should now probably be more captious about Stevens than I was when I wrote this.' This wavering on the part of two of our most interesting critics is a measure, perhaps, of the difficulty of being fair to Stevens and of seeing his quirkiness and gaudiness in relation to that soberer 'middle style' which marks his late poems of meditation in *Transport to a Summer* (1947), *The Auroras of Autumn* (1950) and *The Rock* (1955). 'Middle style' for Stevens, it must be understood, usually implies rather more elevation than for most other poets.

Like Eliot, Yeats and Pound, Stevens was writing his earliest poetry at a time when the poetic idiom stood in need of renewal. Unlike them, he was often content to take over Victorian modes and, simply by the audacity of his use of such modes, to turn them to his own purposes. His subject-matter stands frequently close to accepted poetic conventions and themes, in spite of the whimsical titles, like 'Le Monocle de Mon Oncle' or 'The Comedian as Letter C' from his first volume, *Harmonium*, of 1923. After these, one is a little surprised at the old-fashioned romantic excess in some of the actual writing:

> The dark shadows of the funereal magnolias
> Are full of the songs of Jamanda and Carlotta

> – The son and the daughter who come to the darkness
> He for her burning breast, and she for his arms.

– written so close in time to the composition of Pound's *Hugh Selwyn Mauberley* and Eliot's *The Waste Land*. Poor vintage Keats, Meredith, Browning are the origins of such passages, and the Shakespearian note is reach-me-down Elizabethanizing like 'the unconscionable treachery of fate'. As for Stevens' themes, one of the most important in *Harmonium* had been run ragged by romantics and decadents alike – namely the alliance of Death and Beauty. 'Peter Quince at the Clavier', for all the chic of its title, is a set of variations on this theme, where Stevens wins the day by his sheer imaginative panache and his witty reversal of the traditional Christianizing commonplaces:

> Beauty is momentary in the mind –
> The fitful tracing of a portal;
> But in the flesh it is immortal.
> The body dies; the body's beauty lives.
> So evenings die, in their green going,
> A wave interminably flowing...
> Susanna's music touched the bawdy strings
> Of those white elders; but, escaping,
> Left only Death's ironic scraping.

Stevens, at forty-four (the age when he published *Harmonium*), is self-conscious about his themes in a way romantics and decadents were not. Hence, to a point, the jokes of his titles, establishing (uneasily at times) an ironic attitude to the subject-matter which follows. Thus, in 'Le Monocle de Mon Oncle', Stevens inspects, presumably through his uncle's monocle, the kind of middle-aged romantic poetry his uncle might have written. He considers the theme of spring – 'Shall I uncrumple this much-crumpled thing?' he asks. Both Winters and Davie seize upon this section of the poem which, venturing beyond Keats, Browning and Meredith, results in something that is recognizably Stevens' own:

> A red bird flies across the golden floor.
> It is a red bird that seeks out his choir
> Among the choirs of wind and wet and wing.
> A torrent will fall from him when he finds.
> Shall I uncrumple this much-crumpled thing?
> I am a man of fortune greeting heirs;

> For it has come that thus I greet the spring.
> These choirs of welcome choir for me farewell.
> No spring can follow past meridian.
> Yet you persist with anecdotal bliss
> To make believe a starry *connaissance*.

To the apparently stale topic and into the apparently unusable idiom Stevens brings new life, an awareness of nature that is fresh and individual in this evocation of wet woods, the sounding of bird-song through wind and rain, and the song of the one bird whose 'torrent' is at once a joyful rediscovery of his kind and a release. Perhaps one of the most poignant touches throughout Stevens' oeuvre is his feeling for the way human and animal awareness sometimes overlaps and yet differs (see, for example, 'A Rabbit as King of the Ghosts' and 'Song of Fixed Accord').

Intimations of freshness also impinge through the nostalgia of another early sequence in *Harmonium*, 'Sunday Morning'. A woman is meditating on the fact of death:

> She says, 'I am content when wakened birds
> Before they fly, test the reality
> Of misty fields by their sweet questionings;
> But when the birds are gone, and their warm fields
> Return no more, where, then is paradise?

The phrase 'test the reality / Of misty fields by their sweet questionings' establishes with beautiful implicitness the felt space at the back of bird-song and the sense of the surrounding continuum of nature now no longer clearly seen because of the mist. This power of sensuous evocation, rather than the sensuous particularizing of shapes and substances of the kind one finds in (say) Hopkins, shows itself both in the poems in traditional blank verse and those of a more recognizably modern cut like 'Thirteen Ways of Looking at a Blackbird', also from *Harmonium*, but evidently of a later date than 'Le Monocle' and 'Sunday Morning'. 'Thirteen Ways' strips perception of all imaginative excess:

> IV
>
> Icicles filled the long window
> With barbaric glass.
> The shadow of the blackbird
> Crossed it, to and fro.

> The mood
> Traced in the shadow
> An indecipherable cause.

XIII

> It was evening all afternoon.
> It was snowing
> And it was going to snow.
> The blackbird sat
> In the cedar limbs.

The sharpness of Stevens' evocations of his sensations of the natural scene, and of the loneliness he feels before that scene, recur again and again. Stevens is a poet whose imagination warms to the cold. He wanted to write a 'poetry of earth' and to be the poet of 'a physical universe', praising 'total satisfaction, the moment of total summer'. Yet 'total summer' seems to yield little but rhetoric to Stevens' wintry temperament. True, there are poems of joy in spring and autumn, but the snowscape remains one of his favourite genres, from the desolate compactness of his early and famous 'The Snowman' to the extended meditations of his penultimate collection, *The Auroras of Autumn* (1950):

> The season changes. A cold wind chills the beach.
> The long lines of it grow larger, emptier,
> A darkness gathers though it does not fall
>
> And the whiteness grows less vivid on the wall.
> The man who is walking turns blankly on the sand.
> He observes how the north is always enlarging the change,
>
> With its frigid brilliances, it blue-red sweeps
> And gusts of great enkindlings, its polar green,
> The color of ice and fire and solitude.

This late poetry of the aurora borealis still harks back in a chastened manner to the organ-note effects of the earlier pieces: 'The color of ice and fire and solitude' has a kind of lonely gusto that sorts well with the New England stoicism that watches out winter through yet another March snow storm.

Stevens' conviction that 'The great poem of earth remains to be written' does not quite carry him sufficiently far to write it. He sometimes watches out winter with an answering, icy grandeur. At others, he tries to involve us in a celebration of the physical universe at which he is both priest and organist, the organist's skill in opulent improvisation making up for the priest's uneasy faith when, after moments of reconciliation or truce between mind and matter, the going gets difficult. And, yet, again, and perhaps most acceptably, a Stevens of the middle-style finds a way of telling us that the fiction of the poem, by clearing a space for meaning and fresh apprehension, can reconcile us to a world of fact in a way that the fictions of religion no longer can, as in 'Notes Towards a Supreme Fiction'.

> The death of one god is the death of all…
> Phoebus is dead, ephebe. But Phoebus was
> A name for something that never could be named.

and

> The poem refreshes life so that we share,
> For a moment, the first idea… It satisfies
> Belief in an immaculate beginning
>
> And sends us, winged by an unconscious will,
> To an immaculate end. We move between these points:
> From that ever-early candor to its late plural…

Here, Stevens is following out the implications of one of his earliest poems, 'A High-Toned Old Christian Woman' from *Harmonium*, where the notion 'Poetry is the supreme fiction' first appears and where he tells her that now the church has failed our imaginations, poetry must do the job for us. If the idea that 'Poetry is the supreme fiction' is a frank extension of the ideas of a Victorian like Matthew Arnold in his *Literature and Dogma*, the ideological background to 'Sunday Morning' is also Victorian and a response to conflicts that the Victorians were the first to make explicit. 'Sunday Morning' sets out one of the basic themes of all Stevens' work and this theme was already Tennyson's in *In Memoriam* – namely, the difficulty of Christian faith in a universe where accidental causes seem to nullify the possibility of belief in God. In the opening of the sequence we listen to the meditations of a woman as she reflects on 'the dark / Encroachment of that old catastrophe' which is the death of Christ. She meditates in a setting where the painterly colour of oranges, 'the green freedom' of a cockatoo and a certain leisurely sensuousness are impinged upon by the thought of death and particularly by the death of Christ. Stevens registered this impingement which, one might suggest, underlay his entire dialectic, with a marvellously sure touch:

> Complacencies of the peignoir, and late
> Coffee and oranges in a sunny chair,
> And the green freedom of a cockatoo
> Upon a rug mingle to dissipate
> The holy hush of ancient sacrifice.
> She dreams a little, and she feels the dark
> Encroachment of that old catastrophe,
> As a calm darkens among water-lights.
> The pungent oranges and bright, green wings
> Seem things in some procession of the dead,
> Winding across wide water, without sound.
> The day is like wide water, without sound,
> Stilled for the passing of her dreaming feet
> Over the seas, to silent Palestine,
> Dominion of the blood and sepulchre.

Yvor Winters, in the above-mentioned article, has written well of the passage when he comments, 'The language has the greatest possible dignity and subtlety, combined with a perfect precision. The imminence of absolute tragedy is felt and recorded, but the integrity of the feeling mind is maintained... The calm clarity of tone would be impossible were the terror emphasized for a moment at any point...' This same 'calm clarity of tone' governs the superb last lines of the poem where pigeons make

> Ambiguous undulations as they sink,
> Downward to darkness, on extended wings.

When Harriet Monroe first printed the poem in *Poetry* (*Chicago*), she was troubled by the unappeasing tragedy of these final lines, and moved into final position the penultimate section, one where Stevens' tone is less sure, but where there is a brassy triumphalism which might carry the anxious reader over what is actually being said:

> Supple and turbulent, a ring of men
> Shall chant in orgy on a summer morn
> Their boisterous devotion to the sun,
> Not as a god, but as a god might be,
> Naked among them, like a savage source...

In 'Shakespeare and the Stoicism of Seneca', T.S. Eliot complains about the stoical habit of 'cheering [oneself] up' in the face of absolute tragedy. Stevens' vision of boisterous pagans, or perhaps a future race of supermen worshipping the sun, has a rhetoric which is going to be characteristic of his more willed attempts to 'save the appearances'. The elation soon fades, however, into poetic plangency:

> And whence they come and whither they shall go,
> The dew upon their feet shall manifest.

The lift of the diction in this is banished by the last section and its more subdued stoicism:

> We live in an old chaos of the sun
> Or old dependency of day and night…

This world drifts on, with no divinely sanctioned purpose, through space, an 'island solitude', and the poem with its 'casual flocks of pigeons' enacts the movement 'downward to darkness' and annihilation.

If there is a loneliness in Stevens' poetry which places him close to the European scepticism of Nietzsche – a disbelief that found its most lasting poetic embodiments in the *Duino Elegies* of Rainer Maria Rilke – a certain bourgeois common sense and a taste for the good things of the passing moment kept him back from the frank despair hidden away in Nietzsche's diary entries: 'How have I borne life? By creating.' This might well have been the epitaph of the German poet Gottfried Benn, whose aesthetic nihilism, for which Nietzsche's example was crucial, often reads like a reductio ad absurdum of Stevens' 'belief' in 'the supreme fiction':

> A word, a phrase –: from cyphers rise
> Life recognised, a sudden sense,
> The sun stands still, mute are the skies,
> And all compacts it, stark and dense.
>
> A word – a gleam, a flight, a spark,
> A thrust of flames, a stellar trace –,
> And then again – immense – the dark
> Round world and I in empty space.
>   (Trans. Richard Exner)

Benn, one feel, set the poetic act too far apart from other daily human acts for endeavour, negotiation and ordering, so that the light struck off it illuminates only itself and the waste land spread around it. In Germany, after the Nazi débâcle and the collapse of one practical attempt to create the Superman, no doubt it felt like that to be a poet. But if we are to interpret the world only in terms of 'feeling like that', poetry would soon be in danger of becoming merely an art of mood, hardening into a frigid stoicism. Stevens' 'American Sublime' suggests an American version of something of this kind, but the difference is at once apparent in the play of Stevens' humour:

> ...when General Jackson
> Posed for his statue
> He knew how one feels.
> Shall a man go barefoot
> Blinking and blank?
> ...And the sublime comes down
> To the spirit itself,
>
> The spirit and space,
> The empty spirit
> In vacant space.
> What wine does one drink?
> What bread does one eat?

Moreover Stevens hankers back to the images of Christian sacrament. So the intellectual and emotional need which resulted in his deathbed conversion to Catholicism was always present. At the time of *Ideas of Order* (1935) in which 'The American Sublime' appeared, it was the empty air rather than the sacraments that held the centre of his imagination, as in 'Evening Without Angels' from the same volume. In such a universe, nature reflects back at man the order his imagination has projected on it:

> Sad men made angels of the sun, and of
> The moon they made their own attendant ghosts...

This poet, whose ultimate conversion came as such a surprise to his admirers, had once reserved for the art of poetry the resolution of disbelief and the task of ordering:

> The epic of disbelief
> Blares oftener and soon, will soon be constant.

> Some harmonious skeptic in a skeptical music
> Will unite these figures of men and their shapes
> Will glisten again with motion...

Stevens can pursue his main theme, without the strenuosities implied here in 'Sad Strains of a Gay Waltz', in such pieces as 'A Postcard from the Volcano' (also from *Ideas of Order*), a poem where a hint of historical perspective enlarges the point of view:

> Children picking up our bones
> Will never know that these were once
> As quick as foxes on the hill;
>
> And that in autumn, when the grapes
> Made sharp air sharper by their smell
> These had a being, breathing frost;
>
> And least will guess that with our bones
> We left much more, left what still is
> The look of things, left what we felt
>
> At what we saw. The spring clouds blow
> Above the shuttered mansion-house
> Beyond our gate, and the windy sky
>
> Cries out a literate despair.
> We knew for long the mansion's look
> And what we said of it became
>
> A part of what it is... Children,
> Still weaving budded aureoles,
> Will speak our speech and never know,
>
> Will say of the mansion that it seems
> As if he that lived there left behind
> A spirit storming in blank walls,
>
> A dirty house in a gutted world,
> A tatter of shadows peaked to white,
> Smeared with gold of the opulent sun.

Motifs first established in *Harmonium*, which are to be reintroduced again and again for development and variation, are clearly present here. They begin with the title. Why 'A Postcard from the Volcano'? The poem itself is the postcard, the necessarily arbitrary snapshot of reality (three *could* be thirteen!) from a given angle. A frame is being placed round the chaos of nature. The volcano represents the unordered chaos, the material to be shaped by the intervening human mind. The threat of the sky is there as usual. The opulent sun the ring of men chant their devotion to in 'Sunday Morning' takes its place, as throughout Stevens' verse, as the symbol of renewal and hope of a fresh beginning. The action of the imagination, Stevens' recurrent theme, is present in the suggestions that, though men die, they not only leave behind them their bones, but also transmit their way of looking at things. Even the sky 'cries out a literate despair' because of the poetic faculty of the imagination to imprint itself on it. Similarly with the mansion,

> We knew for long the mansion's look
> And what we said of it became
> A part of what it is...

That other allied theme of Stevens, that the house the imagination builds out of the rubble of reality must fall into decay and return to the primal chaos, thence to be rebuilt by a fresh act of intuitive construction, is embodied in the fate of the shut mansion that becomes 'a dirty house in a gutted world', then – with the possibility of new life and coherence appearing through old decay –

> A tatter of shadows peaked to white,
> Smeared with the gold of the opulent sun.

In many poems of a similar scale, one feels that Stevens found the best outlet for his talents, where the lightness of touch revolves a theme that is treated humanly, delicately and with a nice balance of tone: the postcard, the poet's fiction, restores a freshness to the world we live in, though the moments of order are provisional and threatened by time and the death of both individuals and cultures. Humour and the play and inventiveness of language can keep these moments bright in the mind, moments that serve to open up the mind, 'The way, when we climb a mountain, / Vermont throws itself together.'

'The Idea of Order at Key West', another poem from the same volume, shows us once more the less wintry side of Stevens' imagination. This mid-period Stevens has a woman singing by 'the ever-hooded, tragic gestured sea', and the sound of her voice confronts 'the meaningless plungings of water and wind', so that a kind of ordering seems to take place as song measures its own ambience:

> It was her voice that made
> The sky acutest at its vanishing.
> She measured to the hour its solitude.
> She was the single artificer of the world
> In which she sang. And when she sang, the sea,
> Whatever self it had, became the self
> That was her song, for she was the maker. Then we
> As we beheld her striding there alone,
> Knew that there never was a world for her
> Except the one she sang and singing, made.

Even when the speaker of the poem and his companion, Ramon Fernandez, have turned towards the town, and the singing has ended, an 'idea of order' seems to have spread out from it to all they see:

> ...The lights in the fishing boats at anchor there,
> As night descended, tilting in the air,
> Mastered the night and portioned out the sea
> Fixing emblazoned zones and fiery poles,
> Arranging, deepening, enchanting night.

'The Idea of Order at Key West' tells us much about one aspect of Stevens' imagination – an aspect Helen Vendler acutely, even harshly characterizes in *On Extended Wings. Wallace Stevens' Longer Poems* (1969), when she writes, 'Stevens' self seems to have presented him with a world excessively interior, in which the senses, with the exception of the eye, are atrophied or impoverished...' It is less the impoverishment than the interiority which strikes one in the poem under discussion:

> And when she sang, the sea,
> Whatever self it had, became the self
> That was her song, for she was the maker.

'She was the maker'. So in some sense, the singer is the poet and what she does he does. His words, like her notes, spilling out over nature or 'reality', annex it to human needs. Here her music virtually compels it into ordered significance. Yet, curiously, Stevens himself stands apart with 'pale Ramon', as if he cannot quite believe in the woman's opulent solipsism. ('The American Sublime', placed next in the book, even seems calculated to take the wind out of her sail.) Frank Doggett, in *Stevens' Poetry of Thought* (1966), introduces into a discussion of the poem a passage from Schopenhauer's *The World as Will and Idea* on the nature of the lyric: 'Schopenhauer says of the singer or pure lyrist "the subjective disposition, the affecting of the will, imparts its own hue to the perceived surroundings, and conversely, the surroundings communicate the reflex of their colour to the will".' In this act of absorption and expression Schopenhauer sees nature, through human consciousness, speaking to itself. Perhaps the most extreme example of this notion is the Wagnerian one when Isolde, in the final Liebestod, so imparts the hue of the lovers' situation to the conclusion of the opera that, as 'pure lyrist', she converts all elements to her own 'subjective disposition' and, indeed, knows

> that there never was a world for her
> Except the one she sang and, singing, made.

Wagner's other protagonists here virtually fade away beyond the veil of Maya by the final bars of Isolde's outpouring. Stevens, however, both in the poem and elsewhere, notes a recalcitrance in the situation – that which refuses to be wholly dissolved away into the conceptions of the mind keeps moving in from the peripheries to challenge the lyric accord. Thus in *The Rock* (1955), the last poem in this last gathering of poems is entitled 'Not Ideas About the Thing but the Thing Itself' and that 'world excessively interior', of which Vendler speaks, is once more beset from beyond itself:

> At the earliest ending of winter,
> In March, a scrawny cry from outside
> Seemed like the sound in his mind…
>
> That scrawny cry – it was
> A chorister whose c preceded the choir.
> It was part of the colossal sun,
>
> Surrounded by its choral rings,
> Still far away. It was like
> A new knowledge of reality.

'A new knowledge' implies a new person. Thus if there is something waiting to get into us, there is also something waiting to get out of us, 'the auroral creature musing in the mind', and the two are enabled to interact because, as Stevens says, 'Two things of opposite natures seem to depend on one another, the imagined and the real.' 'The auroral creature' finds release as 'the imagination pressing back against the pressure of reality' ('The Noble Rider and the Sound of Words').

So Stevens concludes *The Rock* by a variation on one of his earliest poems, 'Le Monocle de Mon Oncle', his listening outwards remembering back to the red bird 'that seeks out his choir'. This seeking out of the choir demands a continual poetic readjustment, a readjustment that Stevens in a note *On Poetic Truth*, possibly written in 1954, sees as a guarantee of novelty. His transition from this thought to the role of modern theology is at once unforeseen and yet characteristic of Stevens' leanings towards religion:

> Novelty must be inspired. But there must be novelty. This crisis is most evident in religion. The theologians whose thought is most astir today do make articulate a supreme need, ... the need to infuse into the ages of enlightenment an awareness of reality adequate to their achievements and such as will not be attenuated by them. There is one most welcome and authentic note; it is the insistence on a reality that forces itself upon our consciousness and refuses to be managed and mastered.

This presumably was what Stevens meant when he declared, of the supreme fiction, that 'it must change'. His hope was that it was a mask of the real. But so often the real seemed illusively distant and difficult to situate within the body of the universe.

I have said that Stevens is a poet of evocations rather than patterned inscapes. He hovers above and about his subjects rather than entering into their life co-extensive with his own. 'The American Sublime' may complain of 'The empty spirit / In vacant space', yet no square inch of American space is really empty or unpatterned. Desert or forest will both give back to the eye enough particulars to nourish and sustain if the demands of subjectivity are not too exorbitant. The singer in 'The Idea of Order at Key West', in singing beside the sea, does not explore, say, her relation as a woman to the sea through the lunar cycle, or meditate on the fact that 'human tears' as the scientist tells us, 'are a re-creation of the primordial ocean which, in the first stages of evolution, bathed the first eyes' (R.L. Gregory, *Eye and Brain*). Hugh Kenner (*A Homemade World*, 1975), contrasting Stevens with William Carlos Williams, argues that the latter, unlike Stevens, 'was untroubled by any sense of [Nature's] remote exteriority because he sensed his own biological kinship with processes of struggle and growth':

> Compose. (No ideas
> but in things) Invent!
> Saxifrage is my flower that splits
> the rocks.

And Kenner goes on: 'A way to be part of the world is to consider that through the world as through yourself moves the energy of a cellular dance.' He quotes Williams' prolonged meditation on the unfolding of a flower, 'The Crimson Cyclamen', and concludes:

> Helped out by experiences Wordsworth couldn't have – time-lapse films of opening flowers, and a biology of dynamics, not of classifications – this kind of writing about natural processes belongs to a new phase in the history of poetry. To a reader of professional books on nutrition and mitosis, 'Nature' meant something both intimate and thrusting.

Stevens' sensibility was formed in a previous era and from sources other than these. For all the differences, his was a sensibility far closer to Wordsworth's than to time-lapse photography. Yet Stevens, too, relishes the idea of the dance. It was this that drew him towards the end of his life to write his introduction to a translation of Paul Valéry's *Dance and the Soul*. Why was Stevens drawn to Valéry's conception of the dance and in what way does it differ from the cellular dance of which Kenner speaks? To try to answer these questions reveals further evidence of Stevens' persisting inheritance from the nineteenth century. *The Rock*, the final section of *Collected Poems*, appeared in 1955. To this late phase belong also his two Valéry prefaces – the one already mentioned and another to *Eupalinos*. In some of the poems of this phase Stevens often seems to be content with the pleasures of simply not knowing, of being unsure. And this acceptance produces some of his most quietly impressive poems – 'Long and Sluggish Lines', 'To an Old Philosopher in Rome', 'Song of Fixed Accord', 'The River of Rivers in Connecticut', 'The World as Meditation'. *The Rock* itself is more austere than these, swept clean of all gaudiness. The Valéry prefaces seem almost to have stepped back in time from these works towards a more aggressively aphoristic stance.

At the end of his preface to Valéry's dialogue *Dance and the Soul*, 'Man,' says Stevens somewhat unexpectedly, 'has many ways to attain the divine and the way of Eupalinos [namely the architect, the supreme constructor, in the dialogue of that name] and the way of Athikte [the dancer in the other dialogue] and the various ways of Paul Valéry are a few of them.' One wonders if Stevens meant something just as vague here by 'the divine' as Valéry by 'the soul' in his title *Dance and the Soul*. The way of Eupalinos was the knowledge of his craft – architecture, and, by analogy, poetic construction. What of the way of Athikte, the dancer who gives herself to the pattern of the dance as the stylist gives himself to his style? In Valéry's dialogue, Socrates, who is present at her performance, exclaims, 'Is not the dance, O my friends, that deliverance of our body entirely possessed by the spirit of falsehood, and of music which is falsehood, and drunk with the denial of null reality? – look at that body, which leaps as flame replaces flame, look how it spurns and betramples what is true.' This conception of the dance recalls one aspect of Stevens' conception of poetry as the supreme fiction, and of style as a fine excess, the panache that makes life bearable as against 'the sorry verities' that trouble 'the weeping burgher', in the poem of that name. Valéry's 'null reality' and Stevens' 'sorry verities' seem closely related. So Athikte's dance, in the face of all that, is scarcely a dance of biological kinship with a cellular universe but rather a drunken solipsism. This is, of course, Paul Valéry speaking and not Wallace Stevens. Yet this Nietzschean metaphysic of the self-expressive and self-consuming flame that dances before a meaningless universe must have appealed to Stevens in certain moods – why else this late tribute to Valéry's prose? There had even been a touch of Valéry's ninetyish bravado in Stevens' use of the word 'exquisite', when he had once written: 'The final belief is to believe in a fiction, which you know to be a fiction, there being nothing else. The exquisite truth is to know that it is a fiction and that you believe in it willingly.' A more persuasive formulation of Stevens runs, 'We accept the unknown even when we are most skeptical' ('The Irrational Element in Poetry').

But poetry qualifies in subtle ways such declaring utterances about the supreme fiction and *The Rock* goes on to qualify much that Stevens had said in prose. (By the same token, the prose Valéry is not the great poet of 'Le Cimetière marin'.) If, in *The Rock*, 'The World is Mediation' is 'about' the supreme fiction, it is also 'about' an attitude of mind that is content to repose within its own uncertainty – one close to that 'negative capability' Keats admired, 'when a man is capable of being in uncertainties, mysteries, doubts, without any irritable reaching after fact and reason'. This is a scepticism that nourishes rather than undermines. In the poem, in Penelope's meditation, the world has gone on renewing its promise and she has awaited its revelations. Her waiting could as well be that of a religious discipline as of a meditation on that supreme fiction which can be approached only by way of 'notes towards', but is never to be finally apprehended:

> Is it Ulysses that approaches from the east,
> The interminable adventurer? The trees are mended.
> That winter is washed away. Someone is moving
> On the horizon and lifting himself up above it.
> A form of fire approaches...

'*Je vis un rêve permanent, qui ne s'arrête ni nuit ni jour*' is the epigraph this poem carries from the violinist and composer, Georges Enesco. Penelope has lived this dream out of a kind of animal faith, in a world that exceeds her and yet promises more than its exhaustible present:

> The trees had been mended, as an essential exercise
> In an inhuman meditation, larger than her own.

For Stevens, the world itself must be expressed with the image of an interiority, as if he remembered from his reading of Schopenhauer that notion of nature speaking to itself, and meditating through the human consciousness. But such philosophic notions are provisional, and so are all 'final' certainties:

> But was it Ulysses? Or was it only the warmth of the sun
> On her pillow? The thought kept beating in her like her heart.
> The two kept beating together. It was only day.
>
> It was Ulysses and it was not. Yet they had met,
> Friend and dear friend and a planet's encouragement...

The phrase 'It was only day' seems a massive and miraculous understatement, massive and miraculous enough to sustain that pulse beat of her heart and imagination:

> She would talk a little to herself as she combed her hair,
> Repeating his name with its patient syllables,
> Never forgetting him that kept coming constantly so near.

If, to borrow Winters' word, the woman in the peignoir amid coffee and oranges in 'Sunday Morning' is a hedonist, Penelope, in her patience, is a stoic but not of the inhuman kind. As she takes cognizance of a world that exceeds the human, she feels within herself a 'barbarous strength' that 'would never fail'. Stevens, too, lived out his last days, from all accounts, in exemplary and stoic calm, through the final stages of the stomach cancer which an operation had failed to remove. He had imagined a self to meet that, also, in his meditation on the last days of one of his chief mentors, George Santayana, 'To an Old Philosopher in Rome':

> It is a kind of total grandeur at the end,
> With every visible thing enlarged and yet
> No more than a bed, a chair and moving nuns,
> The immensest theatre, the pillared porch,
> The look of candles in your ambered room...

This final variation on that early theme of Stevens, 'Downwards to darkness on extended wings' allows the wings to extend with a convincingly majestic sweep. What is contemplated here is not the image of a solipsist dancing on the brink of the void, but

> The human end in the spirit's greatest reach,
> The extreme of the known in the presence of the extreme
> Of the unknown...

This poem also is a late triumph of Stevens' middle style which seems to have survived that hedonist's progress Winters once lamented. So do many of the fine late poems that appeared after his death in *Opus Posthumus*.

The Integrity of George Oppen

I first came across George Oppen's work in 1962 when, after a poetic silence of over twenty-five years, he published *The Materials*. His first book, *Discrete Series* of 1934, had long disappeared from view. An involvement in politics and membership of the Communist Party took Oppen away from poetry: he did not feel that art could or should be made to 'serve the cause', and it was not until after war service, when he was seriously wounded in France, and exile in Mexico where he fled during the McCarthy era, that he returned to writing. His early work, that of the period of *Discrete Series* and the New York of the 1930s, involved a rejection of the English literary tradition and an attempt to find a style through the absence of 'style' that could cope with Oppen's sense of exile in a large city where human and cultural possibilities seemed severely delimited – like the motion of an elevator in one of his poems:

> Up
> Down. Round
> Shiny fixed
> Alternatives
>
> From the quiet
>
> Stone floor…

If the alternatives were fixed, that 'quiet / Stone floor' was not itself devoid of meaning. It was bare and it was there. The quiet it exuded seemed to extend the invitation to meaningful words. But at this stage they had to be few, and also true to Oppen's sense of exile from the received tradition. He was increasingly drawn to political action on behalf of the poor and already his poetry itself had embraced a kind of poverty, stripped-down, ascetic, sharing the walls and streets of ordinary living. The more he sought to define the place and the people in it, the more he quietly – that word again – determined to find an image of them that was free of idealised notions of proletarian insurrection of the kind popular with

The Integrity of George Oppen

'committed' artists of the 1930s. So to be a poet meant for Oppen truth to 'the materials' (the title of his second book), and to be committed meant that he could no longer follow the vocation of a poet until people were fed. This was why he opted for party membership and poor relief. But *Discrete Series* had already sketched the groundwork for a beginning in this territory where the human faced the inanimate or the mechanical, shut in by buildings or behind car windows, and where poems might spring up with difficulty like seedlings between cracks in the pavement.

A continuity is signalled by the epigraph to *The Materials* derived from Maritain, 'We awake in the same moment to ourselves and to things.' This second book, with the great gap behind it, contains a sense not only of self and of humanity as they are in the present instance, but of time:

> Against the glass
> Towers, the elaborate
> Horned handle of a saw
> Dates back
>
> Beyond small harbors
> Facing Europe ...

This poetry of intuitive measurements finds its analogy in the craftsmen of the seaboard settlements:

> ... Who is not at home
> Among these men? who make a home
> Of half truth, rules of thumb
> Of cam and lever and whose docks and piers
> Extend into the sea so self-contained.

Oppen's best things, like the products of the men, wear the appearance of having their parts 'End-for-end, butted to each other / Dove-tailed, tenoned, doweled...' 'Workman', from *The Materials*, sets this awareness into perspective with the resistant world which (in both senses) contains it—a world that exceeds the merely human, with its cruelty, beauty and vastness:

> Leaving the house each dawn I see the hawk
> Flagrant over the driveway. In his claws
> That dot, that comma
> Is the broken animal: the dangling small beast knows
> The burden that he is: he has touched

> The hawk's drab feathers. But the carpenter's is a culture
> Of fitting, of firm dimensions,
> Of post and lintel. Quietly the roof lies
> That the carpenter has finished. The sea birds circle
> The beaches and cry in their own way,
> The innumerable sea birds, their beaks and their wings
> Over the beaches and the sea's glitter.

I first met George Oppen in New York shortly after reviewing *The Materials*. The poems impressed me as a lesson in complete integrity and so did the man, back in Brooklyn and looking like a Jewish sea captain. It was now that Oppen's Jewishness struck me – another element in his sense of exile, though one which only gradually entered his full consciousness. First it came as a faint infiltration during adolescence. It grew to a sharp urgency when, as he lay wounded before the German positions, he buried his identity tag with its H for Hebrew. Finally he was to arrive at a fuller historic possession of this sense of Jewishness when, toward the end of his life, he visited Jerusalem for the first time. Interestingly enough, a late volume, *Seascape: Needle's Eye* (1972), begins on a phrase from another Jew with an acute sense of displacement – Simone Weil. Like her he chose to work in a factory and to repudiate the standards of his middle-class background. He similarly embraced the world of the commonplace, 'somebody's lawn' confronting the 'edge of the ocean', as he had already said in *Discrete Series*. Perhaps more so than in Weil's work, we are aware in Oppen of always being in touch with a specific place (a common place in another important sense) and thereby engaging with the whole, starting out from New York, Maine or San Francisco. Oppen may feel he is living in a Waste Land, in the aftermath of the religious centuries, but like Weil – and unlike Eliot—he does not look to religion as a way 'beyond' all that. He embraces the Waste Land too and there would seem to be a direct challenge to the episode of the typist's squalid sexual encounter of Eliot's poem, in the title poem to *Of Being Numerous* (1968). The common place, the sidewalks of the Waste Land, might somewhere be the place of hope for someone coming home from her first job in a city grown beautiful under its evening lights:

> Phyllis – not neo-classic,
> The girl's name is Phyllis –

> Coming home from her first job
> On the bus in the bare civic interior
> Among those people, the small doors
> Opening on the night at the curb
> Her heart, she told me, suddenly tight with happiness –

I spoke of integrity and this is part of Oppen's desire to reject 'style' and also the sort of pose where the poet's work seeks merely to present the psychodrama of a writer's egotism, a common enough failing of much mid-century American poetry. In this sort of poetry, one may be setting oneself outside and above the commercial ruck, but what one is selling is oneself. Oppen, without naming names, implies all this in the form of a question:

> The question is: how does one hold an apple
> Who likes apples
>
> And how does one handle
> Filth? The question is
>
> How does one hold something
> In the mind which he intends
>
> To grasp and how does the salesman
> Hold a bauble he intends
>
> To sell? The question is
> When will there not be a hundred
>
> Poets who mistake that gesture
> For a style.
>   ('The Gesture' from *This In Which*)

Oppen opposes to the poetry of the ego the figure of, not the worker, but the workman, which may mean the carpenter (Oppen's own chosen craft) or the poet who, as Hugh Kenner puts it, 'fits a poem intricately together, testing each strut, each joint', his mind on what he is making and not on the coruscations of self-presentation. What he is making may long survive the transitory flutter of the ego. Or, as Oppen says in *Of Being Numerous,* in a poem in prose:

> I would want to talk of rooms and of what they look out on and of basements, the rough walls bearing the marks of the forms, the old marks of wood in the concrete, such solitude as we know –
>
> and the swept floors. Someone, a workman bearing about him,

feeling about him that peculiar word like a dishonored fatherhood has swept this solitary floor, this profoundly hidden floor – such solitude as we know.

'This profoundly hidden floor' goes back to 'the quiet / Stone floor' of almost forty years previously and it is the consciousness of its existence which supports the structure of four more gatherings of verse, the last of these, *Primitive*, written out of more than usual difficulty – Oppen never composed with fluency and ease – since he had now entered that phase of illness which destroyed his mind. Signs of Alzheimer's disease had begun to show in the mid-1970s and Oppen, confined to a nursing home, was to die of this, compounded by kidney failure, in 1984 at the age of seventy-six.

Oppen detested mystification: he disliked the cult of Jung and also that mysticism that would offer the ghost of the world, as he said in a letter to his sister June, in place of the world itself. Clarity was always his aim and he attained it or fell short of it along 'the arduous path of appearance', in Heidegger's phrase which is quoted in *This In Which* (1965). Alzheimer's is an especially cruel disability for a man who had consciously prized and worked for 'the beauty of clarity'. Yet the mind has unexpected recesses, even as it undergoes destruction. We are told that when he was visited, late on in his illness, by his sister, he suddenly said to her, 'I don't know if you have anything to say, but let's take out all the adjectives and we'll find out.'

A Rich Sitter: Lorine Niedecker

Lorine Niedecker wrote to me in 1966: 'England is dear to my heart – notice of LN so much stronger there than in this country.' Ian Hamilton Finlay had published her *My Friend Tree* in 1961 at the Wild Hawthorn Press and the same press also offered a tape of her poems read by Sharon Cooper. The two editions of *My Friend Tree* sold out and are now, I suppose, collectors' items. Collectors apart, I had been wondering whether English readers had forgotten about her, as they seem to be forgetting about Marianne Moore, Williams and many other American poets who were briefly and fruitfully available here in the 1960s.

In a second letter, she sent me a biographical note for an anthology of American poetry I had edited. The anthology never appeared, for Louis Zukofsky who occupied a major place, had by this time quarrelled with two other of his objectivist friends, and refused to appear in it. The biographical note still puts the basic facts into succinct order:

> Born 1903. Permanent home 3 miles from Fort Atkinson, Wisconsin, on a river at the point where it empties into a lake (and we have spring floods!), educated Beloit College and forever thru reading at home. Jobs: library, radio and hospital cleaning...My husband and I (married name is Millen) live at present in Milwaukee, Wisconsin, city of big boats from all over the world, taverns, Art Center.

The chief focus for her writing lay in Wisconsin in that region of dangerous waters, and it was the pressure of vast provincial American space that brought the content of her highly individual style to bear. 'Space,' writes Charles Olson in *Call me Ishmael*, 'has a stubborn way of sticking to Americans, penetrating all the way in, accompanying them. It is the exterior fact.' The space of an environment, sparse in detail and mocking the trite inadequacy of the names that American locations so often bear, stands at the back of Miss Niedecker's terse formulations – they are fragments shored against long winters, spring floods and literary isolation. Distant from the literary centres, she did not embrace isolation morosely or willingly but wrote:

> How impossible it is
> to be alone
> the one thing humanity
>   has never really
> moved towards

Faced by those yearly floods, she draws on a steady, uneffusive optimism:

> Springtime's wide
> water –
>   yield
> but the field
> will return

These tiny poems are not the fruit of an anxious isolation. They are rather points of patience: in Zukofsky's *'A'*, section 12, she is characterized as 'a rich sitter'. When *My Friend Tree* appeared in 1961, Jonathan Williams, writing in *Kulchur*, recorded something of her Wisconsin background. He notes 'a tiny green house out at Black Hawk Island, three miles from town. Right out in back is the sparkling Rock River, on its way to Lake Koshkonong. No phone, almost no neighbours… The river is a major fact in her life – lying there sparkling and running, often flooding and worrying people. It's in the poems.' 'I've wasted my whole life in water,' as one of the poems says and in another a character wonders should he have built a boat rather than the four houses he put up in a lifetime. It is a world where 'self-reliance' carries no Emersonian uplift with it:

> Fog-thick morning –
> I see only
> where I walk. I carry
>   my clarity
> with me.

Moral persistence, confronted by space and wide water, does not entail a Whitmanian art that would equal or outdo them. Quantity can be a poor measure. The artistic risk Miss Niedecker often takes is to get all that is needful into half a dozen lines. And the risk is real. In his Notes on Poe, Baudelaire, seconding Poe's remarks on the short poem, says: 'It must be added that a poem that is too brief, a poem which provides insufficient *pabulum* for the excitement created, and which is unequal to the reader's natural appetite, is also very imperfect.'

Perhaps sensing this risk of 'insufficient *pabulum*', when she came to write *North Central* (1968) she included two longer sequences, 'Lake Superior' and 'Wintergreen Ridge'. They are two of her finest. The first is a mosaic built up from – to adopt Ed Dorn's phrase – 'her beautifully random instances' which coalesce in a common subject. They range here from snippets of history –

> Radisson:
> 'a laborinth of pleasure'
> this world of the Lake
>
> Long hair, long gun
>
> Fingernails pulled out
> by Mohawks

– to unexpectedly lyrical pieces of geological information, presented with her quiet certainty of touch. In the second long sequence, 'Wintergreen Ridge', developing a measure she first used in 'Paul' from *My Friend Tree* (a three ply measure, though very different in effect from that of Williams) she unites the entire stretch of the piece into a structure of sound that is completely her own, despite the debt to Louis Zukofsky:

> Andromeda
>   Cisandra of the bog
>   pearl-flowered
>
> Lady's tresses
>   insect-eating
>   pitcher plant
>
> Bedeviled little Drosera
>   of the sundews
>   deadly
>
> in sphagnum moss
>   sticks out its sticky
>   (Darwin tested)
>
> tentacled leaf

> towards a fly
> half an inch away

Space which touched her excellent short poems at every point from the outside, has now 'penetrated all the way in' to become part here of a new, flowing and sustained music.

One returns readily to these two fine sequences, but what one carries in the memory are the inimitable short poems. They have the inevitability of epigram or epitaph. Now she is no longer with us, I find myself reading one of her epitaphs for someone else, as though she had written it for herself:

> Hear
> where he snow-grave is
> the *You*
> > *ah you*
> of mourning doves

Tucked into the inside fold of the wrapper of *My Friend Tree*, one discovered its unbound introduction. This is by Ed Dorn, written in a dense prose, the ponderings of which repays. The snatch I have already quoted from it, occupies part of a much longer sentence in which Dorn summarizes the attraction these brief, clear yet mysterious poems hold for him: 'I like these poems because first they attach an undistractable clarity to the word, and then because they are unabashed enough to weld that word to a freely sought, beautifully random instance – that instance being the only thing place and its content can be: the catch in the seine.'

Elizabeth Bishop

English readers began to make the acquaintance of Elizabeth Bishop with the appearance, thanks to Chatto and Windus, of her selected *Poems* in 1956. The same publishers have now honoured their early commitment with *The Complete Poems 1927–1979* which splendidly vindicates them. F.W. Bateson once described their author to me as 'Marianne Moore and water'. Reading these lucid, witty and sometimes sad poems, I wondered how often this sort of dismissal had slowed down the spread of her reputation here.

Marianne Moore, whom she first met in 1934, was clearly decisive for Elizabeth Bishop's work. She did not, however, water down that astringent and humane tone, but learned from it in a way that words like 'influence' do not greatly help us to understand. Behind Miss Moore was the prose of Ruskin. It suggested to her, perhaps, that if only Ruskin's wit could be rescued from his eloquence, the twentieth-century poet could write of nature free of the egotistical sublime. Ruskin witty? Take his pine trees – 'each like the shadow of the one beside it – upright, fixed, spectral, as troops of ghosts standing on the walls of Hades, not knowing each other ... The rock itself looks bent and shattered beside them, – fragile, weak, inconsistent, compared to their dark energy of delicate life, and monotony of enchanted pride – unnumbered, unconquerable.' The shadow at the beginning of this passage, that fantasy of the ghosts, the pre-Lawrencian 'dark energy of delicate life' all pull against the miscalculated organ notes of 'unnumbered, unconquerable'. In her collage poem 'An Octopus' Miss Moore sheers away at all this with:

austere specimens of our American royal families,
'each like the shadow of the one beside it.
The rock seems frail compared with their dark energy of life,'
its vermilion and onyx and manganese-blue interior expensiveness
left at the mercy of the weather ...

Elizabeth Bishop builds her own variations on that in 'At The Fishhouses':

> Back, behind us,
> the dignified tall firs begin.
> Bluish, associating with their shadows,
> a million Christmas trees stand
> waiting for Christmas. The water seems suspended
> above the rounded grey and blue-grey stones.
> I have seen it over and over, the same sea, the same,
> slightly, indifferently swinging above the stones...

This is like a darker, post-imagist, version of the kind of writing one finds in the prose of Sarah Orne Jewett's little masterpiece, *The Country of the Pointed Firs*. Yet the suggestion of threat in it is something that makes Miss Bishop's evocation of northern latitudes and dying sea-side towns, of Maine, New Brunswick and Cape Breton, different from Jewett and also from the pastoral atmosphere of a similar setting in Miss Moore's 'The Steeple-Jack'. There 'the hero, the student, the steeple-jack, each in his way, / is at home'. For Miss Bishop people are only provisionally at home. When she travels south (Nova Scotia and Brazil are her two extremes) she asks

> Is it lack of imagination that makes us come
> to imagined places [...]? Should we have stayed at home,
> wherever that may be?

Nearer home, at Cape Breton, the place is depopulating, there is an idiot, a dwarf dressmaker, a student who, unlike Miss Moore's Ambrose in 'The Steeple-Jack', is a morose giant. Not that Miss Bishop lays all this on with Faulkner's palette knife. But hovering over her northern sea-vistas and her Brazilian jungles, there is a hint of the darkness about to fall, a margin of the sad and the inexplicable that refuses to be exorcised by her brave wit. At times the brilliant surface of her work reminds one of Hemingway, the Hemingway of *Big Two-Hearted River* (she, also, was an enthusiastic fisher). Style never becomes for her, as for him, a ritual of self-congratulation, though there are one or two Martian indulgences. Yet one senses that her objectivity is governed by enormous reticences and her precision comes from an effort at self-control that refuses to be more explicit.

It is curious that *The Complete Poems* does not contain the long prose section 'In the Village' from her third volume *Questions of Travel*. This can hardly arise from a policy of excluding the prose, for we have half a dozen uncollected prose pieces gathered together here. 'In the Village' derives from her own childhood. Born in 1911 – the year of her father's death and her mother's committal to an asylum – she is brought up 'in the village' in Nova Scotia. Here 'in the middle of the view', we are told, 'like one hand of a clock pointing straight up, is the steeple of the Presbyterian Church'. A background of pain and alienation (the mother comes home from the mental institution and disappears again) contrasts with a bright particularized foreground seen through the child's eyes and this, to some extent, shuts back the pain. The mother's scream is driven out by the clang with which Nate the blacksmith shapes a horseshoe:

> Nate is shaping a horseshoe.
> Oh, beautiful pure sound.
> It turns everything else to silence.

On first reading *Questions of Travel* years ago, I felt there was some evasion in this silence. But, since then, the strip-tease of Lady Lazarus, and other less-practised stunts, have made me wonder whether there was not a justifiable degree of self protection in this elected silence. The inclusion of 'Poems Written in Youth' in *The Complete Poems* bears out this feeling. Among these very interesting pieces – some written in the poet's sixteenth year – recurs a devastated sense of inner division – in the elf, for example, who appears there and whose 'singing split the sky in two'. This poem, and several more, could well have been the results of merely juvenile Angst. But the theme of division is taken up again in later work, as in 'The Weed', distantly but distinctly modelled on George Herbert's 'Love Unknown'. In 'Love Unknown' a hard heart is dipped in a bloody font, suppled in a cauldron marked 'Affliction' and pricked into new life by thorns. A voice at the end of the poem interprets all this to the poet and the saving nature of his experiences. At the close of 'The Weed', the interpreting voice offers less reassurance:

> The weed stood in the severed heart.
> 'What are you doing there?' I asked.
> It lifted its head all dripping wet
> (with my own thoughts?)
> and answered then: 'I grow,' it said
> 'but to divide your heart again.'

In *Sonnet*, which comes over thirty years later and in the last year of her life, she is still pursued by this theme:

> Caught – the bubble
> in the spirit-level
> a creature divided;
> and the compass needle
> wobbling and wavering,
> undecided ...

Poems like this are peripheral to the main body of Elizabeth Bishop's work, and the pain which brought them forth – her sense of isolation, her sexual inversion, perhaps – is checked and counterpoised by her steady outward glance. Could a larger poet have confronted the pain more directly and have brought it to bear more tellingly on the scope of her 'objective' style? Perhaps. yet there is a courageous reaching-away from the luxuries of self-enclosure in her best work and towards the life that is going on around her or the life that is absent, as in 'Crusoe in England', where the returned castaway reflects:

> And I had waterspouts. Oh,
> half a dozen of them at a time, far out,
> they'd come and go, advancing and retreating,
> their heads in cloud, their feet in moving patches
> of scuffed-up white.
> Glass chimneys, flexible, attenuated,
> sacerdotal beings of glass ... I watched
> the water spiral up in them like smoke.
> Beautiful, yes, but not much company.

Miss Bishop admired a quality in George Herbert that she calls 'almost surrealistic'. She is thinking of the narrative of the heart's mysterious adventures in 'Love Unknown'. That poem, with its tight allegorizing, is not in any very exact sense 'surrealistic', but one sees what she means. She spent a year in France during the 1930s, 'where I had read a lot of surrealist poetry and prose'. The overheavy, rich soup of the Unconscious seems to have been less to her taste than a surrealist liking for disparities which leaves room for wit. Lautréamont's famous 'chance meeting, on a dissecting table, of a sewing machine and an umbrella' could be comic, as Max Ernst perceived. Miss Bishop came to look for disparities in, she says, 'glimpses of the always-more-successful surrealism of everyday life'. There is her memorable family filling station:

> Do they live in the station?

> It has a cement porch
> behind the pumps, and on it
> a set of crushed and grease-
> impregnated wickerwork;
> on the wicker sofa
> a dirty dog, quite comfy.
>
> Some comic books provide
> the only note of color –
> of certain color. They lie
> upon a big dim doily
> draping a taboret
> (part of the set), beside
> a big hirsute begonia. [...]
>
> Somebody embroidered the doily.
> Somebody waters the plant,
> or oils it, maybe. Somebody
> arranges the rows of cans
> so that they softly say:
> ESSO – SO – SO – SO
> to high-strung automobiles.
> Somebody loves us all.

Or there is nature's own surrealism in 'Florida':

> The state with the prettiest name,
> the state that floats in brackish water,
> held together by mangrove roots
> that bear white living oysters in clusters,
> and when dead strew white swamps with skeletons,
> dotted as if bombarded, with green hummocks
> like ancient cannon-balls sprouting grass. ...
> Enormous turtles, helpless and mild,
> die and leave their barnacled shells on the beaches,
> and their large white skulls with round eye-sockets
> twice the size of a man's.

As Elizabeth Bishop grew older her out-put, never voluminous, slowed down, but her late book *Geography III* contains some of her finest work. 'The Moose', from that collection is a quintessential Bishop poem, returning to beginnings in New Brunswick, summoning up and summing up. Across the vast geography of her northern world travels a bus, the people who join it hinting at the existence of a community behind those woods and along those bays, as when

> a lone traveller gives
> kisses and embraces
> to seven relatives
> and a collie supervises.

Behind the voices of the travellers on the bus we hear the voices of grandparents 'uninterrupted / talking, in Eternity':

> Talking the way they talked
> in the old featherbed,
> peacefully, on and on,
> dim lamplight in the hall,
> down in the kitchen, the dog
> tucked in her shawl.

What suddenly unites all the passengers, drawing them away from sleep, is the appearance of a moose, another witness to those spaces. Unlike the buck that crashes through Robert Frost's poem 'The Most of It' and leaves the poet to his own cosmic loneliness unreciprocated, the moose unites poet and travellers inside the stopped bus. They belong to a common universe along with the animal:

> Taking her time,
> She looks the bus over,
> grand, otherworldly.
> Why, why do we feel
> (we all feel) this sweet
> sensation of joy?

> 'Curious creatures,'
> says our quiet driver,
> rolling his *r*'s.
> 'Look at that, would you.'
> Then he shifts gears.
> For a moment longer,

> by craning backward,
> the moose can be seen
> on the moonlit macadam;
> then there's a dim

>   smell of moose, an acrid
>   smell of gasoline.

    This rich collection concludes with a series of translations of Latin American poems from both the Spanish and Portuguese. These are finely done as one would expect from the translator of the Brazilian prose classic *Minha Vida de Menina*, published under the title of *The Diary of 'Helena Morley'* in 1957. That, too, is an achievement of Miss Bishop's that deserves to be more widely known over here. When, in the Introduction, she goes to look at Diamantina, the setting of the diary, one sees her *translating* the place into the terms of her own art: 'In the cold clear air, the town itself, with its neatness, rockiness, and fine glitter, seems almost on the point of precipitation and crystallization.' In the action of her poems there is also often a feeling of precipitation and crystallization. There is some darkness and some loneliness. But there is humour and humanity, too, which can make of the cold clear air a bracing element in which isolation is in abeyance and the heart is undivided in its sympathies.

Poetry and Friendship

David Kalstone died in 1986 before completing his book *Becoming a Poet: Elizabeth Bishop with Marianne Moore and Robert Lowell* (edited by Robert Hemenway). Originally, instead of a triangular study of Elizabeth Bishop and her relations with Marianne Moore and Robert Lowell, its scope was to have been more general, a study of an emerging poetic generation in the post-war years, 'especially Robert Lowell and Randall Jarrell'. But Elizabeth Bishop became its centre and Marianne Moore and Lowell the not quite equal halves. Jarrell inevitably faded from the picture, for once he had introduced Bishop to Lowell, it was the latter who exercised the far greater attraction and influence over her and Bishop, anyhow, was always in two minds about the success of Jarrell's poetry and there occurred a decided cooling in relations once she had expressed her disapproval of his novel, *Pictures from an Institution*. Robert Hemenway has carefully edited Kalstone's incomplete typescript and James Merrill has contributed a final chapter on Bishop's *Geography III*, her 'last and, in many senses, greatest book', as Kalstone had noted. Merrill talked with him about this and 'without presuming to complete that chapter myself', he tries to suggest why *Geography III* had seemed so important to his friend.

'One of the strange things about poets is the way they keep warm by writing to one another all over the world.' Virgil Thomson's sentence prefaces this book which is so often concerned with letters exchanged by the protagonists. Poets' letters not only serve to keep one another warm, but also seem doomed to steer towards The Big Disagreement or Misunderstanding. For Moore and Bishop this was the latter's long poem 'Roosters' which Moore attempted to rewrite (the curious result is given in an appendix), and for Bishop and Lowell, his use of personal letters in *The Dolphin*. 'The intensity of her response was unexpected,' says Kalstone, just as Miss Moore's had been when she sealed her letter about 'Roosters' with a silver star and warned, 'do not read at mealtime or on going to bed.' Kalstone tells the story of these two friendships with a nice combination of literary criticism and biography, though his book is scarcely the 'full-scale critical-biographical consideration' the blurb speaks of. However, it is full enough and refreshing, too, after the biographical block-busters which seem to have become usual nowadays. Kalstone's dealings with Bishop's poetry and what he has to say about Moore's and Lowell's, are exemplary. He writes crisply and with tact, and the life is never called upon merely to eke out our sense of the works. They stand in courteous relation to each other, which is what Bishop feared Lowell's failed to do once he began explicitly making poetry out of his private affairs while in the act of living through their desperate complications.

The friendship with Moore was a four-year tutelage. Moore (and her mother) corrected Bishop's poems and stories – she originally did not think of herself as principally a poet –, which led to the later major disagreement about 'Roosters'. When they met, Moore was forty-seven and Bishop, still a senior at Vassar, twenty-three. She was attracted by the objectivity of the older woman's style and the mysterious way in which description could become spiritual significance. Description for Bishop meant a sane reaction against what Moore saw as her 'interiorizing'. The temptation to 'interiorize', heaven knows, must have been great, with the early death of her father, her mother's madness and her own orphaned status in the house of relatives. These years of extreme loneliness also brought her a kind of self-possession. 'Please don't think I dote on it,' she said of her unhappy childhood, and later on, when Lowell had incorporated and foreshortened in one of his own poems a passage of Bishop's prose about that childhood, 'I don't want to have it any worse than it was,' came her response. She never, says Kalstone, traded on her losses – unlike, one might add, Berryman or Plath, or for that matter Lowell himself, who had managed to trade not only on his own but on hers too.

Moore's objectivity was the outward sign of her security; Bishop's clarity and sensuous detail, strengths that had to be mastered in face of all the displacements of her youth. Place itself was never a given for her – she had lost the Nova Scotia of her childhood and she had to live in Brazil before she could find her way back to it as a writer. 'I've never concealed this,' she said of her mother's madness, 'although I don't like to make too much of it.' Her mother lived until 1934, the year of the meeting with Moore. One can see why a poet whose steadying attention to the physical world and its surfaces should have been someone Bishop instinctively responded to: if only she could acquire something of that ease, objectivity and daring, she might establish for herself a sense of place and presence in a world where the threat of solitude and dispossession was always at hand – and to be resisted.

Kalstone establishes the terms of the friendship most deftly, with Bishop 'testing herself against the older poet' in 'a mixture of disobedience and dependence'. Moore encouraged and made suggestions. It was not until the 'Roosters' episode that she unexpectedly upset the delicate balance that had assured the persistence and growth of their intimacy and of Bishop's poetry too. The occasion would be comic if it had not been so fraught with dangers for them both. It is hard to be certain of the precise reason for Moore's irrational horror at the poem and her determination to rewrite it – aided and abetted by her redoubtable parent. Was there – one can merely speculate – some subconscious streak of jealousy when she read this, the most ambitious and lengthy piece Bishop had so far attempted? The 'pupil', after all, had beaten her in getting into the pages of *The New Yorker*, a triumph she seems to have resented. And Moore, as Kalstone notes, felt at this time, stalled in her own career. The ostensible objection was to words like 'water-closet' and 'dropping-plastered', with Moore defending herself against possible charges of prudery by reminding Bishop that she had not blenched at Smart's 'to the mermaid's pap / the scalèd infant clings', or Cowper's tame hare that 'swung his rump around'. Nevertheless, 'few of us, it seems to me, are fundamentally rude enough to enrich our work in such ways without cost'. Hence the rewriting, blatantly disregarding the poem's triplet structure, with Moore suggesting a new and comically more ambiguous title, 'The Cock'. This time Bishop was firmly disobedient and went her own way. When the poem appeared in *North and South*, Moore reviewed the book and even brought herself to praise details of this poem that had once unnerved her. It was not literally true, as Bishop later claimed, that she never again sent Moore any of her poems for comment, but politeness must now do the work of generous friendship and, in Kalstone's words, 'Moore's treatment of Bishop's new work was, after "Roosters", gingerly and restrained.'

Both Moore and Robert Lowell wrote reviews of *North and South*. It was now he who became the more intimate and influential friend. They met in 1947, introduced by Jarrell, and their relationship continued for the better part of thirty years. Lowell even half persuaded himself and told his friends (though not Bishop) that he was in love with her. Six years younger than her, he was well ahead in the world of literary connections and able to discover grants for her, persuade her to read publicly and even secured her the post of poetry consultant at the Library of Congress. There was always the threat of what she called his 'ego-maniacy' (she was largely absent in Brazil, however, when some of his worst attacks occurred), but the friendship was fruitful for them both. His letters to her and his busyness on her behalf show a kindness and generosity far removed from the brutality of his manic highs. Lowell believed that Bishop's off-beat style helped him reject the heavy armour of his earlier manner and, as she wrote to him, she found *his* poetry 'so strongly influential that if I start reading it when I am working on something of my own I am lost'. This, of course, also defines the sense in which it couldn't be of help to her, and she always resisted Lowell's tendency to over-dramatize. 'Bishop,' writes Kalstone, 'had a more settled pessimism and was more reticent about expressing it – constitutionally so, but also because in their encounters she was unnerved when Lowell exaggerated his loneliness.'

The major influence, felt by Lowell himself, comes from Bishop's rediscovery and exploration of her own childhood. This was stimulated by her reading of the Brazilian classic *Minha Vida de Menina* – actually written by a twelve year old – which she was later to translate as *The Diary of 'Helena Morley'*. Bishop's own childhood resurfaced in her short story 'In the Village' which tells of her mother's insanity and her early life in Nova Scotia, and also in 'Gwendolyn', the narrative of the death of one of her playmates. Lowell based a poem, 'The Scream', on a passage from 'The Village' – making things worse than they were, according to Bishop – and this whole phase of hers predates his *Life Studies*, a book where his own prose '91 Revere Street' appeared – one piece from a mass of unpublished autobiographical writings – and also the autobiographical poems where he incorporates prose rhythms in a new way. Bishop's rediscovery of childhood seems to have been the catalyst behind this significant and perhaps unsurpassed period of Lowell's poetry.

The Big Disagreement or Misunderstanding came later, when it was Bishop's turn to write a long, uneasy letter about Lowell's use of private correspondence in his poems. It had all really begun when he had worked a letter of hers into verse, drastically simplifying and melodramatizing its content. But *The Dolphin* brought forth the full weight of her disapproval of his methods while trying to be fair also to the 'magnificent poetry ... also honest poetry – *almost*'. There follows her pained and even angry critique with its climax: 'One can use one's life as material – one does, anyway – but these letters – aren't you violating a trust? If you were given permission – if you hadn't changed them ... etc. But *art just isn't worth that much.*' She is not entirely coherent, but one sees what she means.

Lowell thought her letter 'a kind of masterpiece of criticism, though her extreme paranoia – about revelations gives it a kind of wildness'. 'Paranoia' was a two-edged noun for Lowell – one that he did not use to her, but in a letter to Frank Bidart. He stuck to his principles (if that is the word), but changed many details: 'he would quote in italics,' as Kalstone says, 'and attribute many of the lines, changed, to himself.' The friendship of the two poets survived this letter and others reiterating its main drift. Two years later Lowell wrote to her, 'I feel our friendship has passed out of some shadow.'

How could they not have disagreed about such matters as 'revelations'? She wanted to distance her past, to recover it, but not immerse herself once more in all its harrowing painfulness. Lowell, so nineteenth-century and Freudian in this respect, had always burrowed under and re-emerged with magnified exacerbations such as she kept at arm's length. Kalstone comments: 'For Bishop, ... writing must document the literal truth; Bishop would insist on this with a scientific tone to her voice. But part of her meaning was that such literal representation kept almost inconceivable pain within its bounds.' Lowell's pain, she felt, lacked bounds in ways damaging not only to himself but to those who were close to him. Other people have felt differently. A. Alvarez, reviewing Lowell's *Day by Day* and speaking of both Lowell and Berryman, says: 'For readers of poetry the work clearly justified the cost; whether or not the poets themselves and those closest to them thought the same is, mercifully, not our concern.' And yet, reading them, how can we ever quite feel so 'mercifully' remote from the life and lives behind such work?

Bishop exemplified her own philosophy of using a distanced suffering in *Geography III*, her last collection and one that Kalstone did not survive to write about. One is grateful for Merrill's 'Afterword', but hungry for the missing dénouement. The rest of the book, even in its unrevised state, is a measure of what we have lost. Few critics write so unshowily as Kalstone and with such quiet accuracy about poems and their genesis in the poet's life and contacts.

Eye and Ear in the Verse of James Laughlin

James Laughlin's poetry comes mainly in two sizes, short-line poems and long-line poems. He began by writing in short lines and, of course, he has frequently returned to that form. These poems seem to me to belong at the centre of his achievement. Their hold on the exact phrase, intonation, or cadence also makes possible, when he comes to write long-line poems, a flowing distinctiveness and clarity, where many another poet might sound merely diffuse. There is no Whitmanian afflatus: what we hear is the tone of the speaking voice modulated as between friends, the diction nicely adjusted to conveying the matter in hand without overemphasis. But there is a price to be paid. What one misses in these long-lined poems is that exquisite adjustment made possible by the short line as it involves ear, eye and breath in explorative uncertainties of a rare order.

The first poem I ever read by Laughlin happened to be of the short-line variety. Its title was 'Above the City'. I found it quoted whole by Marianne Moore in an essay called 'Humility, Concentration, and Gusto' in her *Predilections,* which I acquired in 1956. At first the poem puzzled me, but rapidly puzzlement turned to delight. There seemed to be two patterns at work, the visual and the oral, each refusing to become reconciled with the other without negotiation and without the reader's active co-operation:

> You know our office on the 18th
> floor of the Salmon Tower looks
>   right out on the
>
> Empire State and it just happened
> we were there finishing up some
>   late invoices on
>
> a new book that Saturday morning
> when a bomber roared through the
>   mist and crashed
>
> flames poured from the windows

>   into the drifting clouds and sirens
>   screamed down in
>
>   the streets below...

And so it goes unstoppably on, until guided into its coda by three deft but unobtrusive internal rhymes – 'realized', 'surprise', 'eyes' – one in each of the three concluding stanzas. One sees why Marianne Moore was taken by this poem, she whose visual arrangement of her verse so delighted in antagonizing eye and voice. She even went as far as to reorder the last two stanzas and wrote to Laughlin, 'Can you condone it?' 'I could indeed,' the poet gallantly responded when he reprinted 'Above the City'. Yet one is relieved that he also retained the poem in its original form where the last stanza violates the line count of those preceding, but has more verbal muscularity than Miss Moore's – despite its extra line, which is empowered, in Doctor Johnson's phrase, with 'more weight than bulk'. Indeed, fundamentally the relation of eye to ear in Laughlin stands far nearer to William Carlos Williams than to Miss Moore. The latter is more interested in arranging her words as if they were patternings on some kind of sampler, elegantly displayed, but not invariably aiming for that precarious unity where the seen and the heard both challenge and reinforce each other, until it is the ear that becomes the final arbiter and measure. In Laughlin one sees the closeness to Williams's playing off the two elements against each other, of (as he says) 'poem against metric'. Williams unfortunately has a weakness for terminology that sometimes renders ambiguous what he is saying. In 'poem against metric' here 'metric' seems to gesture toward the way words lie visually on the page and not to the countable recurrence of a beat. This he also sees as a partnership between the oral or 'verbal invention' and visual layout. 'The poem is here, but the metric *is here,*' as Williams writes to one correspondent, 'and they go along side by side – the verbal invention and the purely metrical invention go along arm in arm, looking for a place where they can embrace.'

In first reading 'Above the City', I liked all the brisk work the eye was called on to do, and I enjoyed that first real shock, the enjambement or stanzaic leap to the famous skyscraper that appears in stanza two. At the same time you heard the speaking voice pulling against stanzaic layout. I could not have known then – long before the publication of Hugh Witemeyer's edition of the correspondence of the two poets – that Laughlin and Williams had been discussing the matter with each other in the late 1930s. 'Damn the bastards,' wrote Williams, 'for saying that you can't mix auditory and visual standards in poetry... What they ... don't know, is that an auditory quality, a NEW auditory quality, underlines and determines the visual quality which they object to.' Laughlin himself had been speaking about 'the tension ... between the strictly artificial visual pattern and the strictly natural spoken rhythms', in opposition to his Harvard associates, who disputed this aspect of his poetry.

The earliest of Laughlin's books that I have in my possession bears the date of 1945. It was poems from this collection, *Some Natural Things,* which opened *The Collected Poems* of 1994. Between these two dates you might imagine a good deal of fame as a poet would have come his way. Yet look into any of the anthologies – into, say, the benchmark *Norton Anthology of Modern Poetry* – and you can be sure of not finding Laughlin there. The same is true of literary histories – *The Columbia History of American Poetry,* for example: silence. As a famous publisher, you might think he would be regarded as a phenomenon, a publisher who writes excellent verse. One of the blurbs on the 1994 *Collected Poems* says, 'Here is America's great popular poet, if only the bastards read poetry.' Perhaps one day, when people tire of all those phoney novels, he will be. But not yet.

Over thirty years ago, I asked Henry Rago, the last of the great editors of *Poetry (Chicago),* why one could trace so few notices of Laughlin's books. 'Because', said Rago, 'he never avails himself of the system of promotion – he even refrains from sending out review copies.' So perhaps Laughlin's own modesty is partly to blame? Clearly he had dubious feelings about being his own publisher and apologizes to and for himself in 'The Publisher to the Poet':

> Right hand blush never
> for left handed brother
>
> action and thought are
> children of one mother

Laughlin's career as a writer began with Latin and Greek at Choate school. Catullus has always been one of his touchstones. In the notes to *The Collected Poems* (called typically 'Not-Notes') he tells us of the next step: 'After a boring freshman year at Harvard I took off for Europe and enrolled in Pound's Ezuversity at Rapallo. He was, by all odds, my greatest professor ... and my education continued for thirty years after I became his publisher.' 'Ezra', a recent poem of some length (and an earlier version of 'Some Memories of E.P.'), charts this formative relationship:

> You said I was
> Such a terrible poet, I'd better
> Do something useful and become
> A publisher, a profession which
> You inferred required no talent
> And only limited intelligence.

One of the suggestions made by Pound for this publishing venture was the work of his friend – and soon to become Laughlin's friend – William Carlos Williams. Williams was just the man Laughlin needed to know and read. More, perhaps, even than Pound, it is the stylistic influence of Williams – with a dash of Cummings in the punctuation or lack of it – that enabled Laughlin to develop his own style. Its form – before he went in for longer lines as the imaginary poet Hiram Handspring – was dictated by the typewriter: 'The rule is that in a couplet any second line has to be within two typewriter spaces of the line preceding it.' The result is a breaking up of those curious things words and sentences and a pleasurable dislocation between what one sees and the cadence of what one reads – you are not meant to pause at the end of every line, as in the verse of Robert Creeley any more than in Marianne Moore's syllabics:

> You know that comical
> puppy has grown up in-
>
> to a marvelous hunting
> dog he's in the woods
>
> all day and brings out
> rabbits by the dozen
>
> but the funny thing is
> he never hurts them he
>
> doesn't even bite them
> just carries them home
>
> in his mouth & leaves
> them on the porch for
>
> us   poor little things
> at first they're much

> too scared to move but
> in a little while they
>
> shake themselves & hop
> away to the woods again

It is out of such domestic incidents and the pleasures and pains of love and of family life that Laughlin creates many of his best poems. He has, of late, written of the suicide of his son Robert and the death of his wife Ann. These are unusually harrowing incidents for Laughlin (he writes about them with never a false note), yet it is often the inevitable painful collisions of family relationships, our violations of one another, that give substance to his poems. Laughlin insists that he writes 'light verse', but it is not of the Ogden Nash kind. The lightness betokens a sensitivity in handling deceptively simple, but tricky subjects. The head in 'Step on His Head' is only a bobbing shadow jumped on by his children, but the incident is fraught with pain to come:

> now I duck my head so they'll
> miss when they jump & they screech
>
> with delight and I moan oh you're
> hurting you're hurting me stop and
> they jump all the harder...

The crucial poem of Williams for Laughlin in helping him towards his characteristic style was the former's 'The Catholic Bells' with its own dislocations:

> ... ring for the lame
>
> young man in black with
> gaunt cheeks and wearing a
> Derby hat, who is hurrying
> to 11 o'clock Mass (the
>
> grapes still hanging to
> the vines along the nearby
> Concordia Halle like broken
> teeth in the head of an
>
> old man)...

It was after reading this that Laughlin wrote 'Easter in Pittsburgh', his longest poem to date, and one in which the subject matter of the family – the uncle who preaches and drinks, the sacked maid and governess, the strike in Pittsburgh and tear gas at the steel mill – all comes into focus and availability. Lowell in *Life Studies* seems to have learned something from Laughlin's poem and also from his 'The Swarming Bees' (on Uncle Willy, another drinking relation). Lowell, writing about William Carlos Williams and also paying tribute to 'The Catholic Bells', says of Laughlin at Harvard: 'our only strong and avant-garde man was James Laughlin.... He knew the great, and he himself wrote deliberately flat descriptive and anecdotal poems. We were sarcastic about them, but they made us feel secretly that we didn't know what was up in poetry.' Williams's two poems on his own parents, 'Adam' and 'Eve' of 1936, appeared to have given food for thought to both Lowell and Laughlin.

It was in 'Easter in Pittsburgh' that Laughlin most energetically carried forward the dramatic qualities that Williams had discovered in the cadences of the natural speaking voice when he had written 'The Catholic Bells'. This was an historic moment. It seemed to Williams that Laughlin had taken what he himself had done and extended its possibilities. The realization and mark of understanding between the older poet and the younger show significantly in a letter Williams wrote to Laughlin in 1939: 'The Easter in Pittsburgh is a milestone. That's a noteworthy poem, a revolutionary poem in more ways than one. I'm thinking of the form of it.... . It gains dignity at your hands, it reveals the possibilities in the form, possibilities for the long sought dramatic unit of speech, of composition that can go anywhere it wants to.' Williams then confesses, 'The one thing that has disturbed me at times is that my studies and labors in the form of verse have not shown a quality susceptible of further development. I've had a few imitators but no one, till now, who seemed to be able to take what I've done and step it up to the next level.'

The marks of Laughlin's poetry are its humanity and its variety of both themes and idiom. Besides the poems in English, there are those in '(American) French', at least one in ski-slopes German, and those that use Italian. The most beautiful of these last form a sequence which recounts a love affair between the young poet and an Italian girl, 'In Another Country':

> she called vieni qua splashing her
> arms in the clear green water vieni
> subito and so I followed her swim-
> ming around a point of rock to the

> next cove vieni qua non hai paura
> and she slipped like an eel beneath
> the surface down through the sunken
> entrance to a hidden grotto where
>
> the light was soft and green on fine-
> grained sand è bello no? ...

A number of the poems have this 'light that never was on sea or land' ('è strano questa luce com' un / altro mondo'), but the majority take place in the world of common experience, as effortlessly unstrained as Williams's poem on the plums in the icebox.

One values these poems for their use of a wide and unexpected subject matter – the small boy, for instance, who fashions cardboard hatchets, bloodstains their blades with red crayon, and lays them affectionately on his father's work desk. 'Anything,' as Williams stated, 'is good material for poetry. Anything. I've said it time and time again.' Laughlin evidently agrees with this contention. Yet there is more to the end result than the sheer randomness of merely 'some natural things' (the title of one of his books). In describing his way of writing ('Technical Notes'), Laughlin explains that he prefers, as against using poetic diction,

> to build with plain brown bricks
> of common talk American talk then
>   set 1 Roman stone
>
> among them for a key

This keystone and sense of cumulative architecture in these carefully assembled structures represent the conversion of everyday matter into the matter of art. 'With me a poem,' says Laughlin,

> is finally just
> a natural thing

And yet, as Guy Davenport has put it, in 'a neat oblong of phrases, squared away on the page, each line [is] a little event in itself'. These events impress us for the shapeliness of their appearance, their having been 'squared' into inevitability and also possessing a keystone. What we listen to is the natural speech with which Laughlin begins now brought to an aesthetic focus by the heard measure of the poems. These are the products of many decades in which 'the shaping spirit of the imagination' combines its forces with those of nature.

Black Mountain Revisited

'In most books, the *I*, or first person, is omitted; in this it will be retained.' Thus Thoreau in telling us what to anticipate from him in *Walden* and, 'That', he goes on, 'in respect to egotism, is the main difference. We commonly do not remember that it is, after all, always the first person that is speaking. I should not talk so much about myself if there were anybody else whom I knew so well.' The *I* of whose presence he forewarns us is less talked *about* in *Walden* than confronted by places, situations, irreducible objects, which by making immediate demands on that *I* force it to act in relationship and in a certain self-forgetfulness. The *I* discovers the commonalty it shares with soil, water, wood-chuck, tanager, field-sparrow and whippoorwill. Among its 'grand democracy of forest trees' (Keats in another context) the *I* is both challenged and confirmed.

Martin Duberman prints the above passage from Thoreau as epigraph to his exploration of the educational venture at Black Mountain College, *Black Mountain: An Exploration in Community*. It is an odd choice for someone with such an uncertain awareness of his own self – someone who, a few pages further on, confides in us that 'a posture of bland agreeableness ... unfortunately comes rather naturally to me even when the social pressures are not exceptional'. He wants both to warn us about himself and to complain that historians have previously failed to do this kind of thing. His attempt is to dramatize the impact of the data on the historian and the historian on the data. The data are often fascinating, but the drama, as W.C. Fields would have put it, is a corny little thing. Either Mr Duberman's *I* is not of tantalizing interest, or he lacks the artistic gift to make it so. He parades it before us not only in an introduction, but also in a preface. If this show of frankness were to have succeeded, it would have demanded a style arrestingly grotesque enough to persuade us that, yes, despite all our suspicions of being got at, this is, after all, a way of doing it, and only an American could have brought it off. But instead of a style sufficiently individual to convince *us* and to convey *him*, in all his protesting dither, aggrievement and desire to please, the exploration pushes from shore into a pool of stagnant jargon: 'currently considered innovative ... the singular, shaping talents of our time ... the aura of flamboyance ... skills at information-retrieval ... spotting personal style through the veneer of an interview format'.

Duberman insists that 'to try to show up in one's work instead of distancing oneself from it, to remove the protections of anonymity, can be searing. Yet harnessing one's emotional resources to one's "academic" work can help to release them in one's life – or can make one aware for the first time of how limited those resources in fact are.' But what is a reader to do about it if that final parenthesis turns out to be true? And isn't the whole proposition a cliché? What historian worth reading – Gibbon, Macaulay, Burckhardt, Michelet, Parkman, Carlyle, Geyl – fails to show up in his work? And what writer – it is as a writer that Duberman ask to be judged – would have let pass that 'harnessing one's emotional resources' without realizing how clichés betray? Those emotions may be turning mill-wheels or whatever, but, 'harnessed', they are in uncomfortable bondage, squeezed by a distrustful and preconceiving will, quite at odds with Duberman's conscious formulations about anarchy and community. He shows up more than he knows, perhaps would be both pleased and 'seared' to realize that he does so quite early on in the book. Not *mere* self-revelation, he keeps protesting, and, imprisoned in the mirror of his own self-regard, he ultimately repeats rather than reveals himself. A characteristic touch of the egocentric comes at the conclusion of the preface, poised euphorically over the little typographical abyss of white paper which separates preface and book. After an eight-hour session, in which Duberman tapes Anni and Josef Albers, Albers tells him to make the facts lively facts:

> 'You're encouraging me', I replied, 'to write a book about the impact of Black Mountain on *me* – which is exactly the kind of book I want to write.'
> 'Then, I say, "Good luck!"' Albers answered.

The tape-recorder had been switched off, but conceivably Albers did say that. Maybe he was tired. Or maybe he meant it ironically. At all events, Duberman's intentions could hardly have been more frankly 'harnessed' from the word go.

The start of the book is what its author calls 'traditionally-written history'. as distinct from his ideal interaction of self and subject. In revising the early chapters, he allows them to remain what they were. 'And [they] should so remain', he adds, 'for this book has been process, too, and that, too, should show.' Well, what of unreconstructed Duberman, from the readers' point of view? We get clear of entanglement with him until page 89 (more of page 89 later) and he tells the story of the beginnings of Black Mountain College with perfect adequacy – though I missed the 'style both elegant and casual' that one reviewer reports – and here there are only occasional drops into stylistic jabberwocky ('facets of living' being 'shared', sex characterized as '*an* aspect of relating').

The narrative begins with he charges made against John Andrew Rice at Rollins College, Florida, in 1933. He had called a chisel one of the world's most beautiful objects, public debates 'a pernicious form of intellectual perversion', had an 'indolent' walk, put 'obscene' pictures on his classroom walls, wore a jockstrap on the beach ('running pants', he corrected). In fact, three years of Rice's sharp tongue had earned him the distrust of colleagues and the college president. The upshot was that he and a handful of staff and students left to found, after the inevitable search for site and finances, the college that was to last until 1956. One warms to Rice, despite his admitted arrogance, with his conviction that Harvard *must* be a great institution since, as he said, 'What institution on the face of the earth has been able to endure two college presidents [Eliot and Conant] who were chemists in 50 years?' Rice was convinced that he wanted art at the centre of things, and his courage and intuition nowhere show better than when he decided that he must employ Josef Albers, in flight from the Nazi persecution. Rice had consulted Edward Warburg and Philip Johnson at the Museum of Modern Art, and Albers had been a suggestion of Johnson's. 'But he does', as the latter said, 'have one defect.' 'What defect?' 'Albers doesn't speak a word of English.' Rice's response was, 'I don't think that's a defect. What's the matter with not speaking English? Several people at Black Mountain speak German and besides, we can always put interpreters in his class.'

The early years of the college are dominated by these two men, Rice and Albers. Albers is one of the few teachers whose methods we get a clear idea of, both from the reports of students and his own essay, 'My courses at the Hochschule für Gestaltung at Ulm' (*Form* 4, pp. 8–14). What he primarily did was to shear Johannes Itten's Bauhaus course of its theosophy and to ground the students in the nature of materials. His conception of education is far removed from

Duberman's own: 'Only draw what you see, and train the pencil to do what your eye sees. Don't worry about "self expression".' In short, let eye be *I* and let hand articulate that new awareness – an awareness that belongs to the self but only because earned by not 'worrying about' that self. Reading of Albers transplanting and extending Bauhaus methods in North Carolina, one savours a moment of history. As an eye-witness puts it, coming across Albers in Black Mountain's 'hillbilly setting, in the Southern Baptist Convention country of the Tarheel State, was like finding the remnants of an advanced civilisation in the midst of a jungle'.

With small classes and with some dedicated teachers, a modicum of rather contradictory theory, a desire to show it *can* be done, Black Mountain got under way, its shortcomings appearing like those of most human endeavours, once the unimaginable touch of time had confirmed it as an institution. With savage factionalism; with endless meetings when modest questions (no hot lunch on Sunday, for example) were given all the exhaustive debate of world-changing issues; and with staff and students almost constantly in each other's presence, it is a miracle the place survived so long. For any reader not on the point of leaving wife, family and neighbourhood for a kibbutz, and for anyone less fascinated by Brook Farm or the Oneida community than Mr Duberman, Black Mountain can only be of interest because of the individuals who survived its pressure-cooker when things were bad, and those who, like Fielding Dawson, Ed Dorn, Michael Rumaker, found the right teachers at the right moment. Charles Olson, who put as much into the communal effort as any man, was writing from Black Mountain in 1951, well before its closure: 'I believe in the Chinese system of an active man living where life is, and coming to youth once a month, NOT living in the midst of them, as, here – *dread it, dread – fear it!*' (*Letters for Origin, 1950–1955*, p. 72).

Some of the most fortunate encounters at the college seem to have taken place during the summer sessions, when the visitors came and factional issues were in abeyance. Buckminster Fuller, John Cage, Rauchenberg, Franz Kline, the dancer Merce Cunningham, Willem de Kooning were all summer arrivals and the interactions between these men resulted from an absence of the pressures of full community living.

Olson gave the college a new direction – back to the 'core of the apple ... what Rice said, in the first catalog, was to be her aim – that the arts shall share the center of the curriculum with the more usual studies ... just that was what the LAST BLACK MOUNTAIN WAS...' Until such time as this happened, and people like Creeley, Duncan, Oppenheimer and Dorn appeared at Black Mountain, writers seem mostly to have distrusted the educational methods of the place. Alfred Kazin, for example, visiting in the mid-1940s, has 'no respect for what went on educationally at Black Mountain', is surprised that somebody might have been 'turned out by the place who was not a complete intellectual nebbish'. No one in his class on *Moby Dick* knew who Jonah was, so he instituted a short course on the Old Testament. Duberman explains, as though this were some aberration, that Kazin 'thinks of learning as something that "one has to assimilate", of information to be accumulated' and was thus 'appalled at the lack of information most students had'. But presumably the identity of Jonah *has* 'to be assimilated' – a piece of information, acquired, if you like, in a highly imaginative context, information that releases the mind to understand what Melville is talking about? The visual arts held the centre at this time, and Kazin felt that 'if you were a serious writer, Black Mountain could be in many ways a very half-assed place'. But he found his ill-informed students decidedly interesting: 'it was like a gallery of the higher neuroticism.'

Kazin's elation at the landscape of Black Mountain – Dahlberg's, too, until the college soured on him – reminds one how much those mountained and wooded fastnesses must have contributed to the spirit of that place. Duberman is thin on landscape; he is best in conveying the nag of close-packed enmities up there, or the shabby refusal of the faculty to say farewell to the drama teacher, Bob Wunsch, arrested for homosexuality, ensuring, so Duberman suspects, his self-destruction. Though he adds characteristically: 'perhaps I exaggerate – a function of my own indignation as a homosexual, a potential victim'. Again, feeling that he may have understressed the positive side of things, Duberman draws on the help of 'Peggy Cole, author of the well-received novel, *The Varmints*, and several prize-winning stories'. Miss Cole treats us to a bout of community singing. Of course, happiness is hard to describe. For Fielding Dawson at a later, less puritan, phase in *The Black Mountain Book*, it seems often to have been a question of 'Let copulation thrive': acting as student aid on admissions, he hungrily votes 'yes' when he sees the glossy photograph of a fine-looking blonde: she arrives in her station wagon 'and when we shook hands and she said her name I winked and told her I already knew. That

Black Mountain Revisited

night *we fucked merrily*.' (His italics.) There are a lot of stories like that in Dawson's book. Maybe to have students handling admissions is not a good idea.

One cannot complain that Mr Duberman idealizes Black Mountain, although he may admire things others wouldn't, as when, with the place on the edge of collapse, and things kept going by adeptness at shop-lifting, 'Neither institutional structures', he tells us, 'nor barriers of age and "position" stood in the way of continuous dialogue'. It sounds like Martin Buber gone mad. However, this 'continuous dialogue' can be a brutal process and Duberman is both mesmerised and frightened by the idea of it. His way of telling the story is to inter-leave it with his 'personal reactions', to counterpoint the march of events with a 'Song of Myself'. *The New York Review of Books* found this approach to be 'a pioneer model of how the vexing problem of subjectivity and objectivity in historical interpretation should be handled...' But the result is more a model of tactlessness than of interpretation. Pioneers, O pioneers, beware, if this is the Leatherstocking whose trail you follow. The first personal intervention comes on page 89 with the ominous heading 'My Journal' and the cry, 'The data is taking over again. Or rather, my compulsiveness about being totally accurate...' There is a man-to-man talk about the necessity of the book being written 'for *me*', then exit the author saying, 'Mea culpa'. The next appearance of length is when a faculty meeting that took place in 1936 is reported in full and Duberman inserts his own comments of 1971 as though he were present at the meeting. No one can answer him back, of course, and it is he who closes the debate, putting John Andrew Rice right about dogmatism. Yet even when he makes room for his own *I* in this fashion, he is continually hedging: 'I'd go further', he says dramatically at one point here, 'and suggest that students are usually better off without teachers...' But comfort follows in the form of a parenthesis '(at least as we know them)' and dramatic challenge wavers into didactic tautology with, 'for they serve not as facilitators, but impeders'.

There is one instance in this book where 'the problem of subjectivity and objectivity in historical interpretation' gets the treatment it deserves — a genuinely funny one. This occurs with the attempt to reconstruct what actually went on at the neo-dada or proto-Zen happening, staged by John Cage and Merce Cunningham at Black Mountain in 1952. Satirizing his own 'compulsiveness about being totally accurate', Duberman gives five versions from eye-witnesses, with a bizarre range of disagreement as to detail, often essential detail. You really do end up, for the nonce, feeling that history must be the supreme fiction, and Mr Duberman obliges, as a historian, by trying to give us an 'objective' distillation of all five points of view:

> We now know there was a ladder – or at least a lectern – and if M.C. wasn't on it... then Rauschenberg or Olson was. Except that Olson was also in the audience. But possibly that was after he delivered his poem; or maybe he came down and sat in the audience in order to deliver his poem, since that, as you'll recall, was broken into parts and it may be that he himself delivered only one of those parts (the part that was in French, perhaps). As for Rauschenberg, we know he exhibited something, either as backdrop or foreground – and something he himself had made. Except, of course, for the Gramophone: clearly he couldn't have made that – nor those discs, which were something from the twenties, or thirties, or Piaf. Clearly, too, there was an audience, and clearly it was in the center, though its exact arrangement – whether broken into triangles, squares or not broken at all – is less clear. Yet it had to have aisles since, as everyone agrees, Merce danced down them, followed by either a barking or a silent dog (and maybe by the previsionary spirits of a dance company due to arrive the summer of 1953). We know that there were other activities as well: Cage read – something (yet another account insists it was Emerson and Thoreau); and David Tudor played – something (maybe even something by Cunningham, who might also himself have played); and visuals of some kind were definitely shown, like slides, or movies, or montages, or hand-painted glass. As we know everyone loved it. Except Wolpe and Johanna Jalowetz (who at least loved all the people involved in it).

It is a pity there are no pictures of all this to confuse the issue a bit further. The book carries a good selection of photographs of people and places during different phases of the college's history. I should have liked more, not out of a compulsive desire for totality, but because they exist. Mr Duberman wonders if Alexander Schawinsky's production of 'Danse Macabre' at Black Mountain in 1938 was the first mixed media event in the United States, rather than the above-mentioned Happening. Speculation about this matters less than knowing what it all looked like. We get no sense of the visual impact of 'Danse Macabre', nor does Mr Duberman reproduce the intriguing photographs taken of Schawinsky's abstract theatre. One would have liked, too, the pictures of the architectural models Gropius and Breuer made for buildings, projected but never realised. This was one of the first important schemes to come of that famous partnership, and Black Mountain made it possible. It was in the end rejected for financial reasons and replaced by a tamer building, designed by Laurence A. Kocher. Besides the models and drawings for the Gropius-Breuer, there are also the Jean Charlot murals done in 1944. Mr Duberman does not include illustrations of these.

One of the impressions left by this book is that its writer is more interested in process than in Art – hence the passing over of this visual evidence and hence the refusal to take full measure of the kind of literary sensibility Black Mountain produced in the 1950s – for here is the moment in the book when literary criteria are most needed. Duberman ends up admiring Olson's human qualities rather than 'his talents as poet or essayist'. Uneven Olson may have been, but this is short shrift. It is clearly personality that chiefly appeals to Duberman, and personality with which he can (his own verb) 'empathize':

> This chapter about *him* [Olson] is in style closest of all those in the book to being *me*. Somehow in writing it, without any conscious attempt to hold Olson's precepts before mine [sic] eyes, I've found the words coming out closer than ever before to the way I breathe, the way I sound when talking. The broken rhythms, the jets of energy, the tumbling sequences that overleap chronology and violate canons of orderly narrative are where I am – and want more to be.

The palpitation that Olson excites in Duberman gets tiresome for the reader; what the empathy produces is mainly pastiche, and the attempt to 'get close to the writing' in Olson's sense issues as self-consciousness of the sort that concludes the book: 'I completed the book a few minutes ago. I'm strangely, idiotically, near tears... But I've tried, too – that I do know; tried for a personal search to match theirs...' All this protesting sincerity is what Duberman offers us as the basis of relationship between author and reader – a bit like those dreadful moments when Whitman is threatening to kiss us. The personal search of which he speaks is related to his own methods as a teacher and the theory of education he seeks to put into practice in his 'unstructured seminars'. Behind the book looms his resignation from Princeton. We never quite know what went on there, but Mr Duberman does very explicitly parallel the experimentalism of Black Mountain with his own mode of teaching. Since he insists so strongly on our knowing about this, it would be ignoring his intentions to pass over the notions of education involved.

I think myself they are emotionally vicious. They share the same premises as the book – for education is seen as a kind of therapy, just as writing here, with the self making explicit emotional demands on the subject and encouraged to make them since the first question always seems to be 'What does this mean to *me*' – me being invariably italicized. In his Princeton course in 'American Radicalism', Duberman looks, he says, for 'a way of bringing' – and here come those italics – '*ourselves* to a topic'. He believes that in 'unstructured education' one should combine topic and group therapy. On one occasion a therapist was present, on others the therapist was presumably Duberman. The aim is *not*, he will insist, to make ourselves the topic, but how is a teacher who is not a saint, surrounded by students whose libidos are at the popping stage, to avoid this happening? And by what extraordinary presumption does one assume that one's students all *need* therapy? The inevitable seminar on 'sex roles' turns up and one senses the almost masochistic self-interest of the teacher as he seeks both to diminish his 'authoritarian' role and his desire '– a self-destructive urge, I suspect – to be up front about my homosexuality if the topic comes up…' A wraith of good sense keeps warning him and he calls this 'caution'. All along, the attempt 'to establish the superiority of [the group's] collective authority over that of any single individual – and especially over me' seems sentimental in its attitude to authority and sinister in its political implications. In this type of group where 'we expressed to each other our accumulated feelings, positive and negative', one of the measures of success 'in getting in touch with our own feelings' was that 'B. literally cried'. R., on the other hand, 'left almost immediately, threatened by the directness of the communication, and that saddened me'. One feels for R. Perhaps it was just decent reticence.

Reading through this in the chapter 'New Definitions of Community', I found two quotations kept coming to mind. The first was from Donald Davie's poem, *Against Confidences*:

> Candour can live
> Within no shade

> That our compulsive
> Needs have made
>
> On couches where
> We sleep, confess,
> Couple and share
> A pleased distress.

The other was Joseph Conrad's demanding ideal in *The Mirror of the Sea*: 'To forget one's self, to surrender all personal feeling in the science of one's fine art, is the only way for a seaman to the faithful discharge of his trust.' Conrad is talking about the realities of seamanship. He is also talking about the demands an art or a subject makes on the self before that self has a right to urge 'personal feeling' as a criterion. 'Quand je vous parle de moi, je vous parle de vous.' That old humbug, Victor Hugo, didn't really mean it. He had designs on us. So does Duberman's theory of history teaching and his manner of writing a book. The writer can keep trying to persuade his reader, 'Look, I'm being sincere. B. literally cried.' The reviewer exists to refuse the complicity of such compulsive needs.

From Amateur to Impresario: Charles Olson

Olson began to write his poetry in the aftermath of war, challenged to extend his scope by the appearance of *The Pisan Cantos* in 1948. He acknowledged these as Pound's greatest achievement so far, approving their abolition of chronological time in favour of imaginative juxtaposition, but firmly opposed to their politics. He had begun visiting Pound in St Elizabeth's Hospital back in 1946, recording bits of his conversation and leaving among his papers a remarkable account of his ambivalent feelings towards the master who was to outlive him (*An Encounter at St Elizabeth's*, 1975). As he wrote:

> His power is a funny thing. There is no question he's got the jump – his wit, he speed of his language, the grab of it, the intimidation of his skilfully wrought career. But he has little power to compel, that is, by his person. He strikes you as brittle – and terribly American, insecure. I miss weight and abundance. He does not seem – and this is a crazy thing to say in the face of his beautiful verse, to appear ungrateful for it – but I say it, he does not seem to have inhabited his own experience.

The poet who, for Olson, had inhabited his own experience more cognizantly was his other mentor, William Carlos Williams. Olson lets Pound express the measure of Williams's self-consistency.

> Said he: 'Bill has always been confused. He's one of the reasons I make so much of race. It's hard enough for a man to get things clear when he's of one race, but to be Bill! – french, spanish, anglo, some jew from Saragossa...' And though I left Pound that day and shall not see him again, he went on to say something which is true, that what has made Bill important is that Bill has never said one god damned thing that hasn't first circulated entirely through his head before it comes out his mouth.

A certain ungainliness in Olson (an awkward sailor, 'Even at sea I was slow, to get the hand out, or to cross a wet deck') and the fact of his Swedish-Irish parentage, clearly permitted a degree of identification with Williams's insecurities, justifying his own hard-won insights and his late start as a writer:

> The sea was not, finally, my trade.
> But even my trade, at it, I stood estranged
> From that which was most familiar.

Here the ugly, expressive jolt of 'at it', counterpoised by the fluent enjambement after 'estranged', earn him the membership of his trade. It is a verse that does not seek to please, but which permits him to inhabit more securely his own experience.

Opposed to Pound, Olson's aim was to go on to write poetry where history would not be distorted to fit personal whims, nor by the wish, as he said, 'to return America to its condition of a small nation of farmers and city-state patricians, all Boston brahmin, and Philadelphia brick'. In Pound, Olson detected 'a kind of blindness to the underground vigour of a present'. Hence his turning to Williams who had chosen to stay at home and tap that vigour in New Jersey.

Like Williams's *Paterson*, *The Maximus Poems* would ground themselves in a single locality and their history would be underpinned by geography – that of Gloucester, Massachusetts. Williams, Olson felt, had chosen from the annals of Paterson violent and anecdotal instances that won their place in the poem on account of their picturesqueness rather than for the meaning they brought to bear on the present. Olson's own annals of extraordinary individuals would gain admittance for what they had to teach of the nature of rule and change. And there would be no burning of the library, as in *Paterson*, Book 3 – a destruction Williams half persuades himself to welcome. Olson knew the value of books and his was to be a history interpreted with care: he would have the candour to let his errors stand, if need be, but correct them in a later episode. Before long, still conscious of moving little-acknowledged in the shadows of Williams and Pound, he would be writing of them as 'these two inferior predecessors'.

A few years ago, Marjorie Perloff in 'Charles Olson and the "Inferior Predecessors"' (*ELH*, Summer, 1973) gave a hard look at Olson's essay 'Projective Verse' and at some of his more gnomically unintelligible utterances, placing damagingly side by side his poem 'From the Song of Ullikummi (translated from Hurrian and Hittite)' and Hans Güterbock's text of the original. I think myself that the

Song is bad – it was given its first public reading in Pound's presence at the Spoleto Festival in 1965, a peace-offering, and there is some pathos in that. I would also agree that many of the utterances from the 1960s, the nadir being represented by *Poetry and Truth, The Beloit Lectures and Poems* given in 1968, make baleful reading. But 'Projective Verse' still seems to me, for all its unevenness, a genuine attempt to measure where things stood with verse in the late 1940s. It is certainly a work of discipleship and one can track many of its formulations, as Professor Perloff does, to Pound's 'Treatise on Metre' and to Williams's manifesto statements. But Olson knew this: his intention in 'Projective Verse' was not originality, but the extending of a tradition forward from the two masters he acknowledged and quoted as openly in his work as Pope did Dryden and Milton.

Olson wrote 'Projective Verse' when he was unknown. The earlier *Maximus Poems*, printed in Stuttgart (1953–6), found fit but limited audience. Later Olson passed from the élite public grouped round the Black Mountain experiment to the over-exposure of a fame that seems to have followed the publication of *The New American Poetry*, edited by Donald Allen, in 1960. In the prose, you can trace the path from the dignity and care of essays like 'Human Universe' or the conversational epistolatory style of *Mayan Letters*, to the garrulous improvization of 'The Beloits' as he called *Poetry and Truth*. In *Muthologos: The Collected Lectures and Interviews*, Volume 1, Olson's every stammer is tape-recorded and there are stage directions to indicate what he is physically up to. George F. Butterick, the editor, stresses the impromptu 'intended for the moment only' quality of these addresses, but here they are, for all time. What Butterick calls 'the poet's *tour de force*', 'his most significant public appearance', printed as 'Reading at Berkeley', strikes me as a tragic document. Olson comes on with a bottle of whisky and, very conscious of being Charles Olson, reads and talks for fifty-nine pages, exchanges kisses with someone's girlfriend, gets steadily drunker, asks helplessly for his companions, Duncan and Creeley. We even get the intermission on the tape.

> Olson: ... I'm drunk on youse guys. And I mean it.
> Welch: ... Hey, don't you have to pee too?
> Olson: ... Nah, shit, pee? I never pee.

Whatever happened to the writer of *Call Me Ishmael*? America discovered him, absorbed him, made of him – the man who had distrusted the ego of Pound and who wanted to remove the afflatus of 'personality' from verse – a public figure with a whisky bottle in his hand. To large, ignorant audiences he played Charles Olson, with his friends often in the cast. Indeed, it is one of them, Allen Ginsberg who in the first exchange in *Muthologos*, sees part of what is wrong with public performance of this kind: 'Actually ... we're talking all the time at home, so half the conversation is now elliptical here.' Olson's attempt to fill out the ellipses leads to more non-stop talk, Ginsberg trying to put on the brakes but finally giving up in face of the logomania of Duncan and Olson himself. *Muthologos* bears out Hugh Kenner's diagnosis in *A Homemade World*: 'From amateur, Olson became impresario. ... We may guess that in his later years, when his bear hug embraced a vocation as itinerant campus catalyst, he spent too much time talking to students who were too gladly impressed.'

Muthologos apart, are these volumes under review, as one current bookseller's catalogue dolefully and with a perhaps too precipitate honesty fears, evidence of the Olson industry going into full production? They may well be, but in themselves they are never merely that and might even stem the tide for a bit. They leave little room for reduplication and already begin to overlap in their concerns.

George Butterick's *A Guide to The Maximus Poems* is fat and factual. In its own way it attempts to do for Olson what Edwards and Vasse, with their *Annotated Index to the Cantos*, did for Pound. Butterick's method is different, and reminds one of Guy Davenport's in his excellent 'Scholia and Conjectures for Olson's *The Kingfishers*' (*Boundary*, Fall-Winter, 1973–4). That is to say, Butterick reveals the width of Olson's borrowings and background, often quoting sources in full, and thus assembling something like the sort of commonplace book that Olson might have compiled but didn't. You can read it, which is more than you can say for Edwards and Vasse, whose annotations are of the variety of 'Paris: the French city'. Butterick is good enough to explain for us foreigners what Eskimo Pie and Necco wafers are.

Besides people, places, books identified, there appear photographs of Olson throughout his life, beginning with one of the infant Charles in his postman father's mail sack (it makes a splendid cover illustration for Olson's touching memoir of his father, *The Post Office*, written in 1948 in the same unselfconscious style as his Pound memoirs).

Photographs also adorn Paul Christensen's *Charles Olson: Call*

Him Ishmael. One hopes that this careful young scholar did not caption them: 'Robert Duncan in the dining-room of his ornately furnished home...', 'Paul Blackburn was often lured to Mediterranean cultures'. The book is not at all of the *Time* magazine sort. Chronological and critically interpretative, it deals not only with all the *Maximus* but many of the shorter poems, too. The quickies in the last chapter, 'Olson and the Black Mountain Poets', a rapid glance at the principals, could most readily be dispensed with. It's hard to know who benefits from these little 'over-views' – not always the principals: Ed Dorn gets trounced for his 'stuffy and half-private witticisms' in *Gunslinger*, but 'the poem creates the sense of a new era for poetry.' What sort of criticism is that?

Some overlap occurs between *Call Him Ishmael* and Sherman Paul's *Olson's Push: Origin, Black Mountain and Recent American Poetry*. There are more photographs, this time of places not people. Like Christensen, Paul surveys the outlying writings and the historic context, devoting the longest section to *Maximus*. There are many insights here, though little of Christensen's sense that, ultimately, the vision comes apart and the craftsmanship deteriorates.

It is an awareness that something changes radically in the second volume of *Maximus*, once Olson has shifted ground from the historic to the mythical, that unites Christensen's book and Robert Von Hallberg's *Charles Olson, The Scholar's Art*. This last rapidly impresses the reader as being the most brilliant of the three studies, and one puts it down with the conviction that it is also one of the most remarkable books on any post-war poet. An immediate gain in focus and concision comes from Von Hallberg's decision to limit his area of enquiry to the earlier work, where Olson is least wayward – up to, that is, the second volume of *Maximus* and with some consideration of this, too. The book is more conspicuously an account of Olson's poetics than of his poems – though there are fine readings of 'The Kingfishers', 'The Praises' and of many crucial passages from *Maximus*. Von Hallberg believes we should know what sort of a poet Olson was and points out that 'he begins as though the offices of poetry and of expository prose have not been separate and distinct for two hundred years', substantiating this with Tolstoy's 'Where the boundary between prose and poetry lies, I shall never be able to understand'.

Olson's 'is first of all a referential poetics', writes Von Hallberg: 'hence subject matter is primary for him as it was not, through the forties and fifties, for most of his contemporaries'. Like Pound he saw himself as a teacher – hence 'The Scholar's Art' – and, also like Pound, 'actually expected his readers ... to go to the library and read the books'. Poetry, for Olson, was as much concerned with the preservation of knowledge as aesthetic self-sufficiency. One might begin with some suspicion of a book which aims to first establish the nature of a poetics rather than leading us there via the poem. But both Von Hallberg's contention that Olson's poems 'cannot be adequately appreciated within terms of recent poetic theory', and his subsequent exploration of alternative theory, powerfully remove our preconceptions of what a poem *ought* to be and so enable us to see with a new clarity the nature of Olson's achievement. 'He was trying', says Von Hallberg, 'not to contrive a tradition out of which he might write (which is more or less what Pound did in *Guide to Kulchur* and Yeats in *A Vision*) but to call attention to what was and still is there'.

In the early 1960s, in a scribbled P.S. at the end of one of his higgledy-piggledy letters, Olson asked me whether the old ship canal was still open south of Gloucester (England). I had no idea, having my eyes mostly on the limestone escarpment above that, and forgot the question till after his death. Then walking along the Severn one day, I climbed up the embankment to discover, hidden behind it and parallel to the river, the canal of which Olson had spoken. A barge was travelling up it with a load of mud dredged out of Sharpness docks. It was instantaneous, dripping evidence of 'what was and still is there', something that Olson's poetics could have rescued from the status of a mere image, bringing to bear the factual poetry of a whole region.

Some Americans

A Personal Record

In the following pages, I have tried to tell of the way certain American poets, together with a painter, helped an English poet find himself. I wanted also to convey to the reader what some of them were like as people. My first three chapters deal almost exclusively with America. In my fourth and last, where the mediating figure is Ezra Pound, Italy and America become an inextricable concern. The first chapter was written between 1976 and 1977, the second and third in 1978 and the fourth between 1978 and 1979. I am more than grateful to Hugh Kenner who suggested the making of this book.

Ozleworth Bottom
Wotton-under-Edge
1979

1: Beginnings

A boy from the provinces, going up to read English at Cambridge in 1945, as I did, will have learned little of American poetry from his university teachers. None of them seemed to mention it. While still at grammar school, I had invested half a crown, that no longer extant coin, in a copy of the Sesame Books selection of Ezra Pound. This was published by Faber and Faber and is not to be confused with the *Selected Poems* edited by T. S. Eliot. We had been studying a book at school which purported to be *Modern Poetry*, introduced by the now forgotten essayist Robert Lynd. The Pound was very different from what one found there. Puzzled, I read it through many times; tried to scan the opening lines of 'E. P. Ode Pour L' Election de Son Sepulchre'; tried the same with 'The River-Merchant's Wife". Evidently it couldn't be done. This was a naïve discovery, no doubt. Scansion had figured prominently in one's education – in English, French, and Latin. I am grateful that it did. But here its only use was to point the difference, to suggest, with the Mauberley extract, that perhaps some type of syncopation was at work. What held my attention in the book was the prosaic phraseology of poems like 'The Garden':

> And she is dying piece-meal
> of a sort of emotional anaemia

and

> ... is almost afraid that I
> will commit that indiscretion

That stress and pausing on 'I' before the line break was also arresting. As for the poem's opening, 'Like a skein of loose silk blown against a wall,' nobody that I knew of could have written more cleanly than that. It was a sense of cleanliness in the phrasing that drew me, still puzzled, to Canto II toward the end of the book. I returned many times to

> Lithe turning of water,
> > sinews of Poseidon,
> Black azure and hyaline,
> > glass wave over Tyro.

and

> Salmon-pink wings of the fish-hawk
> > cast grey shadows in water,
> The tower like a one-eyed great goose
> > cranes up out of the olive-grove...

The canto closed on the word 'And...' That was also something to think about. But nobody told me where to go next, either at school or at Cambridge. I carried these talismanic fragments at the back of my mind. After all, there were other things to think about – practically the whole of English literature from Chaucer to the end of the nineteenth century. I was also reading French and German.

The talismanic fragments somehow did their work, for what they had to teach survived the only other reading of an American that I accomplished in bulk at Cambridge. This was Whitman. He, along with Nietzsche, formed the style of the earliest unfortunate poems that I wrote on going down in 1948. Before that, shortly after my arrival at college in fact, I put out six shillings on a secondhand copy of Michael Roberts's *Faber Book of Modern Verse*. It was here I first encountered Gerard Manley Hopkins, and along with Hopkins the handful of imagist poems by T. E. Hulme – these seemed to have something in common with the clean surfaces of Pound, but I had no notion of the history of all that. There was also Marianne Moore and, again, I think I found the right talisman in 'The Steeple-Jack". Prompted by this, my eye caught sight of a review of her work in an old copy of *The Criterion* which quoted from 'The Jerboa':

> > it stops its gleaning
> on little wheel castors, and makes fern-seed
> foot-prints with kangaroo speed.

'Rum stuff,' said my roommate, when I showed it to him. 'Pretty self-conscious, I should say.' Perhaps he was right. He knew more about literature than I did at that date. I went on admiring the rhyming of light against heavy beat, along with the perception the lines contained, but in secret. When I came across 'The Fish' (in Anne Ridler's *Little Book of Modern Verse*), I kept it to myself. What would he have thought of the way that title became the subject of the first sentence of the poem?

The Fish

> wade
> through black jade.

No, I couldn't possibly have this doubted and discussed. I would have to explain also the appeal of the splitting of article from noun on two occasions and in two ways:

> ... the submerged shafts of the
> sun,
> split like spun
>   glass, move themselves with spotlight swiftness
>   into the crevices –
>   in and out, illuminating
>
> the
> turquoise sea
>   of bodies...

The dividing off of parts of language, the perceptual accuracy, the unexpected addition – 'of bodies' – to that apparently complete 'turquoise sea,' the deft rhyming – these taught me more than I could yet confess to have learned. Why, when I admired this sort of thing, and when I was looking at Cézanne in the Fitzwilliam Museum, did I imagine I was a Whitmanian vitalist? The conscious mind is a shallow thing. Or rather, it is seldom conscious enough at the right moment.

The next step was Wallace Stevens. It should have been Stevens and William Carlos Williams. I will explain. I muffed the thing badly. One evening, late in 1947, my new tutor – my earlier tutor had passed me on as a hopeless case – read to me, in a pub in Trumpington, Williams's 'Tract' from Oscar Williams's *Little Treasury of Modern Poetry, English and American*. I thought it delightful. He handed me the book to reread it and, as he did so, the pages fell open at Stevens' 'Thirteen Ways of Looking at a Blackbird'. I gazed through this rapidly then moved back to 'Tract.' It was 'Thirteen Ways' that stayed in mind. However, as I didn't possess the anthology, and as Stevens was unpublished in England, I did not reencounter the poem for two or three years. The Williams sank from recollection. He also was unobtainable and I was not to read him seriously until 1956. And, besides, there remained the paper on Spenser to be prepared, Aristotle's *Poetics,* Book Ten of Plato's *Republic* to read. The name of my new tutor was Donald Davie. At the time, I do not think he knew much more about American poetry than I did. In quantity, perhaps less. He hadn't laboured through all that Whitman.

On going down from Cambridge in the summer of 1948, I found myself reading a lot of poetry I'd previously not had the time to explore. The Americans as yet were no clear enthusiasm, and poets whom I was to find increasingly intriguing as I read them in extenso – Moore, Stevens, and Williams – were simply not available. These stood to one side of the metaphysical tradition which was still very much in the air, vouched for by Eliot and F. R. Leavis, whereas a poet like Allen Tate could be recognizably associated with that tradition. His selected *Poems, 1920–1945* appeared in 1947. William Empson was also coming forward into renewed prominence and – diverse as they were – one could read him side by side with Tate with little sense of incongruity.

This training in the metaphysicals, whatever else it did for one, gave little help for recognizing the kind of thing that a Williams was after. Between 1948 and 1951 I read a lot of Augustan poetry. This provided a good antidote to the effects of Dylan Thomas's romanticism, for Dylan Thomas was still the voice which sounded in one's ears as one sought for a contemporary style or, quite literally, if one switched on the BBC. Pound and his 'sinews of Poseidon' was also an antidote, and with the publication of *The Pisan Cantos* in 1949 a returning presence on the scene. I also acquired, on loan, a precious copy of Miss Moore's *Selected Poems* of 1935, and from the same source (the poet, Ronald Bottrall) Hart Crane's 1933 *Collected Poems.* This was a book that, round about 1950, stopped me in my tracks. The sequence that laid hold of me was not 'The Bridge' (except for 'Cutty Sark', which I already knew from Roberts's anthology) but 'Voyages':

> Meticulous, past midnight in clear rime

– that was a voice that appealed to me, and:

> The bay estuaries fleck the hard sky limits.

At the same time I recognized something else in Crane besides this sharp, perceptual view of the sea – an ache that took me back to my growing dissatisfaction with Whitman, an ache that, if I read the poems correctly, was suicidal. Of course, one had the evidence of Crane's own life. In 'Voyages' itself, as in the apostrophe to the 'bright striped urchins,' there seemed to be a clear recognition that, with the sea,

> there is a line
> You must not cross nor ever trust beyond it
> Spry cordage of your bodies to caresses
> Too lichen-faithful from too wide a breast...

Yet, at the same time, Crane yearned for a sea imagined as an experience of paradisal unity where 'sleep, death, desire' merged into one as 'a floating flower.' As I read it then – and wrote an essay in 1950 to try to argue the matter out – Crane saw the choice as one between individual, self-responsible life and non-individual death, and he chose the latter. He dreamed of some understanding only to be felt in 'the vortex of our grave' or 'the seal's wide spindrift gaze toward paradise'. This paradise seemed to be reached, as in Whitman, by a surrender of self, a violation of the limits of the self, in a communion with impersonal forces, and must involve not just the death of the self, but the death of that sense of individual responsibility which conscience bids us never to violate even for the most obsessive idea or the most spiritual ideal. Besides Whitman, Crane reminded me of Emerson's 'shudder of awe and delight with which the individual soul always mingles with the universal soul', and also of Poe's 'Think that the sense of individual identity will be gradually merged in the general consciousness' in *Eureka,* where a pseudo-scientific vision of the universe striving back into original Oneness seemed to supply the rationalization of a wished-for psychic state. At the same time, I admired the writing of 'Voyages', grudgingly, feeling a schism in the contrast of exact description or evocation (what the human eye can, humanly, see, the ear hear) and the more indefinite synaesthetic mode of apprehending things (what is felt in the process of an imagined union with nature).

The way I then read Crane was undoubtedly prompted by D.H. Lawrence's diagnosis of Whitman in *Studies in Classic American Literature,* as 'always wanting to merge himself into the womb of something or other'. It was that desire to merge, common also to Poe and Emerson, that seemed to be active in Crane's case. Perhaps I identified him too closely with Poe, whose *Eureka* I had just read and in which Poe's desire to merge suggested a wish to reject all personal responsibility and, simultaneously, to stand in some kind of rapport with others and with nature. Hence, conceivably, the recourse to drugs and alcohol, as in Crane's case, with the attendant feeling of release from his own ego. I had also been reading Baudelaire during this period, and a quotation from his 'Of Wine and Hashish' appeared to fit Crane's 'Voyages': 'Il ne serait peut-être pas bon de laisser un homme en cet état au bord d'une eau limpide; comme le pêcheur de la ballade, il se laisserait peut-être entraîner par l'Ondine.'

So I extrapolated my view of Crane from his poem, finding my way closer and closer to my own basic theme – that one does not need to go beyond sense experience to some mythic union, that the 'I' can only be responsible in relationship and not by dissolving itself away into ecstasy or the Oversoul. Crane brought this theme to bear for me more decisively than any poet I had read before. My talismanic fragments – Pound's 'lithe turning of water', Miss Moore's penetration of the sea in 'The Fish' while refusing to merge with it – were also working for me; and their way of writing was working for me in its attention to word and thing.

Rereading, soon after Crane, Stevens' 'Thirteen Ways' – an American friend had procured *Harmonium* for me – with its sharp, discrete fragments, I saw all at once a possibility of writing that would release me from the rather predictable stanzas that were to make up my first pamphlet, *Relations and Contraries*, in 1951. In the title of that pamphlet I already had my theme, yet perhaps only in one poem there did I start out along the path into which American writing was leading me. It began:

> Wakening with the window over fields
> To the coin-clear harness jingle as a float
> Clips by, and each succeeding hoof fall, now remote,
> Breaks clean and frost-sharp on the unstopped ear...

This very English scene – yes, milk was still delivered by horse float just over twenty-five years ago – was intended as a piece of Poundian syncopation, modelled on that 'Ode Pour L'Election de Son Sepulchre' which I could not scan. 'The unstopped ear,' quoted from the same poem's 'caught in the unstopped ear,' implied in my own variation that the ear was unstopped not to the sirens' song, but to the sharpness of sense experience – to the sort of sound you might hear 'meticulous, past midnight in clear rime', though this was in broad day. Reading Stevens' 'Thirteen Ways' led me for a

1: Beginnings

while to look from different angles at separate instances of the meticulous:

> Pine-scent
> In snow-clearness
> Is not more exactly counterpointed
> Than the creak of trodden snow
> Against a flute.

This, too, was the fruit not only of reading Stevens: 'pine-scent in snow clearness' had been one of my talismanic fragments for years, and if I had possessed Miss Moore's scrupulousness, it would have been printed in quotation marks. At eighteen I had seen a reproduction of a Chinese landscape with precisely that title. The two sensations, perfectly combined, perfectly separated, seemed even at eighteen to be an instance of extraordinary purity, a possibility for right feeling. Years later I recognized their implication in Pound's 'radiant world where one thought cuts through another with clear edge, a world of moving energies, magnetisms that take form…'

I imitated Stevens' 'Thirteen Ways,' but the poem I chose to write an essay on in 1951 was 'The Comedian as Letter C' – another poem of the ocean, and one in which the hero Crispin suggested an alternative to Crane's mystical approach and to his sea-merge. I rather regretted the fact that, after leaving the sea a different man, Crispin came to a somewhat bourgeois Gemütlichkeit. However, he did not attempt to lose identity in the ocean, but rather to allow himself to be changed by the experience of it – to see the world afresh rather than take off into the absolute. The challenge of Crane's 'Voyages' made me see how often my own preferred American poems had been sea-pieces. Pound's second Canto, Miss Moore's 'The Fish', 'The Steeple-Jack', 'A Grave', Stevens' 'Comedian', and, retrospectively, Whitman's 'Sea Drift' – all these seemed to propose a moral terrain where you must confront nature, and they implied for me a moral atmosphere that itself partook of the sharpness of brine and sea breeze.

I sent my paper on 'The Comedian' to Stevens as well as a commentary on his 'Credences of Summer'. His reply concerning the second piece appears on page 719 of *Letters of Wallace Stevens*. Acknowledging the account of 'The Comedian' in an unpublished letter of 3 July 1951, he drew my attention to something I had failed to take account of and that, so far as I know, subsequent critics have also ignored:

... this poem exploits sounds of the letter c; hence its title. These sounds include all the hard and soft variations and pass over into other sounds, or, rather, the sound of other letters, for example in the line

> Exchequering from piebald fiscs unkeyed,

where ex contains the c sound. So, too, do ch, que, scs and k. This grows tiresome if one is too conscious of it, but it is easy to ameliorate the thing.

An odd way to write poems, I thought, but a regard for such minute particulars of language was, anyway, a healthier sign in a poet, perhaps, than the desire to lose himself in the Oversoul or spin away into 'the vortex of our grave'.

The 1950s were an unpropitious time to write the kind of verse that interested me, and England an unpropitious place in which to publish it. An heir of Pound, Moore, Crane, Stevens must inevitably appear an odd fish in English waters. I wrote the poems that comprise my short book *The Necklace* between December 1950 and March 1953. They first appeared, with a small press, in 1955 and would not have appeared then, had Donald Davie not contributed an introduction. It was Hugh Kenner's review of this booklet for *Poetry* in the summer of 1956, and the subsequent interest in what I was writing by the editor, Henry Rago, that sustained me through a state of mental emigration and led to a first visit to the United States. Simultaneously, I could also count on and received the criticism and encouragement of Donald Davie. By the date of Kenner's review in 1956 I had virtually completed a full-scale collection, *Seeing Is Believing,* adding a few more poems to the manuscript in the following year. This book found no English publisher – I tried most of them – until 1960. It was to appear in New York.

Critics have spoken of the presence of Williams in both *The Necklace* and *Seeing Is Believing,* but I did not seriously begin to read Williams until the autumn of 1956 – his *Desert Music* and *Journey to Love* – and I doubt that very much could have percolated. Soon afterward I went through *Paterson,* unconvinced of its success except for certain passages. I had also been reading *Light and Dark* by that underestimated poet from upper New York State, William Bronk. It was pressed on me by Gael Turnbull, who had lent me the Williams volumes. At that period he was running Migrant Books, in Worcester, an organization for circulating recent American and

1: Beginnings

Canadian works which appealed to him. From the same source I early acquired Robert Creeley's *The Whip* and his stories, *The Gold Diggers,* also the two-volume Stuttgart edition of Charles Olson's *Maximus Poems.*

The distinguishable American presences in my own work, so far as I can tell, were, up to then, Pound, Stevens, and Marianne Moore, and yet, if through them the tonality sounded American, the tradition of the work went back to Coleridge's conversation poems. At the same time, I had absorbed from Eliot's criticism what he had perhaps absorbed from Santayana's 'The Poetry of Barbarism', namely a suspicion of the romantic ego and of the notion that poetry can be carried through by the gust of personality and intensity. All this – and I shall not tax the reader's patience much longer with the search for 'influences' – worked together with my own painting and with the sort of visual and literary discipline I had learned from passages like Ruskin's famous description of the fir tree:

> The Power of the tree ... is in the dark, flat, solid tables of leafage, which it holds out on its strong arms, curved slightly over them like shields, and spreading towards the extremity like a hand. It is vain to endeavour to paint the sharp, grassy, intricate leafage until this ruling form has been secured; and in the boughs that approach the spectator the foreshortening of it is just like that of a wide hill-country, ridge just rising over ridge in successive distances.

I read this to Hugh Kenner twenty years ago, and recently (in *A Homemade World,* 1975) he has quoted and applied it very justly to the development in modern American poetry effected by Marianne Moore. I am certain that Miss Moore knew the passage and that Ruskin is one of the texts that she and I had in common.

On first meeting Kenner in England in November 1956, I was moved to learn from him that Miss Moore had read his review of *The Necklace,* had been interested in his quotations, and had remarked: 'I think there is as much Moore as Stevens in them.' In visiting her on his way through New York, he had had in his possession a copy of her latest book, *Like a Bulwark,* intended for myself. When he delivered this in Somerset, it was inscribed in her hand:

> For Mr. Charles Tomlinson
> from Hugh Kenner
> and might I say? from

Marianne Moore
November 10, 1956

I was cheered that anyone could take an artist's position as seriously as Kenner in his generosity took mine, once I had shown him my paintings and also the new manuscript – the bulk of *Seeing Is Believing* – which I realized was certainly unpublishable in England. He even spoke of the matter to Wyndham Lewis, and reported him as saying, 'Tell him by all means to go to America.'

After receiving *Like a Bulwark,* I wrote almost immediately to Miss Moore, enclosing a copy of *The Necklace* and writing out for her the Victorian notice from the tower of the Clifton Camera Obscura at Bristol:

> ... the camera obscura to those unacquainted with it has a magical effect, the movement of persons, animals and carriages, the waving of foliage and the coming and going of ships being caught in the picture with the distinction and vivid colouring of nature and affording a high gratification to the observer from the continual changes and varying effects of light and shade upon the landscape.

Her reply, gratifyingly swift, was written on 24 November 1956:

Dear Mr. Tomlinson,

    I thank you for your good wishes, for the Victorian notice outside the Bristol tower with a camera obscura at the top – *indeed* a poem – and I thank you for The Necklace. I am complimented that you think your work resembles mine. I shall now see if I can make mine resemble yours: i.e., The Bead, The Art of Poetry, 'the facets of copiousness', the sea 'rolling and unrolling fringes from submerged rocks' and the 'bee's wing.'

    I cannot, alas, match your address, shall have to be content with writing it.

    It was a little aggressive of me to seize the opportunity to join Hugh Kenner in giving you my book which was *his* gift...

Sincerely yours
Marianne Moore

Late in February 1957 I wrote my first poems in emulation of the three-ply cadences that Williams used in the two books of his I had read. I completed, to begin with, 'Sea Poem', 'Winter', 'Le Musée Imaginaire', and 'Letter to Dr. Williams'. Shortly afterward I made an exchange with Hugh Kenner – in return for the correspondence of Hilaire Belloc, he sent me Williams's *Collected Earlier Poems* and *Collected Later Poems*. For the time being, however, it was the three-ply poems that appealed to me most, perhaps because they afforded the possibility of a more meditative movement. They served also later on when, with the help of Henry Gifford, I came to translate Antonio Machado and needed a form that would progress at a speed resembling that of thought, while avoiding the rather facile rattle that occurs if one translates Spanish octosyllabics directly into English with end rhymes.

When I began imitating Williams's measure and applying it to the cadences of an Englishman's English, I was still finding it difficult to place poems in my native country and this new, apparently odd layout was hardly going to be a recommendation in the eyes of editors. A number of my things had found a home for themselves in *Spectrum*, a little magazine published by students at the University of California at Santa Barbara. Hugh Kenner served on the advisory board and, in 1957 when he was teaching at Santa Barbara, so did Donald Davie. I sent 'Letter to Dr. Williams' to *Spectrum,* and it came out in the autumn number, 1957, immediately following a poem of Williams's own. Seeing them together, I wrote to Williams to establish contact.

In the meantime, thanks once more to Hugh Kenner, the much refused manuscript of *Seeing Is Believing* had gone off to a new publishing house in New York, McDowell Obolensky. On Christmas Eve 1957 two things occurred: I received news of their acceptance of the book and also a postcard from Williams promising a letter 'in reply to your poem in *Spectrum'* and ending, 'Take care of yourself. Poetry is a tough racket.' A few days later the letter arrived:

Dear Tomlinson:

> Through Hugh Kenner l have just become acquainted with your name, God be praised! for to meet an Englishman to whom my name is not anathema is almost to be classed by me as an event. Not that I give a damn except as it signalizes the advent of someone who may turn out to be a friend.
>
> That poem which has been printed in *Spectrum* seems to clinch the matter. What you have written in that poem is high praise for me and I am all the more impressed that you have allowed yourself to copy (in this instance) my form. Anyone who is influ-

enced by a verse form which liberates English verse is my friend.

Let's not go into that at the moment. I am amazed that your lines fall so easily and beautifully into the pattern of my verses in Desert Music and Journey to Love. It makes me feel that my deviations are valid and not mere eccentricities – and that they may be susceptible of proliferation. There is no room for rancour in any serious study of English verse, your attitude shows a light hearted spirit which is tremendously encouraging to me. As you may know I have not many friends among the scholars in this country as well as England. A small clan makes for penetration in the attack when our front must be consolidated at all costs...

It was encouraging for me in return to find myself so suddenly one of a clan whereas previously my sense had been of almost complete poetic isolation. A new clan had also been preparing itself in England – this was the group of poets known as the Movement. I shared their feelings about the need to displace the last of the 1940s neoromanticism and the uncritical admiration for Dylan Thomas, yet I felt the whiff of Little Englandism in their manifestos and in some of their verse to be a symptom of that suffocation which has affected so much English art ever since the death of Byron. Though Davie rode with the Movement, their ranks and their anthologies were closed against my own work. He, too, curiously enough, was producing poems at the time influenced strongly by an American model – namely, the verse of Yvor Winters. But Winters was more easily assimilable among English notions – after all he wrote in quatrains – than was my own choice of American poets. That Davie was a Poundian – though not noticeably in his verse as yet – was to lead him eventually to an interesting and fruitful state of literary schizophrenia.

With the Movement then at large in England, to be admitted into Williams's clan lent me a renewed sense of confidence. Perhaps this was slightly unreal, for the main body of the work I had already accomplished had very little to do with Williamsite procedures, though I could see that it intersected at certain points with his concerns. Williams, after all, had to face out a sense of cultural deprivation and overcome alienating forces very different from the day-to-day experiences of a European. When Kenner says that his chief technical discovery was 'that words set in Jersey speech rhythms say less but mean it with greater finality', he makes a valuable formulation. But that is hardly a task to which a European could

1: Beginnings

pretend to address himself.

In listening to Jersey speech rhythms and to what he calls 'the American language', Williams evolved his theory of 'measure'. 'Measure' – by which I take him to mean those structural principles that still subsist in the language of poetry when one has abandoned traditional metrics – he seems to have supposed, in his more polemical moments, belonged to a specifically American poetry. Already I was trying to prove that 'measure' belonged also to English poetry, though I would have hesitated to define it in terms of Williams's variable foot, that self-contradictory notion which Alan Stephens parodies in the phrase 'an elastic inch'. Yet to be admitted to the clan, on whatever grounds, was an honour, for I felt it to be a platoon in a much larger action, one that would eventually establish the importance of other American poets in England besides T. S. Eliot.

Once I had heard from Williams, I sent to him 'Sea Poem', which struck me as superior to the verse letter. He replied in the New Year:

Dear Charles:

'Sea Poem' is a fine piece that impresses me both for its scholarly composition in the English sense of the term and for its generosity toward the American idiom and all it implies for me…

Did he mean by 'its generosity toward the American idiom', I asked myself, that he took me to be writing in some sort of American? After all, if I was being generous at all, it was toward his three-ply measure rather than any specific idiom. My idiom was Queen's English, deriving of course, in its poetic structure, from an American example. But 'American idiom'? I feared that when McDowell Obolensky brought out *Seeing Is Believing* in the summer of 1958, he would find it uninteresting, because if he read it in the light of its influences, they were clearly pre-Williams and the themes of a decidedly English and European cast.

On this score I was wrong. His enthusiasm for the book brought an immediate letter on its publication and eventually a review in the pages of *Spectrum. I* shall not quote Williams's letter or review in detail since they are mostly adulatory of my own work and, while adulation may sound sweet to the recipient, it is apt to be a bore to any second party. There is *some* adulation in what I shall summarize, but the point that it goes to prove concerns Williams as much as, and perhaps more than, myself. Williams, in his mid-seventies, needed the sense of a clan. He still felt the uphill grind toward reputation in America and was not to find an English publisher till after his death. As late as 1959 the *Times Literary Supplement* for 6 November listed Williams among a heterogeneous 'profusion of talents as yet unnoticed'. But in another article in the same number, one read: 'We have passed the period of aggressive nativeness in American poetry, the sort of thing illustrated so determinedly (and for British readers so bewilderingly) in the poetry of William Carlos Williams.' Williams's aggressiveness, his anti-colonialism, was born of frustration rather than a mindless dislike of England. Indeed, he felt that the British outlook was more civilized, better informed than the American and that the British *ought* to have seen what he was up to and what measure was all about. There exists a certain pathos in this attitude as it shows itself in a letter he sent to Kenner on the publication of *Seeing Is Believing*. 'The new world writer,' he says, 'can now look up to his more cultured brother with complete trust in him.' Kenner had told him of my struggles to get the book into print, and in this he saw not only a reflection of his own long fight but felt, now the book's existence was a palpable fact, that the battle for measure had been carried into England and by an English writer. Both these things – his own remembered frustrations and an Englishman's poems with an American flavour – caused him to describe *Seeing Is Believing* as 'the most moving book out of England that I have ever read', 'a major event in my modern world' (letter of 12 July 1958); and later on he wrote: 'What you are doing with the poetic line ... is a fundamentally important labor in the development of English prosody.' His old-fashioned sense of what England stood for led him to write as follows in the review:

> An Englishman, if he is the guardian of his country's scholarship through an enviable tradition, cannot avoid the issue but with the grim determination of the breed must follow where his betters have led him. If scholarship has led him astray he must reexamine his sources and finding an error correct it.

That was what he took me to be doing, in this collection of poems for which he felt such delight, animated also no doubt by his earlier pleasure at those three-ply verses of mine where his own existence was directly saluted by an Englishman.

In 1959 I was awarded, along with six other European writers, a travel grant to visit the United States. I had been sponsored by Henry Rago of *Poetry,* but heard that Williams and Miss Moore had both written letters of recommendation. My first disappointment on getting to New York, in October 1959, concerned the fact that Marianne Moore could not be visited. She was about to go away, 'so cannot,' as she wrote, 'seem as cordial as I feel. When I have come back, I shall ask if you might then be able to find a time for us to meet. I hope that you are not dismayed by the clatter and noise of New York, or worn out by the journey and the effort of leaving home.' There was opportunity, however, for a telephone call, and I heard for the first time that voice of which Louis Zukofsky was later to say to me: 'She talked like a sewing machine. You could almost count the syllables.' It was an unkind, but not inaccurate, description of her curiously staccato way of speaking while emphasizing certain words. She reverted at once to her theme of the unattractiveness of New York. 'This Sodom and Gomorrah of a city', she called it. 'Chicago is worse,' she added, 'though there's a fascinating Museum of Science and Invention there. But if you say, "I want to go to the Museum of Science and Invention", *they* say, "Not time." Here, it's impossible to look around and *not* notice something unsightly. Why, to find *beauty*, Mr Tomlinson, I had to go as far as British Columbia last summer and I found out about *that* because of a picture in the *Illustrated London News*.'

Miss Moore was leaving town for Pennsylvania to recuperate from what she described as 'a near stroke'. William Carlos Williams, disabled by strokes that had been more than 'near,' could at any rate be seen at Rutherford. Denise Levertov first took me out there to visit him. We would go after lunch, she said. That was the best time and when his mind showed itself most active. Denise was very properly and protectively solicitous for Williams. It would be preferable if my wife and child did not accompany us, for he tired easily. I assured her that the child was most biddable, a product of Europe like herself. But she remained firm – no doubt rightly so – and anyway, I was joking rather than insisting.

We lunched at Denise's apartment on West 15th Street, went by subway to the Port Authority bus station and, for the first time, I crossed that marshy flatland, the Meadows, between New York and Rutherford. Trucks were dumping their fill in the remaining spaces between suburban outcrops. Development was going forward here and there with no distinguishable centre or direction. A touch of civility in the white Lutheran church whose scrupulously painted wooden structure dominated one settlement. Then scattered filling stations, motels, wires, roads, presaging a future, perhaps. Suddenly a river with birds on it, a lost pastoral almost side by side with all this. The tree-lined back streets and the neat, wooden houses of Rutherford came as a surprise. So did the squat church that was built of a durable-looking stone.

'Wherever's your wife?' was the first thing Williams asked, turning to me, after giving Denise a forceful kiss. 'And the child?' This was a good day. Despite his trailing arm, despite the occasional difficulty he had in finding words, which Mrs Williams would supply, he seemed boyishly energetic, even radiant in his eagerness to convey in the flesh that friendship he had already offered in his letters. Both he and his wife moved in their talk between past and present. 'When we came here,' he said, 'the place was surrounded by woods, and now – .' 'One thing I *would* like,' said Mrs Williams, 'is to see a horse-drawn carriage or two back.'

I admired their two plant pictures by Charles Demuth. 'There's something else I wanted you to see,' said Williams and, taking me by the arm, he propelled me upstairs. It was his workroom he wished to display: the desk, the electric typewriter, the papers, the books. What caught my eye, as we stood talking, was a metal letter-clip – Victorian I supposed – in the form of a hand, with long fingers, extending from a cuff, the metal simulating lace here, with a texture of dotted lines, circles, and zigzags. 'In forty years,' said Williams, 'you are the only person ever to have admired that. Look, you're going to cross the continent. When you pass through New York on your way home come and see me, with your wife and child this time, and it's yours. You have a right to it.' I feared I had all too little right to it, that I must merely have sounded covetous.

Returning with Denise down Rutherford's main street to the bus, I could now complete for myself Williams's unfinished sentence about the once surrounding woods. The neons were splashing and trickling their colours over wet sidewalks between buildings whose graceless monotony was made drabber and lonelier by the damp dusk of late autumn.

Three weeks had gone by when we found ourselves, on a Saturday evening, in the Lowells' car, driving through Boston in search of a parking lot. 'Two things out of many things,' Lowell's wife, Elizabeth Hardwick, was saying, 'have brought on the lacks of the last fifteen years – the motor craze and the school laze-craze.' 'Look,' said Lowell – we were driving along the bank of the neoned Charles River – 'that's just about the vista commanded from Olive Chancellor's window in *The Bostonians*.' Yes, James had foretold it all with his 'desolate suburban horizons, peeled and made bald by the rigour of the season'. When I next turned up a copy of *The Bostonians* what struck me about the description of the vista to which Lowell had referred, was how close it stood to being a poem by Williams: 'There was something inexorable in the poverty of the scene, shameful in the meanness of its details ... loose fences, vacant lots, mounds of refuse, yards bestrewn with iron pipes, telegraph poles and bare wooden backs of places.' James one would imagine to be an antithetical writer to Williams. Yet some of the urban poetry James catches out of the corner of his eye, as it were, often contains the kind of detail out of which Williams would construct an entire poem. I am thinking of chapter fifteen of *Portrait of a Lady*: September quiet in a London square, two small children, rusty railings, a dominant red pillar box; or again, in *The Ambassadors*, book seven, chapter two: evening over Paris, a whiff of violets, 'a far off hum, a sharp near click on the asphalt'. Williams would have made a choreographic poem out of these details, 'drawing ... many broken things into a dance by giving them thus a full being'.

Williams was often to come to mind in a journey across America that lasted some five months. In the curious cross-ply of circumstance his name was intricated, for me, with that of another antithetical figure, the poet and critic Yvor Winters. In that same number of *Spectrum* in which Williams's 'Translation from Sappho' appeared side by side with my own 'Letter to Dr Williams' was Donald Davie's article, 'An Alternative to Pound?' It opened as follows:

> The Stanford school of poets, grouped around and schooled by Yvor Winters, seems to me perhaps the most interesting feature of the poetic scene in the U.S. Where other masters – British as well as American – have tried to come to terms with the challenge of the Poundian-Eliotic poetic mostly by diluting, muffling, taking what they want and evading the harder truths, Winters has met the challenge by offering a considered and coherent alternative, an alternative poetic theory grounded in an alternative morality driving through to an alternative practice. And so, while more talent can and does spring up in other quarters of the poetic scene, it is only from the Poundian wing (and by that I mean rather Charles Tomlinson, say, than Louis Zukofsky) or else from this other extreme at Stanford, that one can expect talent, when it appears, not to have to save itself by *ad hoc* improvisations, hairs-

breadth escapes and eleventh-hour expedients. It is especially good, if also ironical, that this most traditional and forbiddingly 'classical' of current schools should be, at Palo Alto, within the orbit of that San Francisco bohemianism which, in its naive reliance on the generous impulse, spells death to any poetic whatever.*

'From the Poundian wing...' Did that mean also Williams? For me, by that time, it must do. At all events, having read Winters and finding Davie's formulation challenging, it seemed absurd to be in California, as we were in the December of 1959, and not to visit the poet at Palo Alto. At some time between his article of 1957 and our advent, Davie, while teaching in California, had shown Winters my poem on John Constable. 'Too concrete,' had been the comment. But, then, one heard he had said the same to an admirer of his own poem, 'A View of Pasadena from the Hills'. A visit seemed worth the risk.

The preliminaries proved more bracing than ominous. I explained to Winters, over the phone, that we did not wish to trespass on his day unduly, or to put out his wife by arriving at their mealtime. 'My wife?' said Winters. The tone was matter-of-fact rather than surly. 'I am perfectly capable of preparing you a meal myself.' So, beginning with lunch at Palo Alto it was to be a whole day.

I had never before driven on an American freeway – and in the England of 1959 freeways did not as yet exist. In a borrowed car, we therefore departed early from Berkeley, determined to arrive on time. The route was unexpectedly simple and Winters's directions turned out to be lucidity itself. You cannot kill time on a freeway and once you are off it, though you fear you may now mistake the road and go astray, it is also possible to arrive at your destination with surprising speed. This we did. We were an hour early.

A tall hedge concealed the Winters's house, equally impenetrable (or so we told ourselves) from either side. We determined to sit out the hour, quietly, under its protection. Almost as soon as we drew up, Winters had appeared at the gate and was striding toward the car. My wife, the first to gather herself together, fell rather than stepped out onto the ground, apologizing, as she did so, for being late. The day had begun and would evidently end in fiasco.

---

*Donald Davie, 'An Alternative to Pound?' *Spectrum* 1 (Fall 1957), pp. 60-63. Reprinted in *Two Ways Out of Whitman* (Manchester, 2000), pp.39–41.

1: *Beginnings*

However, this reputedly unaccommodating man who, it was said, could resist all attempts at conversation with a yes as curt as his no, either took pity on us or simply liked us. We did not speak much of literature, but when we did it was then that constraint entered in. Williams? He has become unreadable. Pound? A complete barbarian. The only poets Winters was prepared to discuss with approval were, all too predictably, those of his own school – Alan Stephens, Edgar Bowers, J. V. Cunningham. Yet the striking thing about Winters's conversation that day was its lack of precisely that quality of ratiocinative abstraction which he professed to admire in poetry. His talk consisted of a celebration of the concrete: Californian wines, Californian trees and the shapes of their leaves, local topography and the changes the vicinity had undergone, the habits of airedales, the migration of birds, the kinds of birds that visited Palo Alto, the distinguishing peculiarities of the older Californian culture.

Later on, in his study, while preparing to sign a copy of his *Collected Poems,* he handed to me J. V Cunningham's most recent book. I turned the pages for a few moments, then saw that he was looking at me. 'Well, what do you think of *that?*' I paused before speaking. Did he really expect an instant judgement? All that I could summon up was: 'It looks – er – more original than *The Helmsman.*' 'Original?' said Winters; 'there is no particular virtue in originality, you know.' One could imagine a tone in which that could have sounded crushing, yet it was offered not coldly but rather as advice, something to be pondered. I hesitated to subject this gift to the argument it invited, for, after all, it was being made simultaneously with that of his own poems. What formulated itself in the mind, without ever reaching the tongue, was something like, 'There *are* certain obviousnesses of tune and movement, too smoothly homing rhyme sounds, which suggest a merely passive echoing of traditional forms and...' The thought, however, was prompted less by any immediate consideration of Cunningham, than by a weakness that I had always felt marred a number of Winters's own poems, along with certain quaint inaptnesses of diction. Here was a poet, all rigour and closed forms, who could yet describe a military rifle as 'with carven stock unbroke', an attempt at archaism as ungainly as (of the same rifle) 'your bolt is smooth with charm' was insipidly lax.

The day was an entire success. The dignity and dimension of the man unmistakably communicated themselves, as did a capacity for friendship, rather than friendliness. Winters showed no desire to please, but, as in his urging one to try a particularly fine wine, he was eager to share what he deemed best. The same eagerness appeared when he offered for one's meditation, as it were, his distinctive vision of things Californian. That vision was, further, tinged with a kind of elegiac sadness, as in his poem 'California Oaks', an awareness that the place had changed and was changing now beyond all recognition. Like Williams, he complained: 'When we first came here, this was the country.'

I was never to see Winters again, yet I have often had cause to think of his tie with another part of America. In northern New Mexico, there is a ghost town called Madrid – the first syllable of the word takes the accent. The coal mine, the town's sole *raison d'être,* had closed long ago round about Christmas and, for many years, the desert dryness preserved the Christmas decorations intact, including a life-size but faceless Joseph accompanying a Mary, whose features the sun had similarly obliterated, with the Christ child on an ass. On the further side of the town, the school still remains, locked and empty, its walls fissuring apart. It was here that Yvor Winters taught, after spending three years bedridden with tuberculosis in Santa Fe.

New Mexico, Atlanta, the Deep South, Baltimore, Washington, and at last, by April, New York once again. Miss Moore was now home, I imagined, and having written to her ahead from Washington, received the reply: 'Monday afternoon the 25th Mr. Tomlinson? about half past 3? I was dejected thinking I had missed you. Am just making a train, – not very ceremonious.' On 23 April a second note arrived:

> Would it tax you too much to come to see me Monday morning the 25th about eleven or quarter of eleven? – talk for half an hour or longer; and at about twelve go with me to a small restaurant nearby for lunch – (a reliable little place, – though far from peaceful or spacious.) So please pardon that.
>
> I do wish on *no account* to miss meeting you having managed so badly as to have been disabled for more than a month, – with deferred promises now multiplied and tasks which are *said* to be peremptory, crowding me uncivilly – I find Monday morning the most leisurely of any day afterward, until you would be leaving New York. Evenings are not so good for visiting... I seem toward evening to have a froglike croak, and other vestiges of the fever and laryngitis I have suffered the past month.

(I am not contagious or physiologically a menace, however, I am glad to say)...

Indeed, Monday morning, it was her vivacity and not her laryngitis which proved contagious. It was an intermittent vivacity that had to struggle against the lingering effects of illness and the increasing debility of old age. At times, her face seemed completely and fadedly inert, as if all energy had far withdrawn from it. Then a smile would transform her frailty and she was back in the current of life. I have never visited her part of Brooklyn since that morning in April 1960, and have often wondered whether the wood-fronted houses there, and the houses with colonnaded balconies, have survived. The apartment building at 260 Cumberland Street was stone-faced with a massively heavy front door. Miss Moore lived five floors up in pleasantly cluttered quarters. Among the pictures were three reproductions of works by Blake, Dürer's rhinoceros, a photograph of T. S. Eliot as a boy and, beneath these, myriads of animals, including a ceramic leopard and an elephant, and a wooden alligator paper-knife, a work of therapy by a mental patient. To add to these, I gave her a small black turtle modelled in the New Mexican pueblo of Santa Clara.

For some reason – perhaps because I had written of him and she had quoted him in 'An Octopus' – Ruskin was the writer of whom we spoke most. 'He knew everything, didn't he!' she said. She recalled going as a young woman with her mother to see Ruskin's house at Coniston, her mind's eye still retaining the memory of a peacock's feather he had owned and of a watercolour of the Tyrol he had painted. I thought immediately of 'The Steeple-Jack' and 'as Dürer changed / the pine tree of the Tyrol to peacock blue ...', wondering whether the memory had also reinforced the writing of that. 'There is a lovely portrait of Ruskin,' she was saying. 'I think it's in Millais's *Memories*. Ruskin is the man who has said it all. Let's see if we can find that book.' We searched, fruitlessly as it turned out, among many dusty volumes while she aired her literary likes and prejudices: 'I never did care much for Mallarmé... Samuel Beckett? There's nothing to *find* in Samuel Beckett... *Time* magazine? I really abominate the existence of *Time* magazine for betraying my whereabouts. I telephoned directions on how to find this house to their interviewer, and when the interview appeared they printed the directions too. Since then I've been haunted by school children demanding information. And look at this mimeographed sheet!' It was a poem headed, 'This is better than you can do, Miss Moore.' 'Now, Mr Tomlinson, have you kept perfectly *well* during this lengthy journey of yours?' The question was asked with such suddenness, so intently and intensely, that I heard myself replying, very much to my own horror and against my will, that I had had dental troubles. Perhaps it was not entirely her solicitude, but also the fact that I was suffering at the very moment from toothache, that forced the answer out of me. 'Then, Mr Tomlinson,' she returned, 'I shall give you thirty dollars. I know what our dentists are like.' I assured her that there was no need to do that, I should soon be home where things were cheaper. 'I shall send it anyway,' she replied; 'I am sure it hasn't been cheap for you and Mrs Tomlinson to cross this continent.' I was relieved when our talk turned back to poetry. She explained to me, in great detail, which of my poems she liked – these included the Ruskin piece. 'You can bring them to a conclusion without forcing it – that has always been my problem. And so I cut relentlessly.' This seemed the opportunity to mention something I had long had on my mind. 'I was surprised,' I said, 'having known "The Steeple-Jack" for so long, to find the flower passage missing from the 1951 *Collected Poems.*' She looked at me almost guiltily: 'Then I may put it back,' she blurted; 'I get embarrassed about my own digressions and I probably cut too drastically. Yes, I may well put it back.' When A *Marianne Moore Reader* appeared the following year, 'The Steeple-Jack" was the first poem to appear, as in the 1951 *Collected*. This time the poem bore the subheading 'Revised 1961'. The flower passage had returned and in a far more extended form than that which I remembered from *the Faber Book of Modern Verse*. Five more lines of flowers had been inserted with some tinkering to follow, to tie them in.

The little restaurant was not, as she said, spacious, but it turned out to be peaceful. She was recognized at once, as how could she not be in one of her broad-brimmed hats among that soberly dressed clientèle? When I left her back at her apartment, I received a subway token, as did all visitors from Manhattan, out of a bowl of tokens, to pay my way back to town from the Lafayette Avenue station. She asked me, as I was leaving, if I had enjoyed New York. When I replied that I had, her face kindled with a smile that seemed unexpectedly like gratitude: 'I was afraid you wouldn't like it – it's gotten so ugly. As for England – I could sing the praises of England from now until doomsday.'

In the middle of the week a card arrived at the Van Rensselaer where we were staying – the grand name though not the grand place. It stated:

> The picture of Ruskin is in J. Ernest Pythian's *Pre-Raphaelite Brotherhood* (F. Warne) by Sir John Millais; and Ruskin is *alone* not with anyone – standing by a torrent with one foot on a bowlder [*sic*] – and might have been about twenty five or thirty years old.
>
> (I had the book away at the top of a recently acquired bookcase in the dining room.)
>
> The turtle is one of my most precious mascots. I think I'll call it for my brother.

Before leaving New York, I took the bus out to Rutherford once more, accompanied by my wife and Justine. It was shortly after Easter, and the tractable European child played with the chickens that had been the decoration on a now-eaten Easter cake. These she was to carry back over the Atlantic. Williams, for all his ills, exuded a sort of holiday gaiety. He told how he had once thought he might have married the poet Mina Loy. Mrs Williams, unimpressed with this item of news whether real or fictional, replied drily: 'She wouldn't have taken you. You didn't have enough money.'

That evening, I found myself once more in Williams's workroom upstairs. 'Well,' he said, 'here's your letter-clip.' And he presented me with the Victorian metal hand reaching out of its elegantly turned lace cuff. I hardly deserved the gift. After five months travel I had completely forgotten it. When I had been in Rutherford before, I had imagined *he* would forget it. But here was the old poet, broken by strokes, whose memory had served him better than mine had served me.

Our last meeting took place that day. Williams wrote soon after our return in reply to a letter of my own:

> Your view of your delapidated garden is entrancing if sad but not irretrievable after hard work – came just at the time I was heartbroken at the failure to take away the trash from our curb during our trash removal week. They did finally come just in the nick of time but the men did a very slovenly job of it. The only good work is left for our artists to do... The artist must be a good craftsman which no one among the plumbers and carpenters it seems is today. Maybe we're too impatient, maybe it has always been the same.

> I'm glad you found something on which to let yourself go in America even if you had to go back to the primitive Indians of the canyons to find it – Mesa Verde fascinated me too though I did not see the dances as you did.

The letter closed with enquiries after the rest of the family, ending: 'The Easter Chickens weren't seasick were they?'

We continued to exchange letters. One from Williams in December 1960 contained the following:

> Certainly I know that it is winter and that is a season inimical to me. It is always unpleasant from December through March, the only thing I ever heard cheerful about it was my mother in law's annual prediction for New Year's Day, January first, now it's Spring!

It was after a silence of over a year that I received a short note in January 1962. It said simply:

> Dear Charles:
>
> I have been ill for over a year and unable to communicate with you. I picked up an old copy of the magazine Poetry and stumbled on a poem that you had written. It had a familiar ring, called to mind something over which we had been working together.
>
> It's a theme familiar to me which we had not worked out by half. Go on developing the theme for there is much good grist still in it.
>
> Hope you can make something out of this.
>
> > Affectionately
> > Bill

I never discovered what poem it was he had stumbled on. He lasted through that winter, but died the following year in March, the month when his winter thoughts had usually reached their crisis and the poems were stirring towards hope. He died just too early for us to meet when, after a second spell in New Mexico, I returned through New York that summer.

Miss Moore – or Marianne M., as she had signed her note on Ruskin – survived him by nine years. I had written to her from Taos in the June of 1963. Alas, she was to be away on our return East, in Connecticut and then in Maine, but she replied warmly:

> The Taos turtle reminds me of you daily; and I wish I might see

the children and Mrs. Tomlinson... We depend on you, and read you with such pleasure in POETRY. I value your caring about my changed text – of the Steeple-jack.

We were, however, to meet again before her death – twice, in fact. In April 1966 I did a reading tour of New York State, accompanied by my wife, for the Academy of American Poets. A reception was arranged by my publishers at the Oxford University Press. At George Oppen's place where we were staying, a letter awaited us from Miss Moore, telling of her move up to 35 West 9th Street. Not only were we to go and see her, but she would be present at the reception. A second message arrived a week later, specifying Sunday 1 May for our meeting. I noticed that the address label she had pasted over her old letterhead bore her name and middle initial for the first time – 'Marianne C. Moore' – C for Craig.

When we arrived at Oxford with George and Mary Oppen on the afternoon of the reception, no one else had turned up as yet, or, at least, my immediate impression was that no one had. Then, on the far side of the large room, I suddenly caught sight of Miss Moore sitting alone in a small recess, utterly still and utterly silent. I thought at first she had gone blind, for she had that look of blank withdrawal that one sees sometimes on the faces of the blind. Afterwards, I realized that her expression represented only an intensification of that strange look of inertia I had noticed when I first met her six years before. Six years had aged her into a frailer, smaller, more helpless old lady. What was startling was the thought that she had crossed Manhattan on her own to come to this gathering. She was as old as Williams had been in the year of his death, seventy-nine. Glancing at her from time to time during the course of the reception, I often feared that her frailty could never withstand so much boisterousness and I knew that the sight of so much liquor could have been no pleasure to her. 'This drinking!' as she was to say at the tea party in her new flat; 'They even do it at Bryn Mawr now, I hear.'

At the tea party she was more herself, fragile but unexpectedly light-hearted and mercurial, in her neat white dress dotted with blue. The presence of her niece, Sally Moore, a capable and kind young woman, evidently set her at her ease. Her ease also meant that she could air her opinions. She was speaking of what she called the size of poetry. 'And by poetry,' she added, 'I mean *La Vita Nuova* and *The Divine Comedy*. We don't come that big these days, as Mr Blackmur says.' For some reason or other she had taken a great dislike to the English critic A. Alvarez. I am not sure whether her contempt for him was greater or less than her contempt for Robbe-Grillet. 'Mr Alvarez,' she said, 'is a snake in the grass, but the practitioners of the new French novel are idiots – simply idiots.' I ventured a few diplomatic words in mild defence. She sniffed and said tartly: 'You make every allowance.' The point of her dislikes was that she conceived 'these people' lacked 'seemliness' in what they wrote. Seemliness for her had become almost a war cry, and she held forth with a puritan energy on the subject in that high room with the grimy cowls of the ventilator shafts revolving outside the window on the roof below. 'William Carlos Williams often lacked it, you know. He once gave a reading of an unfortunate passage from his poems here in New York. There were two ladies in the audience who were clearly shocked by it. So I went up to them afterward and said to them: "He isn't *always* like that."'

We added a Mexican toad – a seemly toad carved in onyx – to the animal collection and it took up residence beside the pottery turtle. Leaving the apartment, I caught sight once more of a photograph that had arrested my attention in Cumberland Street – that of T.S. Eliot as a boy, the man clearly distinguishable in those features, which also possessed an unlooked-for insouciance that years of suffering were to veil and transform.

When *The Complete Poems of Marianne Moore* appeared in 1967, the book opened at those exemplary verses, 'Poetry'. They had been cut back from twenty-nine to three lines – the first of these shortened by ten words – though the original version was printed in the notes at the end. I turned anxiously to 'The Steeple-Jack'. The tinkerings of six years before had been allowed to stand as had the information 'Revised 1961', though minor changes had crept in since then. I may have been responsible for second thoughts in 1961, but I regret the addition of 'The climate / is not right for banyans' in place of the more direct, 'There are no banyans...' And also the coy 'if you see fit' after 'snake-skin ['snakeskin,' as it reads in 1967] for the foot'. No, I prefer the poem as I first read it in *The Faber Book* when, on a day thirty years ago, I realized there was a kind of probity possible in verse for which seemliness would be no bad description.

Moore, Williams, Winters, and Henry Rago are all dead. They cemented a bond of affection for America I could never have anticipated at the time of my earliest poems or of *The Necklace*. Wyndham Lewis's 'tell him by all means to go to America' has often re-echoed

1: Beginnings

in the memory. My teacher and friend Donald Davie was to follow that course in the mid-1960s, and I have several times contemplated it myself. Time, however, has removed the temptation while perhaps increasing the reasons for it. I have visited the States three times since the stay of 1962-3; with that stay begins a new phase of literary relations. For in the spring of 1963, in Albuquerque, looking disconsolately through a pile of poetry books I had to review for the *University of New Mexico Quarterly*, I suddenly came upon George Oppen's *The Materials*, and as I read these poems the weight lifted. That same spring I also met Robert Creeley for the first time and in the summer Louis Zukofsky and George Oppen himself. But this phase requires a new chapter to itself.

2: Objectivists: Zukofsky and Oppen

'It pays to see even only a little of a man of genius.' Thus Henry James, of Flaubert. I saw Louis Zukofsky four times, corresponded with him – on and off – for seven years, and edited in 1964 what was, I suppose, one of the earliest Zukofsky numbers of an English review for *Agenda:* I was by no means the first islander to discover Zukofsky – Ian Hamilton Finlay had brought out over here *16 Once Published* in 1962 and that had given one something to think about. Indeed, those sixteen poems promised a way in, whereas the translations from Catullus and the sections of *'A'* I had already seen in *Origin* had left me more puzzled than enlightened. Gael Turnbull, who early on had confronted me with Williams, Creeley, and Olson, was also puzzled, though he spoke of Zukofsky the man and also of the holy trinity, Louis, Celia, and son Paul, in a way to arouse curiosity. In 1961 Robert Duncan's poem 'After Reading "Barely and Widely"' had caught one's eye in the *Opening of the Field* –

> will you give yourself airs
> from that lute of Zukofsky?

But the book was simply not available on which to judge that lute, and it was not until August 1963 that I came to own No. 132 of the three hundred copies in which edition 'Barely and Widely' was printed – in a facsimile of Louis Zukofsky's handwriting and published by his wife. The year 1963 proved in many ways an annus mirabilis. I met both 'objectivists', Zukofsky and George Oppen. And those meetings were preluded by two others – with Robert Duncan and Robert Creeley.

Yet it was not to these previous meetings that I owed my introduction to Zukofsky's poems: the meetings confirmed what I was now ready for. What remains difficult to explain in retrospect – in any retrospect – is the way one's scattered awarenesses suddenly fuse and focus. Perhaps it was further talk with that indefatigable and indispensable negotiator between cultures, Dr Turnbull, whom I had last seen in Gloucestershire and who now turned up in

Albuquerque where I was teaching at the University of New Mexico. At all events, in the autumn of 1962 I began to realize once more the extent of my ignorance about the work of Zukofsky and about what had been going on when in 1930, as Williams tells us in his biography,

> with Charles Reznikoff and George Oppen in an apartment on Columbia Heights, Brooklyn, we together inaugurated, first the Objectivist theory of the poem and then the Objectivist Press... The Objectivist theory was this: we had had 'Imagism' (Amygism, as Pound had called it), which ran quickly out. That, though it had been useful in ridding the field of verbiage, had no formal necessity in it... It had dribbled off into so called 'free verse' which, as we saw, was a misnomer... Thus the poem had run down and become formally nonextant... The poem being an object... it must be the purpose of the poet to make of his words a new form... This was what we wished to imply by Objectivism, an antidote, in a sense, to the bare image haphazardly prescribed in loose verse.

Present at that meeting on Columbia Heights (the apartment in question had been George and Mary Oppen's) was Louis Zukofsky, and it fell to him to outline in his essays a set of working principles. Since then he had gone on writing but was still largely unread.

Late in 1962 I tried interlibrary loan and early in 1963 the system disgorged a pristine copy of *Some Time*. This was the handsome edition put out by Jonathan Williams in 1956, and one thing a quick glance confirmed was that, though this was the seventh year of its existence, no one had ever cut the pages. This realization blinded me – quite literally as I was to discover in a few minutes – with sudden anger, and rushing into the kitchen for a sharp knife, I carved the pages apart in a crescendo of fury: such was the fate of poetry in a public library – once obtained, it was left unread. When calm returned and I sat down to lose myself in the book, I was surprised to discover that every time I turned the page two blank pages appeared. Anger and surprise, combined, had so reduced my faculties that it was quite some minutes before I realized that what I had carved apart was Jonathan Williams's beautiful intentions, and that the immaculate candour of these backs of pages printed on only one side had never been intended to be read. Shame replaced surprise, then shame too gave way as my eyes were invaded by the lovely and exact pleasure of

> Not the branches
> half in shadow
>
> But the length of
> each branch
>
> Half in shadow
>
> As if it had snowed
> on each upper half

— as visually precise as, over the page (or rather over the page and two blanks), the following was aurally meticulous:

> Hear, her
> Clear
> Mirror,
> Care
> His error.
> In her
> Care
> Is clear

— a weighing of tones to be reechoed, perhaps, in the 'Ears err for fear of spring' passage from Basil Bunting's *Briggflatts* ten years on.

In these two pieces, one had both sides of Zukofsky's gift, as stated (in reverse order) in '*A*' 6:

> The melody! the rest is accessory:
>
> My one voice. My other: is
> An objective – rays of the object brought to a focus…

I had the clue and so I read on, but it is difficult to disentangle the effect of that reading from the experience of another book which came unexpectedly and almost immediately after to hand. This was George Oppen's *The Materials* – his first for twenty-five years. Was this dual discovery what André Breton meant by objective chance? In actuality, it was a treble discovery, for out of the same, largely depressing pile of books that lay on my desk for review, emerged Reznikoff's *By the Waters of Manhattan*. I could begin now to reconstruct what had happened in those far-off days in Brooklyn and to see how it was still an active, though temporarily forgotten force in the America of the 1960s. Zukofsky and Reznikoff had gone on publishing, but their books had been hard to come by. It was Oppen who was the real mystery – a mystery that has subsequently been explained – since all that one could find out about previous publication was that volume of 1934 ('Oppen's first book of poems', as it said on the cover of *The Materials*), which had earned the praise of Ezra Pound: 'a sensibility ... which has not been got out of any other man's books'. The existence of that first book – instanced but unnamed on the cover – tantalized more and more as I prepared to write the review. On the track of Zukofsky, I had come upon Oppen, whose work showed something of the same terse lineation and exactness I had discovered just before in Zukofsky's 'Not the branches / half in shadow'. On an impulse I wrote to Oppen, who, in replying, offered me one of his three remaining *Discrete Series*, that first book of poems, and said of the writing of *The Materials* (his unaffected eloquence struck me as one of the classic statements of modern poetry):

> I was troubled while working to know that I had no sense of an audience at all. Hardly a new complaint, of course. One imagines himself addressing his peers, I suppose – surely that might be the definition of 'seriousness'? I would like, as you see, to convince myself that my pleasure in your response is not plain vanity but the pleasure of being heard, the pleasure of companionship, which seems more honorable.

Those last two sentences so held my mind, I wanted in some sense to appropriate them, as one does when learning a passage by heart. They were so close to being a poem, I could both appropriate them to my own need and leave them in the hands of their author, simply by arranging them as lines of verse, changing only the pace yet leaving every word intact. This poem ('To C.T.') was to appear ultimately in Oppen's third volume, *This in Which*. It drew the immediate response from him:

> I find myself entranced by the poem with which you have presented me. I see myself – slightly the elder of the two of us – talking to myself – and smoking *my* pipe, which is a shock. I congratulate the three of us on the whole thing.

Another letter, in which he outlined for me the history of the objectivists – an account he much amplifies in an interview for *Contemporary Literature* (Spring, 1969), contains the following:

> We were of different backgrounds; led and have led different

lives. As you say, we don't much sound alike. But the common factor I think is well defined in Zuk's essay ['Sincerity and Objectification']. And surely I envy still Williams' language, Williams' radiance; Rezi's lucidness, and frequently Zukofsky's line-sense.

My mind went back continually to a phrase in that first letter – 'I was troubled to know I had no sense of an audience at all.' If Oppen's sense of an audience had been an absence, what was Zukofsky's in the poems of *Some Time*? Occasionally it seemed to be almost wholly domestic – as witnessed by those valentines and the frequent family references. But, as I was to learn later, Zukofsky could count on an audience among the circle around *Black Mountain Review*, and its editor Robert Creeley was one of his most convinced readers. When Creeley returned from British Columbia to teach at the University of New Mexico in June 1963, I asked him, in a conversation we taped, what he felt had been Zukofsky's principal lesson for the younger poet. Creeley responded to that question in terms rather different from Oppen's own stressing of the value of Zukofsky's critical sense and the stimulus of his conversation, which were what his letters mainly dwelt upon. For Creeley, Zukofsky chiefly ratified in his poetry one side of the teaching of Ezra Pound:

> What Zukofsky has done [said Creeley] is to take distinctions of both ear and intelligence to a fineness that is difficult… It's extremely difficult to follow him when he's using all the resources that he has developed or inherited regarding the particular nature of words as sound… If you read his translations of Catullus in which he is trying, in effect, to transpose or transliterate, or whatever the word would be, the texture of Latin sound into American language, it's an extraordinary *tour de force*. No, I find that in this whole thing that Pound came into – the tone leading of vowels, the question of measure, the question of the total effect in terms of sound and sight of a given piece of poetry – these aspects are tremendously handled by Zukofsky as by no one else.

A couple of days after talking to Creeley, I set out for Kiowa Ranch, on a mountainside beyond Taos. It had been the gift of Mabel Dodge Luhan to D.H. Lawrence and now belonged to the University of New Mexico. In the period I was to spend there, from 22 June to 27 July, I had ample time and quiet to absorb the books Creeley had lent me – Zukofsky's *Anew* and *'A' 1–12*. I copied by hand most of the former and parts of the latter – mainly 'A' 7 and 'A' 11, which still seem to me Zukofsky's two most impressive sections from that long poem. Kiowa Ranch, the sea-wash sound in its pine trees, the slightly inebriating sense of height, the long horizons, the slow withdrawals of the sunset to a band of deep orange above the far mesas – all these entered into my reading and copying. I found myself composing a poem to Zukofsky and enclosed in my first letter to him

> *To Louis Zukofsky*
>
> The morning
> spent in
>
> copying
> your poems
>
> from *Anew*
> because that
>
> was more
> than any
>
> publisher would
> do for one,
>
> was a
> delight: I
>
> sat high
> over Taos
>
> on a
> veranda
>
> Lawrence had
> made in
>
> exile here
> exile
>
> from those
> who knew
>
> how to write
> only the way they

had been
taught to:

I put aside
your book

not tired
from copying but

wishing for
the natural complement

to all the
air and openness

such art
implied:

I went
remembering that

solitude
in the world

of letters
which is yours

taking
a mountain trail

and thinking
is not

poetry
akin to walking

for one
may know

the way that
he is going

(though I did not)
without

his knowing
what he

> will see there:
> and who
>
> following on
> will find
>
> what you
> with more than
>
> walker's care
> have shown
>
> was there
> before his
>
> unaccounting eyes?

In a letter of 1964, Louis was to suggest emending '(though I did not) / without / his knowing / what he' to '(though I / did not) / not knowing / what he,' in order to 'make it even lighter': 'Give it a thought – or more than one – if you reprint in a volume – I may very likely be wrong.' Then he added with characteristic elusiveness: 'I just hope eels will never eat electrons or they might end up in my mad house.' The reply to the poem suggested a meeting in New York on my way back in August. It also told me that he had been reading my work since 1957, 'and I find it valid. I can read it – which is to be moved – as Ez used to say. And for the rest Prospero had better shut up about Miranda's accomplishments – just go ahead and prosper.' But he was to continue trying to improve Miranda's accomplishments. A later poem, 'Gull' – it emerged from seeing one over Brooklyn harbour – which I dedicated to Louis and Celia, was thoroughly relineated and compacted by him from its first version, so that the poem as it now stands is as much a work of collaboration as Oppen's 'To C.T.' In fact, it so bears Louis's stamp, I have wondered sometimes whether it ought not to ride one day in his *Collected*:

> Flung
> far down,
> as the
> gull rises,
> the black
> smile of
> its shadow
> masking its

> underside
> takes
> the heart
> into the height
> to hover
> above the ocean's
> plain-of-mountains'
> moving quartz.

The letter which contained his revised version bore the apologetic 'about *Gull* – I probably shouldn't be doing this, but what do *you* say?' – this ran vertically down the right-hand side of the poem, then vertically down the left: '(And I'm not so sure about alignment, but who's "sure"?).' And beneath the poem: 'Anyway you moved me to do it fast.' I thanked him. He replied:

> Thank me for? If you hadn't made it in potential, the stroke [axshually, as the weather girl says, I did it very fast] of genius (?) wouldn't have been actual. *No* time wasted, considering you agree – to be perfectly bumptious about it, considering your gratitude makes me happy – and I never take any credit from the prime mover. Don't tell anybody I still do such things, however, or I'll be flooded who knows with rafts of stuff from 'pouncers.'

I wasn't entirely sure what 'pouncers' in inverted commas implied. The idiom and rhythm of the letter are very much those of Louis's speaking voice. The bits you didn't understand in his rapid patter (he was often extraordinarily comic) left you feeling you ought to have, but there was no ling/ering for regret or greater comprehension, because what he had gone on to say now demanded your whole attention. You couldn't afford to miss it. And just as you had to read his letters at all angles for the tiny parentheses, you often had to strain to hear his low-toned voice. His whisper might be as funny as the minute postscript down the back of an air letter: 'C just bogged in income tax reports calls from downstairs to ask if we can claim for being *blind*.'

I was to hear that voice for the first time in August. To begin with there had been doubts – doubts that made me realize that Louis was already a frequently sick man ('I'm ill so I can't move my head to left or right, but just to say it will have to improve by August 4, when you pass through'). There were to be several mentions of 'the aches', not further defined, and three years later, in a letter saying that he had refused some teaching at Buffalo, I read the ominous words: 'The emphysema won't bear the traffic.' There had been more than doubts about seeing the Oppens that summer: it was a certainty they would be on Little Deer Isle, Maine. Then, suddenly, their plans were changed and they intended to be in Brooklyn. And, just as suddenly, our postal search for a New York apartment achieved success – that also was to be in Brooklyn. And though Brooklyn is a large place, as we soon knew, it was sufficiently the one place in which we would all coincide, the Zukofskys, the Oppens, and the Tomlinsons.

In *Kulchur* (Spring 1962) Jonathan Williams has an imaginary movie cast to play the modern poets – Edward Everett Horton as T. S. Eliot, Lon Chaney, Jr., as Robert Frost, Adolph Menjou as Edward Dahlberg, Cary Grant as James Laughlin. As Louis Zukofsky he casts Fred Astaire. There was an uncanny accuracy about this. Still showing signs of recent illness, Zukofsky had a curious dancing lightness in his build, movement, and talk. There was also a touch of elegance, given sartorial precision when ten days after our visit to 160 Columbia Heights, he turned up complete with bow tie at our apartment on Ocean Avenue. What did not fit Jonathan Williams's casting was the densely black, thick line of the eyebrows, the continuously relit cigarette, the nervous puckering of the forehead as the face flickered from anxiety to humour, the voluble, mercurial ceaselessly inventive talk. That tenth story of Columbia Heights gave on to a view of the harbour. It was the same spot more or less that had seen the meeting of objectivists – not yet named – on that day in 1930. Through the window, behind Manhattan Bridge, loomed the span of Brooklyn Bridge. You could see it, but only just. The Statue of Liberty rose clear in the sultry August afternoon in the opposite direction. On the balcony the traffic noises floated up from below, often drowning out Zukofsky's soft voice.

We spoke of many things, including the funeral of William Carlos Williams the previous March ('The nicest funeral I ever went to,' said Louis). But what most remains with me is the music of the occasion. By this I do not mean to reduce it to symbolist essence. 'The greatest satisfactions of conversation are probably musical ones,' as Ted Hughes has said. 'A person who has no musical talent in ordinary conversation is a bore, no matter how interesting his remarks are. What we really want from each other are those comforting or stimulating exchanges of melodies.' The music of meeting Zukofsky was exactly right, and one was encouraged to play one's few bars of accompaniment with a sense of satisfaction at having come in at the right place. His stream of talk was not exactly a monologue – he was too aware of one's presence for that – but it flowed and flashed and glowed in such a way that one hesitated to interrupt it. Or, to change the metaphor, one suggested themes on which Zukofsky variated, very much for one's benefit and delight. There was a mutuality in this process which he evidently appreciated and remembered when two years later he wrote to me: 'Hugh Kenner finally got to see us last week – just dropped in on a chance that I'd be at home, and we spent two afternoons together talking, the first talk of its kind I guess since you and I last talked. (The aches have been such we see almost nobody.)'

The talk at Columbia Heights gave place to his reading for us from his Catullus translations. As he did so, one realized that it was not only Pound that lay behind this venture, but principally the Joyce of *Finnegans Wake*. And Joyce came to mind in the quality of his vocal execution which compared with that light tenor rendering of the Anna Livia Plurabelle passage on gramophone record. The *Cats*, as he called them, came over as beautifully comic, though I could not help wondering whether, without the help of his expert vocalizing, and once extended from half a dozen to 116 plus fragmenta, these transliterations could hold the mind and not bring on a feeling of eels eating electrons. Here, he had pushed what he always called 'the noise' of poetry about as far as it would go. Tune was his other favourite word:

> The lines of this new song are nothing
> But a tune making the nothing full

Do the tunes of the *Cats* survive in their author's voice? Did the Library of Congress perhaps tape some of them, when he recorded there? He would surely have wished them to be heard his way, the noise bringing to the surface a ghostly Roman gabble. He had written to Alfred Siegel in 1957 concerning Siegel's transliteration of the Chinese through Pound's Canto 97, 'you mean the English *noises*[?], that would interest me.'

The Zukofskys regaled us with trifle and cake, washed down with root beer, then walked with us through the twilight to find the bus stop. Louis was saying that his last communication from Ezra Pound was about a rabbi, then went on to define his attitude to the world of regular publishing from which he, Zukofsky, was as yet still excluded. 'I don't care,' was his frequent refrain, though I doubted that. There was a certain undertow of bitterness, though it never dominated the conversation. As we walked through the grimy yet reassuring streets of Brooklyn and finally took up our stand under the pole of the bus stop, it was gaiety that prevailed. We must have talked for half an hour before we realized that no buses intended to halt there and that the notice on top of the pole read 'No Parking'.

George Oppen is a man who came by knowledge with difficulty – which makes his Jewishness a very different thing from Zukofsky's. I recognized the latter's as soon as we had entered his apartment. It had the same flavour that had given point and aliment to my adolescence, when the refugees from Hitler's Germany arrived in the English Midlands. Here were people who had records of Bruckner and Brecht's *Dreigroschenoper* at a time when both were unknown to us. Among them I had heard Kant's categorical imperative explained as if it were a fact of daily life, had listened to a description of Thomas Mann glimpsed paring an apple 'with surgical intentness', had discovered that Heine, Kafka, Rilke could still exist among the coal dust and the fumes from pottery chimneys. In this Jewishness one experienced a familial sense at once secretive and hospitable, subtly tenser than one's own involvement in the painful day to day of family bathos, where lack of money and lack of imagination had produced a stale stoicism. That experience of an eagerly tense intellectuality returned as one met the Zukofskys. Not so with the Oppens.

To gain their apartment in Henry Street, one passed the ground-floor window where a pleasant-looking young man sat writing, as George later told me, pornographic fiction. The scarred hallway and stair led up to the top of the house and at the stairhead stood a man with a lined and weathered face like a Jewish sea captain – a man who, as it transpired, owned a sailing boat but no car. This was George Oppen. Like Zukofsky, he saw the humorous side of things, but he listened more. His speech was less fluent, more meditative; it was exact with a pondered exactness like his poetry.

We talked much of Mexico that evening – for we had been there earlier the same year – and of the Oppens' phase of exile in Mexico City and his joinery shop there. In his talk one warmed to a union of the passionate and the deliberate: there was accuracy and there was economy in this, and somehow, in one story he told us, he had managed to carry these to a point where they seemed like miracle or luck. Tired of the way Mexican drivers aimed their cars at you, George, crossing the Zócalo, had once refused to submit to this humiliation and, as the projectile approached, planted his fist square in the windshield: it was not the fist but the windshield that shattered. 'A stupid thing to do,' said George. The owner of the car got out, apparently for the showdown, but looking first at Oppen and then at the shivered glass, could find no way in which *machismo* could account for, admit, or take action against such folly, shrugged, reascended, and drove off. George has a genius for such inevitabilities. They need not always be the fruit of happy violence. In England, nine months after our meeting, the Oppens were at Ozleworth on an afternoon when the vicar called. Conversation turned on the New English Bible, and I expended a good deal of wasted wrath on our pastor's admiration for this moribund document. He explained that in order to make sure that its idiom was truly current the committee had consulted a bishop's secretary. George was far more of a marksman than I with my incoherent rage. As the vicar was about to leave, George said with a sort of courteous finality, 'The next time you translate the Bible, call in a carpenter – and make sure he's a Jewish carpenter.' Later, walking down the nave of Wells Cathedral, he gave vent to another unexpected apophthegm: 'I guess I'm a Christian,' he said, 'but with all the heresies.'

The apartment in Henry Street was very much a presence in our conversation on that first encounter. As we sat eating, the evening moved into possession of the scene outside. High above Brooklyn, we watched the sun go down to the right of the Statue of Liberty, swiftly like a coin into a slot. Light shone from the statue's torch and from the windows of Manhattan – these of a strange greenish hue as if an effect taken up from the water in the summer dusk. Across the bay the Staten Island ferry stitched back and forth, a trail of lights above the milky turquoise it was travelling over. The television antennae on the near roofs of Brooklyn looked like ships' masts drawn up before the harbour below. This was a room and a view we were to revisit several times before the Oppens left for San Francisco in 1969, when Henry Street was threatened with demolition. The place seems a cell in a larger aggregate, from which memory picks out the building in a street close by where Whitman printed *Leaves of Grass*, now a Puerto Rican restaurant; the commemorative plaque on its wall (stolen, sold, and then recovered); the walk past red Edward Hopperish street façades; what *The Materials* calls 'the absurd stone trimming of the building tops'; the site of the old Brooklyn ferry and behind its delapidated stakes the

2: Objectivists: Zukovsky and Oppen

line of Brooklyn Bridge – Whitman superimposed on Hart Crane.

As the shapes of Manhattan hardened into black that evening, I began to realize that all was not well between Oppen and Zukofsky, and the impression deepened on subsequent meetings with them both. I think I may now speak of this, for George's poem with which I shall close makes no secret of the matter. When I reviewed Reznikoff's and Oppen's books I had wondered why there was no Zukofsky in the series, a joint publication of New Directions (James Laughlin) and *San Francisco Review* (June Oppen Degnan, George's half sister). His exclusion there clearly rankled with Louis. Even before I had met him, I realized the situation was an uneasy one, for, after sending my review to Oppen, I had received the following reply:

> I enjoyed very much reading your review... I will have a copy made for New Directions-SF Review for the mention of Zuk... The first year's poetry schedule consists of Oppen, Reznikoff and William Bronk, in which my advice is obvious enough. My recommendation of course included Zuk, but the suggestion – as you see – has not been acted on. It is by now too awkward for me to discuss the matter with Zuk at all, but it is my impression that they would be more likely to do a Selected than a Collected poems, if only for budgetary reasons. I can't really urge Louis to submit a ms. since I have no assurance at all that they would accept it. But you might urge him to try it if you think it worth the risk – to him – of a rejection. If they had a ms. under consideration I could re-open the discussion.

When I arrived in New York, I had some illusory hopes that I might perhaps be able to negotiate on Louis's behalf. As I stayed on, this hope extended to the possibility of somehow reconciling the estranged friends. But the longer I stayed the more I realized that neither project could be easily accomplished. In the first place, not only his self-respect but also Louis's belief that all his life he had been writing *one* poem (and he was very decided about this) stood in the way of my ever persuading him to submit a selected, and secondly, his feelings toward George had curdled to such an extent that any reconciliation must lie far in the future if it were feasible at all. From hints and suggestions, I gathered that he imagined George had simply failed to act for him, which was not the case. Yet one could not simply *state* this to Louis. He did not live in the atmosphere of simple statement and his aggravated nerves pushed him into more suspicion than was good for him. He was a gentle man, yet his own character and long neglect had created a thorny hedge of self-defence and of self-injury. Years of teaching what he called 'my plumbers' at the Brooklyn Polytechnic Institute cannot have helped: 'My own mess of school etc is proverbial,' he wrote, complaining of chalk fights and 'kids of seventeen who cannot sit on their asses'. 'All I need is to be away from that "job" I guess – the eellecter-monickers, curs, curse.' Perhaps he even resented the fact that George was at last free from the job grind. It is hard to be certain. At all events, he made it clear that no interference, however delicate, could help repair the situation. I unwillingly resigned myself to this fact.

On returning home, I set about sharing my new-found knowledge of things American with my fellow countrymen, or as many of them as read the little magazines. For *the Review*, January 1964, I edited a Black Mountain poetry number in which Louis figured as one of the founding fathers. Ian Hamilton, the regular editor, added his own characteristic postscript: 'The editorial motive of *the Review* in this project has been a documentary rather than, necessarily, a critical one. We believe that the movement ought at least to be known about.' So much for English caution, incapable of surrendering itself to surprise. The following December appeared the Louis Zukofsky issue of *Agenda*. All this time I kept up a regular correspondence with Louis and an exchange of books. He was an excellent critic and immediately perceptive about where another poet's strengths lay. His method of instruction by letter consisted of copying out the individual phrases which had struck him as centrally strong. I mentioned one poem of mine which he had not touched on and he replied, 'I was trying to point at *that* in your work which might now be more useful to you as "craft," when you've extended it *past* your forefathers.' On my *Peopled Landscape* he wrote: 'As for prosody a little nearer Hardy in impulse of song rather than for all I revere his integrity the thought metres of Crabbe – and so on, the old guy's talking too much.' He emphasized that it was 'the "pure" of the craft' he was interested in revealing to one, and on the poem to which I had drawn his attention: '"Craft" as "invention" etc. In itself the poem is nothing to be neglected and in a work like my Test of Poetry would do very well alongside of Crabbe and Marvell ...' He could respond unexpectedly to poems whose premises were very un-Zukofskyan, as when he pointed to one of mine called 'The Impalpabilities' and added '[would be your best defence against

Bottom].' His square brackets managed to be at once intimately playful and also defensive of another's interests, a typical example of the atunement of his epistolatory style and also of his conversation (he was a man who could *speak* square brackets) to the needs of a friend. Of friends' needs he was always studious. His caring ranged from minute, attentive sympathy (on hearing my father was ill, he inquired about him for many letters after) to a sense of troubles taken on his own behalf. It could be simply a question of a meal. Or it could be a friend's luck that brightened his feelings, as when Bunting finally achieved publication with Fulcrum Press: 'I hope Basil gets the garter or sumpin – anything to save him from the dogged silence he's lived. It makes him happy – at any rate he writes cheerfully – to have some attention. *Loquitur* is a beautiful book, and *Briggflatts* is a delayed extension of it.' And there were friends missed. Of Williams he spoke with great affection, for Williams, while not quite getting what Louis was at, had always written of him with generosity. One document of their literary relations I discovered while editing the *Agenda* issue – this was a signed statement of Williams's of 29 June 1948, which ran: 'I hereby grant formal permission to Louis Zukofsky to use whatever he wishes to use of my published literary works as quotations in his writings.'

In the winter of 1964 Louis began to talk of retirement. They were to move to two-and-a-half rooms: 'Kitchen, living room with an L for sleeping. We've been living to pay the rent and income tax. The idea is to get down – to something like a bare table top – and maybe something of the feeling of 30 years ago where we wandered the streets of the same neighborhood, rather young, will come back to us.' By August I heard: 'We're delighted to be in Manhattan again after 25 years… the streets have all the interest of a foreign city to provincials.' The same letter contained the news of acceptance by Norton of his poems ('First publication of poetry since they did Rilke in 1938 …') and of a further bonus that Reznikoff had just telephoned to read out a long and positive review of *Bottom* in the *TLS* – 'very careful and painstaking… So your country gets there ahead of mine.' I hesitated to confess (those were the days of anonymity) that I had written it.

Though Louis continued to feel the loneliness of his position, a period of respite seemed to be ensuing for him. Not that all was plain sailing now. The advance from Norton hadn't, as he wrote, 'covered half the medico's bills'. Yet there was freedom from the plumbers and there was a December visit to Yaddo in 1965 to finish the *Cats*: 'Silence helps – only a handful of reticent respectful guests – so far we can stand the cold. Pines, trails, waterfalls, high views from the foothills of the Adirondacks, and altogether too many good books around with no time to read if I'm to get through with that Guy (Gai).'

In the meantime I had been planning an anthology. If I could not help to reconcile George and Louis, at any rate I could surely get them together inside the covers of one book. And this book would show English readers an area of American poetry with which they were not as yet familiar. The title, *Seven Significant Poets,* embraced the objectivists (Oppen, Zukofsky, Reznikoff, and Carl Rakosi), Lorine Niedecker (characterized in *'A' 12* as 'a rich sitter'), James Laughlin, and William Bronk.

I was in New York in the spring of 1966 and so able to speak with Louis about this idea. Our meeting took place at 77 Seventh Avenue. 'You must come to the biggest Vermeer you've ever seen and you'll find us,' he said over the telephone. The Vermeer proved to be an enormous blowup of one of his paintings used as a mural decoration for the downstairs vestibule of the apartment building. It still looked solidly composed but uncomfortably stretched. The apartment was overheated, at least for English susceptibilities, and Louis seemed ill, though still full of inventive talk. The meeting was attended by a lingering uneasiness. We were staying with the Oppens, a fact not easy to declare, and when the Zukofskys invited us to remain to dinner the awkwardness arose of phoning our hosts from the one room that we would not be back for an evening meal. This I accomplished with absurd secretiveness and put down the phone, having mentioned no names. 'So you're staying with the Oppens,' said Louis. Yet the awkwardness passed and a pleasant meal followed. Louis seemed interested by the idea of the anthology, though he didn't care for the work of Bronk – 'All that Stevensian bothering. You either think with things as they exist, or you give up.' 'Is Oppen in it?' called Celia from the kitchen. Louis seemed to accept that fact as inevitable also. I was not so sure that Celia did. But the way ahead looked clear and there was even a sort of geniality in Louis's contemplation of the prospect.

Back in England I put several months' work into the book and Fulcrum expressed their wish to publish it. When they approached Louis for permission to reprint, there came back a firm no in reply. It wasn't entirely unexpected, but one had hoped that, if reconciliations were not possible in daily life, perhaps literary works could

2: Objectivists: Zukovsky and Oppen

still lie down amicably side by side. I never discussed the matter further with Louis, though obviously, without his presence in the book, it must remain a total impossibility. I'd simply spent a great deal of time to little effective end. We continued to correspond with perfect cordiality though we never met again. I should have foreseen the difficulties in the light of George's letter three years before concerning Louis's diatribes against him to innocent visitors:

> But perhaps I had better say that Louis really has no grievance against me, nor has the world, or no greater grievance than it has against anyone in these times of population explosion. And Louis no greater grievance against me than against anyone who 'gets printed.' Awkward for me, tho. And overwhelmingly ironic to discuss my position as 'a success'... I doubt that I'll produce another book within quite a few years. Maybe that'll heal things.

That was after *The Materials*. Other books followed and finally a collected. But so did books by Louis, including the two volumes of *All*. Clearly he was right to have resisted a selection. He got what he wanted, but what a time it took. And time didn't, in George's words, 'heal things'. When George gave me his *Collected Poems* in San Francisco in 1976 I found in it, toward the close, a poem I had not read before. I thought perhaps I had missed it in his previous collection, *Seascape: Needle's Eye*, but, no, it is not there. The title is 'The Lighthouses' and the subtitle 'for LZ in time of the breaking of nations':

> *if you want to say no say*
> *no if you want to say yes say yes* in loyalty
>
> to all fathers or joy
> of escape
>
> from all my fathers...

and the poem modulates into George's seaboard world where lighthouses flash and the coastal waters are rock-pierced. He recognizes the kinship with Zukofsky – for Zukofsky was in a sense one of his fathers too, a brilliant exemplar and talker in the early days of objectivism. He recognizes also the racial kinship as a motif returns, previously used in the poem 'Semite':

> my
> heritage *neither Roman*
> *nor barbarian*...

I do not know whether Louis ever read the piece or whether, had he done so, he would have recognized George's continuing plea for clarity in relationship. 'The Lighthouses' is a final document in a long and saddening history of misunderstanding, a misunderstanding which a common experience of a time, place, and race might have outweighed but did not. It reminded me of the fact that from both their windows in Brooklyn they had shared the view of the same 'lighthouse' – the beam from the statue shining back in the dusk towards the windows of Manhattan.

3: A Late Greeting: O'Keeffe

The envelope was addressed in a strong hand which might have been masculine. The dictionary defines calligraphy as elegant penmanship. This was certainly calligraphy, but it was forceful rather than elegant, and the diagonal 'Do Not Bend', with its firmly scalloped underlining like an ideogram for 'choppy sea', proclaimed authority. No one had bent the contents of the envelope despite its ample size. The card within carried the message 'A late greeting / I hope it reaches you' and the monogram 'G. O'K.' Georgia O'Keeffe's Christmas card – or was it a New Year greeting? – had been mailed on 20 January 1964, and arrived in England in time for spring, having been readdressed from Albuquerque, where we were no longer residents. The illustration consisted of one of her early watercolours, *Starlight Night* of 1917, scarcely a couple of years after Alfred Stieglitz's discovery of her with his celebrated remark, 'Finally a woman on paper.' It was the sort of starlight night you might find six thousand feet above sea level in the crystalline air of Abiquiu, New Mexico, from where the card had been mailed.

This was the second postal communication that I had received from Miss O'Keeffe – always 'Miss O'Keeffe,' never 'Mrs Stieglitz' ('Why should I take on someone else's famous name?'). The first – before we had met – had been a Western Union telegram: 'Please come Sunday at eleven for lunch.' That unexpected summons to the high village forty miles north of Santa Fe in January 1963 marked a stage on a journey that had begun seventeen years before – also in January – when Donald Reid had sent me (it was my nineteenth birthday) *An Illustrated Handbook of Art History*. In a postwar England not rich in exotic books and in Blackpool, not conspicuous for its bookshops, the unaccountable presence of the compilation by Frank J. Roos, Jr., had caught his eye. What caught mine, on receiving it, was the unknown quantity, American art. Thus, when long afterward I came to read Lowell's poem 'For the Union Dead', Augustus Saint-Gaudens's Shaw Memorial, which is in question there, was no stranger to me, though I had never seen it in the flesh, or more exactly, in the bronze.

Not that the Saint-Gaudens had ever made for me a forceful image. What held the eye was the outline of American painting – Homer, Ryder, Eakins, then (approaching the present) Marin, three Demuths, and a single O'Keeffe, *The Mountain*. This last, indifferently reproduced like all the plates, two by three inches and in monochrome, entered one's meditations. In it, all the sinews of the mountain stood revealed. It seemed to have heaved upward and fallen sideways like a sleeper who has just turned over. And yet it was not in any way personified. The colours, reduced uniformly to grey, except for some darker tree shapes and was it the sky above or a larger mountain containing this smaller one? – the colours could have been those of ice or fire. What the printing could not eliminate was the firm articulation of the musculature, the rock-thrust, the held declivities, the sense of an even light bringing the whole to bear. This was my first glimpse of the landscape of New Mexico, although I had no way of identifying the place or the painter. Indeed, *The Mountain* was flanked by Eugene Speicher's *Portrait of a Girl,* which memory misread as *Portrait of an Irish Girl,* so that for years I carried with me this quite erroneous picture of O'Keeffe. More profitably, I came to associate *The Mountain* with Marianne Moore's poem 'An Octopus', where an entire mountain mass is 'gone over', with its octopus of ice on top '"Creeping slowly as with meditated stealth, / its arms seeming to approach from all directions."' So evidently it was ice colour the grey reproduction had suggested. Wrong again, but the wrongness scarcely injured the picture of the landscape it essentialized although both were the colour of fire. The form rode in the mind unimpaired until it was to blaze back at me from the outside at a first sight of the Sangre de Cristo Mountains abrupt above the New Mexican desert.

'Please come Sunday at eleven for lunch.' It seemed a generous invitation. Whoever heard of going to lunch until twelve-thirty? I had not expected such a wide margin for talk. To begin with, I had expected very little. For whenever I had raised the question of trying to see O'Keeffe, people had shaken their heads. 'You will find it difficult to get in. She sees very few except her friends.' Yet the desire persisted. Having carried that image in one's head for the better part of twenty years, having come through it to an aspect of modern painting one's countrymen had never inspected, one had perhaps earned a meeting. It was my friend, the poet Winfield

3: A Late Greeting: O'Keeffe

Townley Scott, who brought it about. I had been admiring a book of photographs of ghost towns in his house at Santa Fe. The photographer was Todd Webb – 'a close friend of O'Keeffe's,' as Win added. I reiterated my half-forlorn hope. 'I'll call him for you and see what he suggests.' The next thing I knew, a week later, was that I had in my hand a telegram from the great lady.

That winter had been relatively mild. There had been snow and sleet on Christmas Eve, but one had driven with comparative ease, though through clinging mud, to mass at the pueblo church of San Felipe. After the service, there had been dancing, the dancers entering at the huge west door preceded by the soft-timbred music of their ankle bells, their coyote yelps sharp on the snowy air. One was aware of the vast space behind them, and then the explosion of a Kiowa war dance, all energy and feathers, blotted it back into the cold night as six drummers and chorus accompanied the dancers into the resonating church. Christmas Day saw deep, brilliant snow. Then the weather turned kind once more. A week before the visit to Abiquiu I sat in warm sun watching the deer and antelope dances on the plaza of Cochiti pueblo. It seemed like summer and the whole ceremony took on a mesmerically summery glow to the beat of a single drum. The light sought out the white tunics and the red headbands of the line of male dancers in their doeskin boots. The two Deer Mothers, one at either end of the line, flared in red blouses, the left shoulder bare, turquoise round their necks, head-feathers, black kirtles, white puttees. Under the full sun of morning, the two women advanced from the line of dancing men to be met by two deer – male dancers whose forelegs were completed by their bending over on sticks. They moved in fascinated dependence on the Deer Mothers, behind them two bright-blanketed priests. The Deer Mothers drew them without noticing them, with solemn, lowered eyes and an impersonal, sexless dignity. In their hands they carried bunches of feathers and the deer imitated their circular gestures with identical motions of the neck. The weather was part of the ceremony – a slow hypnosis of pulsating sunlight. But it wouldn't last.

The day before I set out for Abiquiu followed a night below zero in the Albuquerque valley. Someone going home drunk had entangled himself in barbed wire and frozen to death. The next night would be even colder, we were told, and it was – down to thirty below, just north of Santa Fe; and at Albuquerque, the breathtaking rareness of snow air and snow light in a snowbound city.

The car was immoveable. Even had it been otherwise, who could say what the weather would be like at Abiquiu? Thirty below. But that was at Tesuque. Also north of Santa Fe. But Abiquiu lay further to the west. One would be late at all events. The generosity of 'come at eleven' put one in the wrong from the start. But what was the use of going back and forth over the situation? The weather was immoveable, too. The air seemed to encase one in a suit of ice. There was not even a whisper from the car battery. Other cars stood on their driveways like stranded boats. The streets were empty.

But one had failed to take into account the desert sun. Once it was above the mountains, the snow began to melt until it lay only in the shadows, a white geometry at the edges of buildings reproducing gables and rooflines on the shining black streets. The immoveable car was dragged, pushed, coaxed into motion, coughed a little, jerked, came unjammed, faded dangerously, was forced back into life by a diligent foot. It was impossible to get there by eleven, if one could get there at all. But the car was moving, the snow was sliding off the roofs, the way through town was clear, and out into the desert the paved highway shone and steamed as the sun drew off its snow. The oranges and reds of the desert were seeping back now through the retreating white. Water sang and flashed through the *arroyos* under the road. The sun was feeling once more for the shapes of the immense arid landscape in which the wet from the snowfall had flushed up the dusty colours like water thrown over a mosaic floor. Among the ghostly greys of the winter cottonwood trees, behind the tin-roofed adobes, along the banks of the snow-filled Rio Chama, everything rekindled, glittered, sending up mica showers, crossing blades of light. Light that had been snow. Snow that underscored the reefs of orange rock. It was the dance of fire and ice. The tall blue of the sky was reestablished, though even the sun could not entirely blunt the sharpened air.

Abiquiu, or Santo Tomás Apostel de Abiquiu, lies twenty miles from the town of Española. Before Highway 84 was paved, it must have seemed fifty. Within living memory the journey there and back took at least three days, and coming to each *arroyo*, a wagon would need to be unloaded and reloaded on the further bank. The story is told by Gilberto Benito Cordova* of the horse-drawn wagon stuck and abandoned in El Arroyo de Oso. Two cousins, inhabitants of

---

*Abiquiu and Don Cacahuate: A Folk History of a New Mexican Village (Cerrillos, New Mexico: San Marcos Press, 1973).

3: A Late Greeting: O'Keeffe

Abiquiu, approaching the spot from opposite directions, began an extended argument about the wagon's real colour, finally threatening each other with physical violence. The son of the cousin who had approached from the Abiquiu side tried the experiment, while the argument was at its height, of tickling one of the horses under its tail with his stick, the result being that the team suddenly started forward and freed the cart, revealing that each side of it was painted a different colour.

Abiquiu still seems set apart. It consists of the crumbling remains of an eighteenth-century settlement of Genízaros, that is, Hispanicized Indians of mixed tribal origins. The word is an etymological relation of the Turkish *janissaries* – Christians turned into Islamic soldiers by the Turks. The car, slithering into the muddy ruts of the village street, found its way by a kind of instinct to a long, low wall behind which sheltered a long, low house, to a gateway adorned by an immense deer skull complete with branching antlers. It brought to mind O'Keeffe's painting, *From the Faraway Nearby,* where the sky is filled with a horned, floating skull, behind it the empty blue, and bare desert hills beneath. Evidently one had come to the right place. Bone by adobe. When I admired the trophy at the gate later that afternoon she replied, 'I swapped a hi-fi set for it.'

I expected a tall woman. She was a vigorous seventy-six, rather small of stature, with a mild but incisive voice, the incisiveness toning the mildness of its sound with a strength that could take itself for granted. She talked readily, easily. She smiled frequently with reconnaissant eyes, so that the lined face of the photographs, with its thin, fine eyelids, possessed an animation that photography in freezing banishes. One saw why Stieglitz had taken his five hundred pictures of her, realizing the practicable part of that dream of his of a photographic portrait that ideally should start with birth, follow out a life to death, and then begin once more with the child of the subject. I was late and I expected her to be displeased, but that day all her guests had arrived late – Todd Webb with his wife, and a granddaughter of Mabel Dodge Luhan with her husband. We had been talking of the great cold when O'Keeffe said to me in the same voice with which she spoke of the weather, 'You got in on false pretences. I am not friendly. I thought you were a friend of Todd Webb's.' I had just met Todd Webb for the first time. The eyes seemed to acknowledge that she was half-joking. I wasn't sure. In retrospect, she seems merely to have been stating the truth of the matter. But neither was she *un*friendly now that I'd 'got in'.

The house was a rambling adobe. The room in which we sat talking, and the adjoining room in which we ate, were painted a stark white. Black vases from San Ildefonso pueblo contained grey twigs, flowerless. She, also, wore black, a masculine-looking trouser suit, and later, when we went outside, a thick black leather coat. On tables and ledges, animal bones of various sizes, stones very smooth and rounded. Dark furniture against white walls, an adobe-coloured mud floor. Under low vigas two Chinese statues, two African masks, no O'Keeffes, no Stieglitz. There was a warren of smaller rooms. They had formerly been used as pigpens, being abandoned as the roofs fell in and then locked. She had bought the derelict house from the church, renovating the rooms one by one and building in each a differently sized fireplace to burn the aromatic *piñon* wood. The rooms had been plastered by local women. 'They do the work best,' she said; 'They did the whole house. Every inch of its surface has been touched by a woman's hand. Now I have to think about the outside. Four years of rainy weather, and the adobe is melting away.'

We ate well. Beef, salad, water-grown tomatoes, pickled onions and curry, prepared by Amelia, her helper; ice cream which she had made herself and apologized for; mangoes which she had never served previously, red wine, coffee. Assisting in carrying out the dishes, one caught sight through the kitchen window of the enfiladed mesas commanding their orange, juniper-stippled spaces with, in the foreground, on the kitchen table, a giant, black grinding-stone, a *metate* that had come from Amelia's grandmother.

Conversation had been easy and unforced at table, but it had been general, and some of it impenetrably local, so that I had the feeling that I had not really been speaking to *her,* that perhaps this was the wages of false pretences. One item of local talk lodged in my ear. It concerned the Indian husband of Mabel Luhan who, as he lay on his deathbed, kept reiterating, 'I want to go to the rodeo at Cimarrón. Why don't somebody take me there?' As the others drifted back to the armchairs, O'Keeffe unexpectedly drew me aside and over to the further end of the dining table: 'And now let's talk. And let me say first of all how much I admire your green English tweed. What a marvellous material.'

We began by talking of the cubists. She had known them early and admired Braque. Was that because of the 1913 Armory Show? No. She had known them before. She had seen them at Mr

Stieglitz's gallery (she invariably referred to him as 'Mr Stieglitz') in an elegant but plain brownstone house – Picasso and Braque drawings, and other things one would wish to see when young, including African things. 'I had no great passions,' she continued; 'I went my own way. I didn't even intend to "live" by painting because there's the danger that you'll try to copy the style of someone else and "work" it.' No, she didn't care for Constable, but loved Turner; hadn't, in fact, known many English people except for Gerald Heard. Thought England would be too green for her, like Virginia, where she had lived for a time. She had toured France – Chartres, Vézelay, Autun; Chartres with its big windows 'like being under trees'. 'I think the architecture is the greatest achievement of the Church – finer than the frescoes, finer than Ravenna.' I wanted to ask about Sheeler and Demuth but she spoke more of the city, of New York, in the 1920s. 'It was the end of brownstone Park Avenue (where you walked when you had a cold). As the skyscrapers took over, high and separate, they made you feel they'd fall on you.' We talked a good deal of Abiquiu. 'It's like living in a novel. Why, there's a mother here who won't let her child have a hearing aid because she's afraid it'll make his hearing worse.' Most of all she spoke of Joe, the Spanish boy, now twenty, she'd been 'bringing on'. 'I've had him get his teeth fixed and scraped. I give him brewer's yeast and molasses and it's improved his complexion and made him stand straight. And, after brewer's yeast, he works better. He's great with cars. He bought an old school bus for twenty dollars when he was eighteen – learned to fix and unfix it, and now he's an expert. I signed for him when he made a down payment on a truck. His uncle and grandfather would have paid off the instalments if Joe couldn't, but they wouldn't *sign* anything.'

Joe was to be in demand that afternoon. The other two guests had departed, and Todd Webb's car wouldn't start. So O'Keeffe asked me to drive her to Joe's place, an adobe house beyond the village, in search of the mechanic. 'I go with him,' she said, 'into the mountains to find watercress. I always find the best, but I'm hoping to teach *him* to find it to save myself.' The afternoon was advancing and deep blue shadows were gathering under the mesas and in the fractures of the rocks, bringing everything to a pitch of vivid abstraction in the sinking light. 'The clarity, that's what I love about this place,' she said, as we took in the lengthening, sharp shadows. 'A pity,' she went on; 'there's no time for you to see my ghost ranch. It's sixteen miles up-country. You'd like the landscape there.' I asked her if it was there she first began painting cattle bones. Her reply was, 'You know why I began painting cattle bones? I used to come here summers, and the question was what to take back to New York which would recall New Mexico. I would have taken flowers, but at the height of summer flowers were scarce. So I took bones and painted them.'

I had noticed that at least once she had painted bones and flowers together in *Summer Days* of 1936. Earlier still, in *Blue and Green Music* of 1919, a much more abstract picture, there was a similar confrontation of growth with death. This picture was fresh in my mind, since I had been examining a slide of it on the previous evening. Out of a concourse of rigid embattled triangles, there emerges in mid-canvas a billowing as if wind-torn area of whitish flame. It resembles, in its involved flickerings and flarings, the unravelling petals of a flower or the skins of an onion bulb. And there, crowning this spectral conflagration, one makes out the pun of a skull shape, squashed sideways, Holbein-wise, like the anamorphosis at the foot of his picture *The Ambassadors*. The whole is immaculately painted, a kind of mask of white death invading the formalized humanism of the cubists. I asked her in the car about this invasion. 'No, I've never seen a skull there,' she replied quietly as though pondering the matter, as though there *might* be a skull there, but unwilling to commit herself to one: 'I didn't *know* there was a skull there.'

Joe was not in. Joe's brother was, and would send Joe over when he reappeared. We drove back. 'When Joe goes into the army,' she said with decision, 'I aim to try and bring on his brother.'

It was getting late and cold and I had to start. First she insisted on showing the rest of the house with its whitewashed adobe fireplaces and Navajo rugs. Then she said in a tone that sounded like Miss Moore's, 'I'll offer you tea before going, but I refuse to offer you alcohol.' Almost her last remark was, 'When you return to New Mexico, you must come in.' Come in? It was an unexpected turn of phrase. 'I am not friendly,' I recalled, but friendly she *had* been, and 'come in' suggested a full absolution from my false pretences, the cordial opposite of 'get in'.

Whenever New Mexico re-enters the mind, it comes in images that are hers and images that are not hers. One which is hers and which I can see clearly with shut eyes is *Red Hills and Bones* of 1941, with its dry vistas, the hill humps with their deep, parched wrinkles full of shadow. Here, a vision that in *Blue and Green Music* flickers

3: A Late Greeting: O'Keeffe

with the underpresence of the skull, grows calm, and the discarded fragments of an animal's skeleton that lie across the foreground of the picture do so in repose, in stillness and light, from the exquisitely segmented spine of the foreground skeleton, through the ghosts of the autumnal chamiso bushes behind to the barrenness of hill and rock mesa. What is missing from the hills and what I saw against the sky on the long drive back that night, rising from the heaped-up boulders, is a Penitente cross. That image also belongs to her, or to one aspect of her work. For, the first summer she was able to pass entirely in New Mexico, that of 1929, saw the painting of *Black Cross, New Mexico,* where the shape of a huge Penitente cross dominates the recession of treeless, rounded hills, the red and yellow bars of the sunset imprisoned between its arms and the horizon of purple land. This black cross, held together by four massive nails, and the blood-coloured sunset beneath it, evoke the ascetic and tragic spirit of Los Hermanos de la Luz, offshoot of the Third Order of St Francis – the New Mexico of the Penitente chapels, the *moradas* where Death armed with bow and arrow sits waiting in its wooden cart. In another picture, *Cross by the Sea, Canada* of 1932, the cross is identical with those one finds in any of the small Spanish *camposantos* of New Mexico; the fence around it resembles precisely the fence of carved wooden pickets, *cuña* or *cerquita*, which surrounds a grave. The image that is not hers is the image of the Indian dance – behind her crosses rises the *morada,* not the church of San Felipe with its explosion of drums and feathers, or the dancing plaza where the drumbeat intercedes between heartbeat and sunbeat and unites them. One critic speaks of *Red Hills and the Sun* of 1927 as 'nature imbued with a pantheistic, transcendent life of its own'. The formula seems an improbable one for O'Keeffe, though it is not a new one, something like it already appearing in the review in *Camera Work* which greeted her first exhibition at Stieglitz's '291' gallery in 1917. If pantheism means anything, it is unitive like the communion of bloodbeat and drumbeat. O'Keeffe's is a separating vision giving her space in which to contemplate the thing before her. The magnified flower paintings and the abstracted interiors of *Jack-in-the-pulpit* in its several versions, though they are symbols for processes that involve and transcend the self, lack the oceanic engulfment of Jackson Pollock's early Indian-inspired totemic pictures and his later kinship with the Navajo sand painters pouring their images. They remain oddly literal in their strangeness and isolation, as irreducible as the black rock that fills three quarters of the canvas of *Black Rock with Blue* of 1970 – like one of Magritte's magnified apples, though there is nothing here to indicate its actual scale or whether, indeed, it is magnified. The blue it bulks against is that which long ago she saw in all its intensity through the holes in held-up pelvis bones, and of which she wrote during the war '... that Blue that will always be there as it is now after all man's destruction is finished'.

She discovered herself during one war and has long survived a second. She was born in the same year as Miss Moore, 1887, a year before Eliot, two after Pound, four after Williams. At ninety-one, she is the last survivor of the great generation. All of these poets had read their Fenollosa. And she, along with Pound, owed much of the direction of her career to his having written. Two statements:

> This man had one dominating idea: to fill space in a beautiful way.

> We find that all art is harmonious spacing under special technical conditions that vary.

The first is O'Keeffe speaking of Arthur Wesley Dow, whose book *Composition* and whose teaching methods introduced the ideas of Fenollosa into American art schools. The second quotation is from Fenollosa's *Epochs of Chinese and Japanese Art*, and it summarizes what he had been saying in the face of a prevailing academicism ever since he had returned from Japan in 1892 to become, first, curator of the Boston Museum of Fine Arts, and then a popular lecturer. O'Keeffe gave up painting in 1912, but in the summer of that year returned to it under the influence of Alon Bement, a follower of Dow's. In 1914-15 she went, persuaded by Bement, to study with Dow in New York, and again in the spring of 1916. Simultaneously, she was discovering the Southwest, teaching near Amarillo in Texas. It was at this moment that the spaces of Fenollosa and the spaces of the desert, of East and West, met in a ground for new harmonies, new dissonances. The stone garden of Ryōanji, the red cliffs of Tomioka Tessai, Hiroshige's red strip of sunset, waited to be rediscovered in America, in Abiquiu. As China's sacred mountain Taishan redeclared its form to an American mind from the mountains beyond the detention camp at Pisa.

'When you return to New Mexico, you must come in.' I have returned to New Mexico twice since then, but I have not 'come

3: A Late Greeting: O'Keeffe

in'. The first time was four years later and the visit was rushed, the second was thirteen and I imagined she would scarcely remember. Perhaps I should have risked it. She hadn't known many Englishmen, and she still recalled Gerald Heard in 1963. Perhaps there is still time. I have written these pages as, in some sense, a late greeting.

4: Dove Sta Memoria: In Italy

Dove sta memoria
> till the stone eyes look again seaward
>> some minds take pleasure in counterpoint

– more talismanic fragments, to set beside 'Pine-scent in snow-clearness.' The book that contains them, *The Pisan Cantos,* I packed in my luggage on our first trip to Italy, 1951. The train passed through Pisa in an autumnal downpour. I looked out for the tower and caught not only that, but what the poem had prepared one for, standing apart from the mass of the cathedral: 'a patch of the battistero all of a whiteness'. The gloom scarcely muffled that whiteness and there was light enough to define the ribs of sharp, projecting stones that punctuate the conical dome and give it the spiky appearance of a sea urchin.

That – *dove sta memoria* – lies the better part of thirty years away. For the past twenty I have experienced, practically daily, another sight which draws the threads together and sets counterpoint into motion – that line of houses, Wortley Terrace, where, when it had not yet spilled beyond itself, Wotton-under-Edge used to end. Sophie Brzeska, Henri Gaudier's companion, lived there after his death and before her removal to the Gloucester asylum. I had passed the house for ten years before I saw at Brunnenberg Gaudier's head of Pound, as whitely commanding as that glimpse of Pisa, its stone eyes looking toward the mountains of the Upper Adige from the garden of his daughter's castle.

Pleasure in counterpoint? Pleasure or pain or both. The young Gaudier – but Gaudier was never not the young Gaudier: the Gaudier who had not yet touched marble used to climb the steps into Bristol Museum to sketch the stuffed animals. I work on the other side of the street and the reminder is always there.

The memory of that death is folded now in the memory of another, a later one. In 1974, going down from the exhibition, Vorticism and Its Allies, to the ground floor of the Hayward Gallery where the photographs of Diane Arbus were to be seen, I met Robert Lowell circulating this latter show in the opposite direction. We strolled out together and took tea beside the Thames.

'You can see why she went mad,' he said, referring to those pictures where nothing is ever quite right even in the most ordinary scenes, and where freakishness puts on such a daily face you could imagine it was the only possibility.

'What did you make of the vorticists?' I asked.

'Oh, pretty inhuman stuff.'

I swallowed down argument, thinking of those early abstracts of Wyndham Lewis, 1912 and 1913, where passion so declares itself, free of all effusiveness, it cannot but get itself mistaken for coldness.

'What about Gaudier?'

'Oh, Gaudier! Gaudier's another thing. Gaudier is marvellous.'

It was Lowell's habit, whenever we met, to recall to me the time before. A decade had elapsed between our drive along the banks of the Charles River and our second meeting in Bristol. 'Do you realize,' he said on that occasion, 'you are the same age now as I was then?' As we sat in the Thames-side cafeteria, he thought back to a charity reading we had both taken part in the previous year at the Skinners' Hall, in the London of Wren and the right worshipful city companies. 'Curious place,' said Lowell; 'you just couldn't get a drink.' I was puzzled, recalling the wine there – its plentifulness had made me fear that the Royal Hospital and Home for Incurables, on whose behalf we were present, would benefit little from our services. Why, even the waiters were drunk – and had been audibly drinking behind the scenes – by the time they came to serve the charity dinner, so that boiled potatoes were rolling in all directions under the feet of the guests. 'You just couldn't get a drink.' It was only afterward I realized that what he had meant was spirits. He had said it with a curious, puzzled, tired little shake of the head. Quite the opposite of that sudden kindling of glance and face at his, 'Gaudier is marvellous.'

From the photograph of Gaudier at work on his bust of Pound, one can see that he had previously envisaged the eyes as diamond-shaped lozenges. In changing these, together with a moustache which he had chalked in as possessing an upward curve, he not only removed a touch of melodrama of the kind which spoils the work of his older contemporary, Jacob Epstein, but realized a head worthy to look, and capable of looking, at the blaze of the Ligurian Sea through its narrowed slits. It had stood facing that sea from Rapallo, a little further up the coast from the spot we had set out for in 1951. It was the same sea that had killed Shelley. Across the bay from which he sailed to his death – 'our' bay – a piano had once been ferried in a rowing boat for Frieda Lawrence to play on in the Lawrences' pink, four-roomed cottage at Fiascherino. The two Englishmen, Shelley and Lawrence, stand incongruously side by side in the mural painting within the Albergo delle Palme at Lerici.

I had gone to work as a kind of secretary at a villa, Gli Scafari, between Lerici and Fiascherino. Its owner was growing blind. Henry James had once described him – the first editor of the master's letters – as 'of long limbs and candid countenance'. Of an age now with James when he had said that, Percy Lubbock was still a tall man and had grown corpulent. The candid countenance was veiled, complicated to read because of the eyes that floated directionless in the heavy features. He had a Jamesian bulk and one fancied at the time – perhaps it was no more than a fancy – that its slack, unmuscular pendulousness stood in the same relation to James the physical man as the style Lubbock had imitated to the master's own. His manners were of an unfailing smoothness, though a certain asperity would occasionally penetrate his voice, as when he reflected on the quality of the Berenson linen at I Tatti – 'both the sheets and the table napkins so much coarser than our own here at Gli Scafari'.

For the first three weeks we received nothing but kindness. To begin with, our meetings with him were few, since he was suffering from a cold and spent most of the time in his bedroom. His friend, Lady Dick-Lauder, present as a house guest, was affable and absent-mindedly good-natured, and in the evenings, when we all met for dinner, there passed between the two of them a certain amount of political badinage. For he, as he described himself and as the regular arrival of the *New Statesman* bore witness, was 'a bit of a Bevanite', while she, with more consistency, recognized that for her better times had gone – she now shared a house with her chauffeur – and had the frankness to regret their passing. One evening we realized that his teasing was directed at us. It was not political, but one heard in it the old, ingrained, slightly querulous asperity. He had been legislating on the pronunciation of the English *a* as in *past* and *castle,* insisting that it should be long also in *ants*. Clearly he had not revisited the island for a long time, for even the English aristocracy would hesitate to lengthen the *a* of *ants*. But what he was evidently indicating – as far, that is, as good manners permitted – was that our mildly Midland *a*'s sounded displeasing to him. But what of that?

4: Dove Sta Memoria: In Italy

One could hardly feel wounded by a man who imagined *ants* should be pronounced *aunts*.

Two weeks later I received my dismissal. It was most mysterious. Lubbock had returned to Florence with Lady Dick-Lauder. The letter came from his stepdaughter, Iris Origo: he no longer wanted a secretary. Could one be dismissed for an accent? It hardly seemed plausible, but we could imagine no other cause for offence. We were penniless and homeless in a foreign country scarcely more than a month after our arrival. I saw myself back in England, once more teaching the recalcitrant children of Camden Town. However, thanks to the diplomacy and kindness of the Marchesa Origo, this didn't happen. We were removed to a *villino* adjoining the gardener's house and stayed there on a small allowance until the following May.

'Now do not forget,' said Lubbock at his return, 'you are still members of the same house party.' This, too, was unintelligible, but he was as good as his word and would bring over his guests to see us.

The shock of dismissal, following on what seemed an escape from three years of teaching elementary school while trying to paint in the evenings, left me not only nonplussed but ill. I realized that I was worn out after three years of incessant work and fell all too easily into a state of increasing energylessness. The Italian doctor diagnosed heart strain. In the struggle back to normality I wrote most of the poems of *The Necklace* and had also begun visiting and drawing the sea caves at the end of that long rocky headland from which Gli Scafari took its name. Those sea caves and the islands visible beyond them have haunted my pictures ever since.

My books had found a home in the little room where the gardener's wife did the ironing for the villa – among them my treasured copy of the Sesame Books selection of Ezra Pound side by side with *The Pisan Cantos*. Both of these now spoke of a world which was close at hand:

> Lithe turning of water,
>   sinews of Poseidon,
> Black azure and hyaline,
>   glass wave over Tyro...

This was the very sea and the light brought home now the exactness of that 'glass wave' as one stood in the shadow of the sea caves and watched the forming and re-forming of the waters. I hadn't at the time associated 'till the stone eyes look again seaward' with Gaudier's bust, of which I knew nothing. The phrase had run together in my mind with the memory of Homer's 'grey-eyed Athena' and also with Pope's 'And laughing Ceres reassume the land'. The line of Pope had even detached itself from its grammatical context so that 'reassume' had dropped its syntactical (though not its prophetic) connection with 'Another age shall see the golden ear / Imbrown the slope... / And Laughing Ceres reassume the land.' In the remembered line, 'reassume' was some unfathomable tense, a subjunctive abiding its full implication until perhaps those stone eyes should again look seaward. The stone eyes were the eyes of a goddess, her statue and her temple restored to that height where the olive groves swept upward from Fiascherino to La Serra, the village on the hill behind us. You knew the way the goddess moved when you saw the upright carriage of those women with bundles on their heads walking down the stony *salita* between the olives:

> ... and from her manner of walking
>
>   as had Anchises
> till the shrine be again white with marble
> till the stone eyes look again seaward.

The poem received its counterpoint every day and the scattered marble shone from the steps of the poorest houses, cheap in that pare of the country, with Carrara at no great distance. Gianfranco Contini speaks slightingly of 'the archaeological nature of Pound's Italy'. Trust an urban intellectual to miss the point. It would be as foolish to label Pope's 'laughing Ceres' archaeological.

A phrase that had defeated me in *The Pisan Cantos,* long before I had reached Italy and used to puzzle out the book on the London tubes, read

>   if they have not destroyed them
>   with Galla's rest, and ...

Part of a list of destructions, its continuation unfinished. But who was Galla? And why 'Galla's rest'? Her remains or her repose or both? The answer arrived unexpectedly. Our real life now faced away from the villa toward the gardener and his wife and through their daughter and son-in-law to the high village above us, La Serra. We had heard there the story that Lawrence had been told when he came to Fiascherino in 1913. *In tempi antichi* when pirates still used to harry the coast, the next village, Tellaro, its church fronting the sea, was saved from attack by an octopus. An octopus? *Sì, sì, un polpo*. Which had caught hold of the bell rope that had dropped its end down over the rocks. And so the village was woken up and rescued from the pirates who were about to raid it while everyone slept. In the version Lawrence heard, the pirates were missing and the people merely terrified by the inexplicable tolling of the bell.

We learned to walk up the *salita* to La Serra in pitch darkness to drink wine with friends – the family of the gardener's son-in-law. We would sit with tearful eyes in the smoke of a wood fire that used the room instead of the chimney for its flue. The wine was copious and one had to exercise a fearful control of the bladder – the Serresi had made of this a fine art – because there was no water closet, and to ask to use the family bucket would have been a breach of good manners and would no doubt have overtaxed the bucket. So one went out at last into the black night and deliciously released a hissing stream among the olive trees, and then blindly felt out with the feet the stones of the abrupt *salita* in the direction of Gli Scafari.

To Gli Scafari came various relatives of the gardener's family to help with the olive harvest, rattling down the olives with long canes. At Easter, Tina, the gardener's wife, was due to visit her father and other relations at Bagnara on the great plain behind Ravenna, and she invited us to go with her. We reached there by train and bus. We descended from the bus in the market square: the weather had remained extremely cold and the male population were still wearing their winter cloaks. Fifty cloaked and hatted figures turned instantaneously, or so it seemed, to watch us in total silence as we crossed the square – strangers and, what is more, foreigners. The front had passed this way, and the village had been blown up and-now rebuilt. The question exercising those silent men was: 'What nationality are they?' A couple of days later, as Brenda and I walked past a group of youths, one of them stage-whispered to the others, 'He's a dirty German, but she's an Italian.' 'No,' I said, facing them, 'a dirty Englishman – *ingle-saccio*.' But they weren't amused. However, no one knifed me.

We were lodged at the house of an ageing widow, and slept in a large, warm bed – *un matrimoniale* – in a large, cold room. The bed was heated by a warming pan filled with hot ash. On the ample dresser stood a single photograph of a young woman. It was slightly unfocused and had turned brown. Buxom and evidently pretty-featured, she smiled out at the guests. 'Your daughter?' I asked the owner of the house. 'My daughter,' she said. 'She disappeared – *in tempo di guerra.*' 'Disappeared?' 'One night armed men came here and took her away. She has never returned. I'm still waiting for her.' 'Armed men? You mean the Germans?' 'No, not the Germans. Partisans.'

The bus to Ravenna left early. Stars were still out and the North Italian plain with its leafless vine stocks waited in dejection for the sun. In Ravenna the puddles lay covered in a fine, wrinkling ice and as the light came back it brought with it not warmth but an aching clarity. We waited, penetrated by the intense chill, for the doors of San Vitale to open, wedging ourselves into the growing patches of sunlight. For San Vitale we had come prepared, as for – later that afternoon – Sant' Apollinare in Classe, 'Vieille usine désaffectée de Dieu' where the poet had assured us that we would still find 'Dans ses pierres écroulantes la forme précise de Byzance.' What took us by surprise, after the hieratic splendours of Justinian and Theodora glistening in mosaic among the herons, ducks, and moorhens of a leafy landscape, was the structure of brick immediately before San Vitale. The material had a simplicity and roughness that, like adobe, could have encompassed anything from a cowshed to a cathedral. The untidy, frosted grass among which it stood gave it the appearance of something distinctly rural, almost reassuringly shabby. This exterior kept the secret of what awaited within: the entire building was covered with mosaic – Christ among his flock of sheep, dressed not as a shepherd but as a beardless Roman soldier; the apostles; Saint Lawrence and, above them against the deep blue of arches and dome, mosaic stars, whose tiny cubes of glass and stone glittered down as sharply as the frosty stars under which we had taken our departure from Bagnara that morning. The light in there possessed an almost submarine phosphorescence and there seemed a touch of gold in it – 'Di color d'oro, in che raggio traluce.' Its source came from windows sheeted with wafers of alabaster: an illumination of glowing calm, the tempered light of a not quite arrived Italian spring, the sort of light the resurrecting dead might find easiest to awake in before they looked out once more at the full light of day. We had wandered almost by accident into 'Galla's rest' and under that vault of which Louis Zukofsky was to write:

> ... the eye can take in
>   gold, green and blue:
>
> The gold that shines
>   in the dark

4: Dove Sta Memoria: In Italy

>of Galla Placidia,
>>the gold in the
>
>Round vault rug of stone
>>that shows its
>pattern as well as the stars
>>my love might want on her floor...

'Butterfly details to glint in his weightless structure,' says Hugh Kenner; 'alertly seen, acknowledged, left in place, barely touched by being named, they pass down a firefly page like clavichord notes, freighted by no rhetoric of "history".' So lies Galla Placidia, or her now emptied sarcophagus, the history she lived through – captured by the Goths, married to their king, exchanged for corn, regent of the western empire – all subdued to this quiet luminosity, these stars 'like a covey of partridges', as Pound says in another context. Once seen, the place was easily recognizable now, and, having read the great work in unchronological order, I finally came upon:

>Gold fades in the gloom
>Under the blue-black roof, Placidia's...

Archaeological? The experience of a diaphaneity that, lost, can be recovered. Brick pierced by an alabaster not merely marmoreal. Alabaster as a touchstone – for light. A structure by no means weightless invaded by its opposite or its complement. Brick and mosaic suffering a sea change. *La cathédrale engloutie*. Not quite: a stay to outlast barbarities. For after Galla Placidia came Attila, burning down Italy in search of her daughter, Honoria, who in a pique with her lovers had offered herself to him.

On our return to the *villino*, Percy Lubbock brought a guest to tea one spring afternoon, a guest whose features I already knew from a photograph in the Penguin edition of *Howard's End*. There, in gloweringly unbecoming close-up, with wide-winged nostrils disapproving of some unidentified moral aroma, the face reminded me of a Staffordshire farmer I had known as a child and whose tart and usually exact tongue I had always feared. Once he dressed me down for swearing when I said, 'What a blooming day', and the sense of injustice I nursed over the years always stung once more whenever I caught sight of that expression on the face of E. M. Forster.

'I want you to show Morgan some of your paintings,' said my ex-employer.

Forster's countenance was mild in comparison with that photograph.

'I have a question I wish to put to you,' he said. 'It will keep till after we have seen the pictures, but I mustn't forget it.'

I showed the paintings one by one. Forster seemed to be bored. Perhaps it was the unasked question that took his mind off these images which he examined so patiently and so absently. Lubbock was in a benign mood. I never knew just how much he could still see, but he made a show of examining the pictures himself, murmuring to Forster, 'I say, what a fancy he has – what a fancy,' and showing all the enthusiasm that the novelist so clearly lacked. I was never to comprehend the mysterious footing on which our relationship stood, or failed to stand. I could no more read his intentions than those of the two benign Chinese figures that graced his library with impassive porcelain faces, their hands hidden under wide draperies.

Before Forster left, we came to his question: 'You have just been to Ravenna, I understand? Now, there is something there I have never seen and have always wanted to see – the mausoleum of Galla Placidia. What's it like?'

'It's a Poundian building.'

'And what exactly is a Poundian building?'

So, almost thirty years ago, I attempted to describe haltingly the effect of that lucid darkness just as I have done now. I could hear myself making my inadequate explanation, realizing, dawningly, in another part of my head, that the effect was one I had been half blindly stumbling toward in the scattered paintings that lay about the room, an effect it was to take another twenty years to begin to convey. Perhaps Forster had been right to be bored. I had a great way to go, and, if these scraps were only beginning to indicate the direction to me, what could they have possibly meant to him?

Before we left that May another meeting occurred – with the poet Paolo Bertolani. He was then just twenty. He had had no regular job since he left school as a boy, yet all his pennies had gone into buying books. One he lent me, *L'Antologia di Spoon River,* came into late fame in Italy, largely, I imagine, because Cesare Pavese had written about it during that phase of Italian culture when an imagined America – for Pavese and his friends had never been there – seemed to offer an alternative to an Italy 'estranged, barbarized, calcified', as Pavese wrote, an alternative, that is, where the mind might come into possession of itself despite the prevailing culture of fascism. Thus, *The Spoon River Anthology* found its way to La Serra and still perhaps seemed to offer a literary model in a village where there was so much unarticulated life under one's windows – like the maid who, late in her pregnancy, aborted herself at the villa, flung her child from the cliff and continued to serve my ex-employer as if nothing had happened; or the cook who acquired a gun and tried to shoot the gardener; or the old, luxuriantly white-moustached peasant who offered a whole history of the modern world through his account of the growth and decline of *i baffi,* the moustache. He it was who, having found a dead eagle, carried it to the front of his house and spread out its wings against the wall. And when, as he said, his communist neighbours had asked what *that* was, he replied haughtily, 'È l'aquila imperiale.' 'A chaste man,' said Paolo. He never married and, having bought the land that had belonged to a local count, was known for the rest of his life as *il conte.* And there were those who *in tempo di guerra* had hidden in holes in the ground to avoid the conscription and now, like Paolo, were faced with the prospect of unemployment and looked to the communists – they had just won the elections hereabouts – to put things to rights.

Paolo showed me his poems – more human than political. I was struck by one phrase – 'una statua di musica' – and I ventured to criticize another – 'deliziosi cipressi'. I could see that the two words made a fine sound, but wasn't sure that 'deliziosi', even if it carried more voluptuous overtones than our 'delightful', quite earned its passage there. Paolo frowned a little. 'Curious,' he said; 'it's been much admired by *una signorina* at Lerici, much admired.' 'But put it,' I said, 'beside *una statua di musica* and hear the difference.' He wasn't quite convinced. The English youth ventured out more boldly: 'Not Petrarch – Michelangelo, he's the man. See how he twists the language to his own uses. He would never say *deliziosi cipressi*. Petrarch might.' There was a deep, deep silence, a wholly uninterpretable silence, in which (and this I did not learn for many years) Paolo was cogitating on the ignorance of his English contemporary who imagined that Michelangelo wrote poems, then deciding that *if* Michelangelo wrote poems, and he, an Italian, did not know this fact, silence was the only possible answer until he came upon some of them. Nor did either of us then realize that in the next town, Sarzana, on the plain beneath the hills where we were standing, another Italian poet, Cavalcanti, had written in exile those lines that Pound translated, 'Because no hope is left me, Ballatetta, / Of return to Tuscany,' and that Eliot had transposed into a poem of his own, 'Because I do not hope to turn again.' Sarzana. *Dove* – in good time – *sta memoria*.

The final meeting with Paolo before our departure took place on the beach. He was leaning against an upturned boat and wore an immaculately white shirt between a blue sky and a purple sea. In his hand he carried a copy of Rimbaud in Italian – *Le illuminazioni*. Evidently he was travelling in the direction of *una statua di musica*. Or so I thought. But his path lay elsewhere. And it was not toward *i deliziosi cipressi* either. I imagined he would surely leave Liguria for Milan and on this assumption, venturing fifteen years later into a Fiascherino the tourists had ruined beyond repair and finding half our friends had gone as migrant workers to Germany, I failed to look for him at La Serra. He had never left the place. His Spoon River? Not exactly. His verse is more intricate than that and less moralistic. But the discovery of American literature, which was largely the work of Pavese and Vittorini, and which brought with it the desire for an accord with reality into Italian writing, remained as decisive for Paolo's art as, in a different way, the contact with America proved for my own.

Fifteen years ... We returned with our two daughters, Justine and Juliet. We were in Siena – 'the most civil city in Europe,' as the friend who suggested it remarked. And so it is, its energies directed toward the yearly horse races for the banner of the Virgin, the *palio*, and its violences also. Pound had recalled the event in his Pisan captivity:

> and down there they have been having their Palio
> 'Torre! Torre! Civetta!' ...
>   and the parade and the carrocchio and the flag-play
> and the tossing of the flags of the comrade

and he too had looked at the 'four fat oxen' that pull the *carrocchio*

> having their arses wiped
> and in general being tidied up to serve god under my window.

He also knew the wells of the city and walked the steep walk up from Fontebranda to the vast church of San Domenico where the black, shrunken head of Saint Catherine of Siena is preserved, 'Narrow alabaster in sunlight, the windows of the cripta.' Had he experienced that other diaphaneity in the stones of Sant' Antimo, south of Siena, where blocks of – not alabaster, insisted the *custode*, but a local onyx – had been built into the walls to conduct a tawny, honied light into the nave of travertine? Onyx or alabaster, certainly not 'that deep but dazzling darkness' of Galla's rest, but an intensity further along the scale of light conceived by the same sensibility which made possible 'Di color d'oro, in che raggio traluce.' And, here, Dante is speaking of the paradisal stair – a Jacob's ladder of translucent solidity – which his own light could not follow out to its end. But, however far the monks of the abbey of Sant' Antimo had progressed along this stair, it soon vanished before them, and history, in the shape of the quarrels of ecclesiastic politics, transformed that place too into a 'Vielle usine désaffectée de Dieu.'

In that year, 1966, a number of coincidental forces had pointed us back to Italy – a parching thirst for the place, a return to its literature, and two new correspondents. I had read *Il gattopardo* by Giuseppe di Lampedusa and went on to read the poems of his cousin, Lucio Piccolo di Calanovella, poems of an entropic history that can only consume, a history turning itself into fable where the Moorish predators of Sicily became 'la forma moresca dei venti', 'the Moorish band of the winds'. I translated a number of his poems and exchanged letters with this strange man, an enthusiast for Hart Crane, who had, further, read all English poetry and, as an investigator of the occult, had been a correspondent of W. B. Yeats: 'In a lecture on myself,' he wrote, 'I have been called a poet of the dead. Very well. The spirits are more human than humans.' An invitation came to visit him at Capo d'Orlando which I always regret I was never able to take up.

My second correspondent emerged after I had received through the post a small volume of poems, *Il diapason*. The author was Mary de Rachewiltz, a name which concealed from me for some time that she was the daughter of Ezra Pound. Her letters displayed a diffidence about her own poetry and, after publishing a second book, *Di riflesso,* she recognized with an unusual certainty that she had come to the end of the emotional need to write poems in Italian and produced, in English, that extraordinary book *Discretions,* the story of her life and of her relationship with her father. Brunnenberg seemed a less exotically daunting place to reach from Siena than Capo d'Orlando, so on our return journey we availed ourselves of an invitation to stay there for a couple of nights.

As we drove through the Italian Tyrol, meeting tanks, lorries, and armed men every few miles, we imagined manoeuvres must be taking place. We were mistaken. The army was out to protect the Italian minority after recent bomb outrages on the part of the

Austro-Germans who had succeeded in killing a policeman called Vogler. Once we realized the situation, we could explain why in Trento, when I had asked an Italian policeman the way, and in that language, he had seemed on the point of embracing me, and why, when north of Merano I continued to ask in Italian for the turning to Brunnenberg, I was given totally false directions.

Mary came out to meet us in a light-blue dress, preceded by her slim and handsome children, Patrizia and Sigifredo Walter Igor Raimondo, both in their teens. Patrizia had recently returned from a stay with her grandfather, who had been shocked at the shortness of her skirt and also by the fact that she had been permitted to go and see Brecht's *Dreigroschenoper*.

Below the castle, the cliff dropped sheer away and one imagined that bringing up children there must have presented similar hazards to the cliff dwellings of Mesa Verde, Colorado. But life at the castle seemed much like family life elsewhere and, though Boris de Rachewiltz was absent, there was a genial completeness in its atmosphere, one difference appearing in an inescapable awareness of the spiritual presence and history of Mary's father, and of the burden of deference due to him. We passed our stay in pleasant talk and in some local sight-seeing along the precipitous paths nearby – principally to Castel Tirolo, once the seat of Margarita Maultasch, regent of the Tyrol in the mid-fourteenth century, the Ugly Duchess of Leon Feuchtwanger's novel and Lewis Carroll's imaginings. The Italian attendant there also appeared relieved when Mary addressed him in his own language and he sighingly lamented the worsening situation and the lot of his fellow nationals. On our walk back to Brunnenberg the subject of Lucio Piccolo arose. Mary told the story of the visit two Italian publishers had made to Capo d'Orlando. The barone of Calanovella had received them, after their fourteen-hour train journey, with an effusive welcome and a portion of ice cream.

Beside Mary's generosity, beside a certain insouciance – the typewriter she had given Juliet to play with 'had belonged to Mr Pound' – there appeared from time to time in that hint of a frown into which her concentration gathered, something of the tension with which a difficult destiny had strung her being. 'A cultural orphan,' Donald Davie was to call her in reviewing her memoir *Discretions*; for the language in which she wrote that book was not the language she had learned to speak first – nor was Italian. A foster-child in the Tyrol, she had grown up using an Austrian dialect. She was now the principessa, wife to a descendant of the Longobard kings. She was also Pound's daughter, and that, through war, through his sequestration, and through the ultimate failure of the attempt to make a home for him at Brunnenberg, had left the deepest mark. 'Do not take your father too literally – or too seriously.' These were the words of Daniel Cory, Santayana's secretary and executor, who was also staying at the castle. His general air of mischievousness about Pound, the privilege of an old friend, served clearly as an attempt to take away the small, gathering frown from her eyes – the same frown that touches the face of Mary as a small girl on the cover photograph of her book. The presence beside her then, with tilted trilby, Bohemian cravat, and energetic beard, still looked down at her from Gaudier's profile on the wall at Brunnenberg.

Outside the window rose the Gaudier bust. The weather was misty. The peaks of the Ziel and Mut hovered invisible beyond the vines. Tourists trickled incessantly across the field path, a right of way for centuries, up to the castle gates. The gates had been placed there merely to prevent them from coagulating in the central courtyard. The bust seemed to attract to itself all the strength from the uncertain light. Whether one would *choose* to live with it ... It asserted now, from its context within a family's history, the massive, male dominance of the image on which Gaudier had based it: Hoa-Haka-Nana-Ia, the giant Polynesian figure in the British Museum. 'I have made a phallus of Ezra Pound,' said Gaudier. Threatening progenitor, it loomed there starkly white, a single mass of thrust stone, the antithetical image to that side of Pound which responded to 'Galla's rest', antithetical also to laughing Ceres.

I had been looking through the notebooks Gaudier kept when he was forming his style, notebooks full of figures evolved from Lautrec but simplified by the bold lines drawn by a sculptor's hand. They must have dated from his Bristol days. It was dark outside. As I got up to return to our own room, I heard a cry and a metallic crash. Brenda coming down the unlit stone stair of the castle, carrying child and typewriter, had missed her footing. The choice of which to let go was no choice at all, and Pound's typewriter had gone bouncing to the foot of the steps to end up there buckled and quivering.

The Pound of Gaudier's bust was unlike the Pound I eventually met. This meeting took place not at Brunnenberg, but at Spoleto in the following summer. Pound's hand felt cold to the touch. The hand of old age. It is strange to have met the innovators of one's time only when age had overtaken them. Except for Eliot –

glimpsed at a London party, crossing the room with intent, beaked features, his movement unexpectedly predatory (or perhaps merely expressive of the concerted desire to escape as soon as possible), the large, butcher's hands clasped behind his back and the shoulders stooping forward into the trajectory of his intended flight. Pound's hand felt cold and, as one took it, returned no pressure. He seemed tired. It was evening. *Don Giovanni* would soon begin in the Teatro Nuovo at Spoleto and I had been introduced to him awkwardly across his companion, Olga Rudge. Mary had spoken to her mother of our visit to Brunnenberg, so conversation came easily. I enquired after Patrizia and Siegfried. 'Siegfried?' she said, 'One cannot possibly call anyone Siegfried at this date. It's the most absurd name imaginable. Why they gave it to Walter, I really can't understand.' Walter was sanctified by Walther von der Vogelweide. Siegfried carried the ineradicable Wagnerian connotation. Miss Rudge, in any case, had no illusions that the romantic 'Siegfried de Rachewiltz' would warrant suffering for in the great levelling down.

The first two acts of *Don Giovanni* followed, unvaryingly stolid. The sets by Henry Moore were also stolid – scarcely sets for *Don Giovanni,* simply sets by Henry Moore. The statue of the commendatore in the final act – and this was where one hoped the sculptor's imagination would come into its own – turned out to be a paltry, plaster thing and the singing no better. During the interval I found myself, with Octavio and Marie-José Paz, in the bar of the theatre. Suddenly Pound came in, Miss Rudge beside him. Photographers leapt forward. Flashes exploded. Pound looked confused, blinded, vulnerable. He stopped blinking, shrunken in stature, unmistakably weary. His pallid fragility darted its helplessness in the same instant at Octavio and me, along with the memory of the great energy that he had stood for in both our minds. We, too, were made all at once vulnerable. Octavio slipped away to the far end of the room, silently mastering his feelings. 'Il est complètement boulversé,' said Marie-José.

Five minutes later, catching sight of Miss Rudge, white-haired yet gaily volatile, eating pizza from a paper napkin at the bar while Pound waited beside her, one saw also the saddening disparity that a difference of not quite ten years will make to two people who have grown old together. But, then, Pound had been aged by more than just years.

After the 1967 Festival dei Due Mondi at Spoleto, I saw Pound once more. This was in Siena in 1970. Crossing the Piazza del

Campo, I met Walter de Rachewiltz, who was about to join his grandparents at the open-air café at one corner. It was the year of the Charles Manson trial, the American phrases oddly disguised by the medium of the Italian newspapers. The trial comes back to mind because Miss Rudge explained that they had been that afternoon to see a rehearsal of Mercadante's opera *Il reggente,* adding that the characters in this piece of 1840s romanticism seemed more like Manson's 'family' than *her* idea of royalty. Brenda, who had been shopping in the same piazza, approached with the two girls, at which Pound rose to his feet, waiting for the ladies to take their seats before he resumed his own. He spoke only when Miss Rudge prodded him into a response – 'Yes or no, Ezra?' – which would be followed by a single syllable from him of decided weight and clarity. But that was all. He sat concentratedly engaged in removing every particle of ice cream from the bottom of his dish with a plastic spoon. Though once the conversation among the rest of us had taken fire and no one was looking at him, he began to examine each face with minute scrupulousness, losing not a word as he leaned forward, picking avidly at the skin on the palm of his left hand. A day later, I saw him, possessed of all the energy he had seemed to lack at Spoleto, climbing rapidly with springy steps the taxing upward gradient of that same sloping piazza. In the evening, he and Miss Rudge wandered past arm in arm, lost in their thoughts, and did not recognize us among the crowd of walkers: they were two old people slowly taking the air of an Italian August whose sultriness the afternoon's rain had freshened.

I told Walter, on our last day, that they had appeared very much at one, unperplexed by and perhaps unconscious of the many walkers along the Banchi di Sopra. With an admiring grandson's exaggeration he replied, 'He's like Oedipus at Colonus.' 'He has his eyes still,' I suggested. 'His eyes,' said Walter, 'are not good now. Olga reads to him. The usual piles of books are sent to him.' 'So it's not worth burdening him with yet another one?' 'Well, he tries to keep up, but probably not. He's eighty-five, you know.' I asked whether Pound had ever known the abbey of Sant' Antimo, that so Poundian building. 'Strange that you should ask,' answered Walter; 'We went there yesterday.' We made our farewells, then Walter paused and said, 'By the way, have you heard? Mauriac is dead.'

A year before Pound's own death the publishing house of Mondadori put out a new literary miscellany, *Almanacco dello specchio*. It contained Cantos 90 and 116 translated by Mary de

Rachewiltz, who wrote: 'Canto 116 can, up to the present moment, be considered the end of the Cantos. The voice is now almost a sigh, but the mind still shines out like a dolphin.' One was in the company of other poet friends: Octavio Paz, Vittorio Sereni, with whom I had long corresponded, and – the realization burst on one out of a twenty-year silence – Paolo Bertolani. Both of us were represented by poems about the Ligurian coast and, more particularly, Fiascherino – I by one composed there all those years ago, he by one telling of its subsequent desecration. So he had continued to write, and in a style that was brusque, compact, fluid. I sent a letter and received in reply a book, a manuscript, and his story of the intervening years.

His job was as rich in variety of human contact as – and rather more unexpected than – that of William Carlos Williams. He was a member of the police force – *vigile urbano*. There had been difficult years, years of depression, poems, part of a novel was due in *Nuovi argomenti*. ★ He was married, with two girls, and had never moved from La Serra. An article clipped from a newspaper reported a prize for verse that same year and carried a photograph. I did not immediately recognize the face, though I recognized the expression, a hard, almost pained concentration, the two sharp vertical lines between the eyes nicked in deep with shade. It was the expression he had worn that day on the beach as he stared seaward, a copy of *Le illuminazioni* in hand.

We exchanged letters – though Paolo is a reluctant if excellent letter writer. He discovered from Vittorio Sereni, who coincidentally owned a holiday house nearby, that I had long ago written a poem called 'Up at La Serra'. This work was something of an embarrassment to me, for in it I had tried to imagine the life of a young poet 'up at La Serra' who

>   knew, at twenty
>   all the deprivations such a place
>   stored for the man
>   who had no more to offer
>   than a sheaf of verse
>   in the style of Quasimodo....

★His remarkable book *Racconto della contea di Levante* appeared in its complete form in 1979.

4: Dove Sta Memoria: In Italy

I wrote the poem at a time when I was experimenting in the use of Williams's three-ply cadences. It was the first of a series in which people are trapped by political or historic situations. Without La Serra – and without Williams – I might not have got these poems under way, so once more Italy and America had combined for me. By the 1970s, however, and by the time I resumed contact with Paolo, I came to wonder whether I had not been tactless in using names – his name, in particular – and presumptuous, even, in venturing to imagine what had been in his mind in the 1950s. When, however, Paolo published a new volume, *Incertezza dei bersagli*, in 1976, Vittorio Sereni introduced it to an audience in Vicenza, in the presence of the poet, by reading his own translation of 'Up at La Serra'. Paolo's approval of that poem, 'a sociological picture' as Sereni called it, made me feel that I could at least look him in the face. And this, before long, I did.

In *Incertezza dei bersagli* there appears a poem entitled 'La casa di Charles' – the house, that is, where we had met in 1952. It records the alterations undergone by that landscape 'of a severe grace', it concludes:

> If you return do not
> return unless riding astride
> a sea-bird's back from some spot
> where even in flight the eye
> can't seize on this scape that men
> and the years have unshaped from the play that was life.

But his letters insisted, 'You MUST come back.' And: 'There are still here and there – especially at La Serra and La Rocchetta – places that keep their old substance.' 'Here (among the alleys, off the roadways invaded by *i prodotti Fiat*) there is a certain peace, an ancient silence. The houses are still those of time gone by with pots of basil in their narrow windows.'

Coming back after twenty-five years to La Serra, I realized that Pound's choice of European exile and of this particular country – for it was not merely a regime he chose – had left its ponderable impression in the literate Italian mind. For no sooner had I sat down to drink the tea specially brewed for me by Sandro Bencini, Paolo's engineer friend with whom I was to stay, than our conversation turned to precisely that theme – Pound's involvement in Italy. Our talk wound its way to where, in England, it too frequently begins – Pound's political culpability: 'Why, when he was part of the whole

European effort toward coherence,' said Paolo, 'he should ever have fallen for – for *that* man.' Paolo worked in a municipal building from the era of Fascism – one that sported a special balcony for speech making by 'that man' or his epigones. I advanced the usual explanations or half explanations: the Great War, when others had lost their equilibrium (Lawrence for example); the death of Gaudier – part of the death of that new renaissance of which he dreamed, the petering out of the great energy that was vorticism. But what I'd wanted to say was that I remembered a time, after the end of 'that man', when you could read on the walls of Italy 'Viva Stalin' – side by side, to be sure, with 'Viva Rita Hayworth'. And I remembered also those in my own country and the States who had trusted Stalin and gone on to be judicious about Pound. Let him that is without fault… In all our attempts to be judicious at his expense, we lack the generosity to wonder why an American should have so desperately thrown in his lot with Europe when he did. Donald Davie, reviewing the memoir by Mary de Rachewiltz, puts us to shame when he reflects of both Pound and Eliot: '[They] acknowledged in effect that, since they had got sustenance from European springs, it devolved upon them as a duty to declare their allegiance when the European centre fell apart. When we think what it meant to make such declarations (what it meant for Pound and what it cost him), the question whether they chose right is less significant than the fact that they chose at all.'

Generosity declared itself when, a few days later, in a remote village in the Appenines, I met the poet Attilio Bertolucci (father of the filmmaker Bernardo Bertolucci), an old enemy of 'that man' and a diligent reader of literature in English. 'It's all very well,' he said, 'for Contini to denigrate Pound's edition of Cavalcanti, but without Pound where would the revival of Cavalcanti be? What did the Italians *know* of Cavalcanti when Pound discovered him? Nothing… And, now, I wonder if you would do me a favour? Would you be so kind as to read to me "Adlestrop" by your countryman Edward Thomas?'

One afternoon Vittorio Sereni drove up to La Serra from his house at Bocca di Magra, bringing with him the young Leopardi scholar Fernando Bandini and the critic Giansiro Ferrata. Over a bottle of excellent wine from grapes grown on the land that had belonged to *il conte,* Ferrata told us two stories of Pound from the 1930s, both of which were new to me. The first concerned a buffet luncheon Pound had provided for literary friends in Florence, and his mounting annoyance as he watched them helping themselves to the cuts of chicken, until he could bear it no longer and burst out, 'It's me who paid for this little feast and there they are helping themselves to all the drumsticks.' The second story recalled the meeting between Pound and the idealist philosopher Benedetto Croce. It had been difficult to arrange and, once arranged, the host was anxious about its outcome. Ferrata described the way the two great men approached each other, bowed, shook hands, transmitted signs of mutual approval and of how Pound pausingly, purringly, almost obsequiously began the conversation with: 'You – you – are the author of the *Aesthetica?* It's beautiful – beautiful … but – but it doesn't work.' 'Lei – lei – è l'autore dell' *Aesthetica?* È bella – bella … ma – ma non funziona' – 'funziona' pronounced, as was Pound's way with certain Italian words, with a strong French accent: 'ma non fongziona'.

Toward the end of my time at La Serra, as we looked out beyond Gli Scafari towards San Terenzo, the place of Shelley's stay, Paolo suddenly said to me: 'In all my years of living here, I never once, you know, actually saw Lubbock until after he'd died.'

'After he'd died? You mean you saw his ghost down there among the pines?'

'Not exactly his ghost, but it felt strange enough. It was one day in summer – a hot, summer morning as clear as a mirror, all blues and greens, brilliant. That day, in my role as *vigile sanitario*, I had to go down to Fiascherino along with the health officer, the doctor who, because Lubbock's body was to be sent back to England, came to inject it with formalin as a preservative. It's a big injection – about a litre of liquid – in the region of the viscera, in the belly. Rather horrible. A kind of short-term mummification.

'We took the cliffside path past the *villino* – I'd never been there since that time I came to see you and forever afterwards marvelled at the way the English eat so very delicately, so very fastidiously. We got to the villa – well, you know the place: right above the sea, just a stone's throw from the beach. As soon as we entered the room where the body lay, what struck me at once was the sheer mass of the dead man. So enormous that he seemed to fill the entire place. Even his face was enormous and very severe, with a decidedly contemptuous look, and it still expressed a very exact sense of security, of command. Yet, despite all that, everything suddenly collapsed into absolute fragility as I felt the great needle – I say felt, because I'd turned my eyes away – start penetrating his abdomen.

And that feeling of fragility grew even stronger as I stood staring out of the window across the garden toward the sea, while the doctor was still going on with his endless injection: I could hear the unconcerned voices of morning bathers echoing up from the beach below.

'There I stood, looking through the window into the blaze of summer, when suddenly – very close, almost as though by stretching out a hand I could have touched them – I saw a couple of field mice leaping from one palm to another, and those lines of Montale from *La bufera* came into my mind: "... e il volo da trapezio / dei topi familiari da una palma / all' altra .." and I quoted them to the doctor – partly to communicate with somebody, and partly to absolve myself from that guilty literary thought coming at a moment like this; partly, also, because I knew of his keen interest in poetry. The reasons hardly added up. And the sense of discontinuity brought on another literary thought – Kafka – and the doctor murmured something about life continuing nevertheless out there despite the presence of this massive corpse, and despite all the other corpses; and he went on about the pure relativity of everything as he continued with his work. And the dead man, when you looked at him after that unforeseen intrusion of the everyday, and even of the banal, into the room and into *us*, the dead man was still enormous even in his fragility, although, as you might say, he no longer carried any weight, any significance. That was the first and only time I saw Lubbock.'

With Lubbock's death, a last survival of James's Italy had gone too. For he, in his day, had married his heiress, whom he had survived, to die in this villa overlooking the sea that was Shelley's, Lawrence's, Pound's, Montale's, and now, for a given time, ours. When Paolo had finished speaking, we could hear beneath us, filtering upward from between the hacked olive groves and the sea, the constant burden of accompaniment of summer Fiats as they circulated past a Gli Scafari overshadowed by hotels, in search of parking space along the once narrow road where the only sound had been the klaxon of the bus passing at morning and at evening.

Sources

'Poetry in America': *The Times Literary Supplement*, 21 October 1994
'On First Reading Pound': in Michael Alexander and James McGonigal (eds), *Sons of Ezra: British Poets and Ezra Pound* (Amsterdam & Atlanta: Rodopi), 1995
'Eliot, Pound and *The Waste Land*: Recorded for University of Keele Tapes, 1992
'Reading *The Waste Land*': Recorded for University of Keele Tapes, 1992
'Williams's Thousand Freshets': introduction to William Carlos Williams, *Selected Poems* (Harmondsworth: Penguin), 1976
'Marianne Moore: Her Poetry and Her Critics': *Marianne Moore: a collection of critical essays*, Twentieth-Century Views (Englewood Cliffs, NJ: Prentice-Hall), 1969
'Wallace Stevens and the Poetry of Scepticism': in The New Pelican Guide to English Literature, vol. 9, *American Literature* (Harmondsworth: Penguin), 1988
'The Integrity of George Oppen': introduction to George Oppen, *Selected Poems*, (Newcastle upon Tyne: Cloudforms), 1990
'A Rich Sitter: Lorine Niedecker': introduction to Lorine Niedecker, *The Full Note* (Budleigh Salterton: Interim Press), 1983
'Elizabeth Bishop': review of Elizabeth Bishop, *The Complete Poems* in *The Times Literary Supplement* , 3 June 1983
'Poetry and Friendship': review of David Kalstone, *Becoming a Poet* in *Parnassus* (vol. 16, no. 2), 1989
'Eye and Ear in the Verse of James Laughlin': introduction to James Laughlin, *Poems New and Selected* (New York: New Directions), 1998
'Black Mountain Revisited': review of Martin Duberman, *Black Mountain* in *The New Review* (vol. 1, no. 3), June 1974
'From Amateur to Impresario: Charles Olson': review of Charles Olson, *Muthologos*, ed. George F. Butterick; George F. Butterick, *A Guide to the Maximus Poems of Charles Olson*; Paul Christensen,

Charles Olson; Sherman Paul, *Olson's Push*; Robert Von Hallberg, *Charles Olson* in *The Times Literary Supplement*, 14 December 1979 *Some Americans – a personal record* (Berkeley, Los Angeles & London: University of California Press), 1981

Index of Names

Albers, Anni 99
Albers, Josef 99, 100, 101
Allen, Donald M. 110
Alvarez, A. 90, 142
Arbus, Diane 175
Arnold, Matthew 57

Bandini, Fernando 192
Barker, George 1, 2
Bateson, F.W. 79
Baudelaire, Charles 76, 122
Beckett, Samuel 9
Belloc, Hilaire 127
Beloof, Robert 46–7
Bement, Alon 172
Bencini, Sandro 191
Benn, Gottfried 59
Berryman, John 90
Bertolani, Paolo 182–4, 190, 191–2
Bertolucci, Attilio 192
Bidart, Frank 90
Bishop, Elizabeth 79–85, 86–90
Blackmur, R.P. 141
Blake, William 137
Bottrall, Ronald 120
Bowers, Edgar 135
Bradstreet, Anne 4
Brancusi, Constantin 35
Braque, Georges 168–9
Brecht, Bertolt 8, 9, 155, 186
Breton, André 146
Breuer, Marcel 105
Brzeska, Sophie 174
Bridges, Robert 18, 22
Bronk, William 125, 160
Browning, Robert 54
Bruckner, Anton 8, 155
Bryant, William Cullen 3, 6
Buber, Martin 103
Bunting, Basil 146, 159
Burke, Edmund 47

Burke, Kenneth 30
Butterick, George 111
Byron, George Gordon, Lord 128

Cage, John 101, 103
Calanovella, Lucio Piccolo di 185
Carroll, Lewis 186
Catullus 93, 144
Cavalcanti, Guido 183
Cézanne, Paul 30, 31, 119
Charlot, Jean 105
Chaucer, Geoffrey 11, 47, 118
Christensen, Paul 111, 112
Cole, Peggy 102
Coleridge, Samuel Taylor 125
Conrad, Joseph 107
Constable, John 134, 169
Contini, Gianfranco 178
Cooper, Sharon 75
Cordova, Gilberto Benito 166
Cory, Daniel 187
Cowper, William 88
Crabbe, George 158
Croce, Benedetto 193
Crane, Hart 2, 120, 121–2, 124, 157, 185
Crapsey, Adelaide 45
Creeley, Robert 34, 94, 102, 110, 125, 143, 144, 148
Cummings, E.E. 94
Cunningham, J.V. 135
Cunningham, Merce 101, 103

Dahlberg, Edward 153
Daniel, Arnaut 43
Davenport, Guy 97, 111
Davie, Donald 11, 53, 54, 106, 120, 124, 128, 133–4, 143, 186, 192
Dawson, Fielding 101, 102–3
Degnan, June Oppen 157
Demuth, Charles 35, 132, 164, 169

Dickens, Charles 24
Dickinson, Emily 3
Dick-Lauder, Lady 176, 177
Di Piero, W.S. 6, 7
Doggett, Frank 63
Donne, John 10, 45
D[oolittle], H[ilda] 2
Dorn, Ed 77, 78, 102, 112
Dow, Arthur Wesley 172
Dryden, John 14, 19, 20, 110
Duberman, Martin 98–107
Dunbar, Paul Laurence 4
Duncan, Robert 50, 102, 110, 144
Dürer, Albrecht 49, 137

Eberhart, Richard 2
Eliot, T.S. x, 1, 6, 13, 16, 17–21, 22–6, 27, 28, 30, 35, 36, 38, 48, 50, 52, 53, 54, 59, 72, 117, 120, 129, 142, 153, 183, 187, 192
Eliot, Valerie 20, 21
Emerson, Ralph Waldo 31, 32, 121
Empson, William 120
Enesco, Georges 68
Epstein, Jacob 175
Ernst, Max 82

Feininger, Lyonel 8
Fenollosa, Ernest 192
Ferrata, Giansiro 172
Feuchtwanger, Leon 186
Fields, W.C. 98
Finlay, Ian Hamilton 75, 144
Flaubert, Gustave 144
Forster, E.M. 181–2
Frost, Robert 2, 84, 153
Fuller, R. Buckminster 101

Gaudier, Henri 174, 175, 187
Gifford, Henry 127
Ginsberg, Allen 52, 111
Gioia, Dana 5, 6
Goethe, Johann Wolfgang von 6
Goldsmith, Oliver 19
Gris, Juan 30, 31
Gropius, Walter 105
Guinness, Alec 24
Güterbock, Hans 109

Hall, Donald 40

Hamilton, Ian 158
Hardwick, Elizabeth 132
Heard, Gerald 169, 173
Heidegger, Martin 74
Heine, Heinrich 155
Hemenway, Robert 86
Hemingway, Ernest 80
Herbert, George 81, 82
Herrick, Robert 34
Herron, Carolivia 4
Holmans, A.M. 47
Holmes, Oliver Wendell 6
Homer 178
Hopkins, Gerard Manley ix, 18, 22, 25, 55, 118
Horton, George Moses 5
Hughes, Ted 153
Hugo, Victor 49, 107
Hulme, T.E. 118

Itten, Johannes 100

James, Henry 39, 132–3, 144, 176, 184
Jarrell, Randall 86, 88
Jewett, Sarah Orne 80
Johnson, Philip 100
Johnson, Samuel 3, 19, 40, 92
Joyce, James 35, 154

Kafka, Franz 155, 194
Kalstone, David 86–90
Kandinsky, Wasily 8, 9
Kant, Immanuel 155
Kazin, Alfred 102
Keats, John 54, 67, 98
Kenner, Hugh 13–14, 19, 31, 43, 50, 52, 65–6, 73, 111, 124, 125, 127, 128, 130, 181
Klee, Paul 8
Kline, Franz 101
Kocher, Laurence A. 105
Kooning, William de 101

La Fontaine, Jean de 38
Lampedusa, Giuseppe di 185
Lanier, Sidney 3
Laughlin, James 91–7, 153, 160
Lavater, Johann Kaspar 49
Lawrence, D.H. 8, 121, 148, 178–9, 192, 194

Index of Names

Lawrence, Frieda 176
Leavis, F.R. 2, 13, 120
Levertov, Denise 131–2
Lewis, Percy Wyndham 126, 142
Lindsay, Vachel 2
Longfellow, Henry Wadsworth 2, 3, 6
Lowell, Amy 18
Lowell, James Russell 3, 6
Lowell, Robert 38, 45, 86–90, 96, 132, 133, 163, 175
Loy, Mina 7, 139
Lubbock, Percy 176, 181, 193, 194
Lucretius 14
Luhan, Mable Dodge 148, 167, 168
Lynd, Robert 117

McCarthy, Joseph 70
McClellan, George Marion 5
Machado, Antonio 127
Maeterlinck, Maurice 9
Magritte, René 172
Mann, Thomas 155
Maritain, Jacques 71
Marvell, Andrew 158
Marx, Groucho 17
Masreel, Franz 8
Matthiessen, F.O. 2
Melville, Herman 102
Meredith, George 54
Merrill, James 86, 90
Michelangelo 183
Middlebrook, Diane Wood 3
Miller, Brett C. 1
Miller, J. Hillis 32
Milton, John 5, 110
Monroe, Harriet 58
Montale, Eugenio 194
Moore, Henry 188
Moore, Marianne ix, x, 2,, 38–52, 75, 79, 86–90, 91, 92, 118, 120, 122, 123, 124, 125–6, 130–1, 136–9, 140–2, 164, 172
Murphy, Francis 4

Niedecker, Lorine 7, 75–8, 160
Nietzsche, Friedrich 8, 59, 118

O'Keefe, Georgia ix, 163–73
Olson, Charles x, 18, 33, 34, 75, 101, 105, 108–13, 125, 144

Oppen, George 7, 11, 70–4, 141, 143, 145, 146–8, 153, 155–7, 160, 161–2
Oppenheimer, Joel 102
Origo, Iris 177
Ovid 4, 5, 14

Parini, Jay 1, 2, 3
Paul, Sherman 112
Pavese, Cesare 182, 184
Paz, Marie-José 188
Paz, Octavio 34, 188, 190
Pearce, Roy Harvey 3, 4
Perloff, Marjorie 109, 110
Picasso, Pablo 169
Pinsky, Robert 2
Poe, Edgar Allan 76, 121
Pope, Alexander 5, 14, 19, 110, 178
Pound, Ezra ix, x, 3, 6, 8–16, 17–21, 27, 28, 29–30, 38, 43, 48, 53, 54, 94, 108, 110, 111, 112, 117, 122, 124, 125, 154, 174, 175, 177, 181, 185, 187, 188, 189, 191, 192–3, 194
Pritchard, William 6

Rachewiltz, Mary de 185–7, 190
Rachewiltz, Walter de 189
Rago, Henry 93, 124, 130, 142
Rakosi, Carl 7, 160
Ransom, John Crowe 2
Rauschenberg, Robert 101
Reid, Donald 163
Rexroth, Kenneth 31
Reznikoff, Charles 7, 146, 157, 159, 160
Rice, John Andrew 100, 101, 103
Rich, Adrienne 3
Ridler, Anne 118
Rilke, Rainer Maria 8, 59, 155, 159
Rimbaud, Arthur 184
Roberts, Michael ix, 2, 118, 120
Roos, Frank J., Jr. 163
Rudge, Olga 188–9
Rumaker, Michael 101
Ruskin, John 39, 79, 125, 137, 138

Saint-Gaudens, Augustus 163–4
Sandys, George 4
Santayana, George 48, 69, 125, 187
Schawinsky, Alexander 105

Schmidt, Michael ix
Schopenhauer, Arthur 64, 68
Scott, Winfield Townley 165
Scrimgeour, Cecil 10
Sellaio, Jacopo del 12
Sereni, Vittorio 190, 191
Sexton, Anne 3
Shakespeare, William 31, 54
Sheeler, Charles 35, 169
Shelley, Percy Bysshe 194
Siegel, Alfred 154
Stephens, Alan 129, 135
Stevens, Wallace ix, 2, 7, 53–69, 119, 120, 122–4, 125
Stieglitz, Alfred 163, 168, 169, 171

Tate, Allen 2, 120
Taylor, Edward 4
Tennyson, Alfred, Lord 5, 57
Thomas, Dylan 120, 128
Thomas, Edward 8
Thoreau, Henry 31, 32, 47
Tolstoy, Leo 112
Turnbull, Gael ix, 124, 144
Turner, J.M.W. 169
Tyler, Parker 36

Valéry, Paul 66–7
Van Doren, Mark 20
Vendler, Helen 3, 7, 63, 64
Verlaine, Paul 10
Virgil 14

Von Hallberg, Robert 112–13

Wagner, Richard 26, 64, 188
Warburg, Edward 100
Warren, Robert Penn 7
Weaver, Mike 1, 28
Webb, Todd 165, 167, 169
Weil, Simone 72
Wells, H.G. 18
Wells, Patricia 7
Wheatley, Phillis 5
Whitman, Walt 1, 3, 31, 105, 118, 120, 121, 157
Whittier, John Greenleaf 3, 6
Williams, Jonathan 77, 145, 153
Williams, William Carlos ix, x, 1, 3, 9, 11, 27–37, 38, 39, 40, 48, 49, 65, 66, 75, 77, 92–3, 94, 96, 97, 108, 109, 119, 120, 124, 126–30, 131–3, 136, 139–40, 141, 142, 144, 153, 159, 191
Winters, Yvor 2, 34, 53, 54, 58, 68, 69, 128, 133, 134–6, 142
Witemeyer, Hugh 92
Wyatt, Sir Thomas 11, 47
Wycherley, William 19

Yeats, W.B. 38, 53, 113, 185

Zukofsky, Louis 75, 76, 77, 131, 143, 144–7, 148–55, 157–62, 180